The Legislators

DICTATED BY THE SPIRIT

JOHN WILMONT EARL OF ROCHESTER

VERA KRYZHANOVSKAIA

Translation to English:

Vanessa Salvador Neciosup

Lima, Peru, August 2023

Beatriz Stella

São Paulo, Brazil, February 2024

Original Title in Portuguese:
"Os Legisladores"

World Spiritist Institute
Houston, Texas, USA
E–mail: contact@worldspiritistinstitute.org

About the Medium

Vera Ivanovna Kryzhanovskaia, (Warsaw, July 14, 1861 - Tallinn, December 29, 1924), was a Russian psychographer medium. Between 1885 and 1917 she psychographed a hundred novels and short stories signed by the spirit of Rochester, believed by some to be John Wilmot, second Earl of Rochester. Among the best known are "The Pharaoh Mernephtah" and "The Iron Chancellor."

In addition to historical novels, in parallel the medium psychographed works with "occult-cosmological themes." E. V. Kharitonov, in his research essay, considered her the first woman representative of science fiction literature. During the fashion for occultism and esotericism, with the recent scientific discoveries and psychic experiences of European spiritualist circles, she attracted readers from the Russian "Silver Age" high society and the middle class in newspapers and press. Although he began along spiritualist lines, organizing séances in St. Petersburg, he later gravitated toward theosophical doctrines.

Her father died when Vera was just ten years old, which left the family in a difficult situation. In 1872 Vera was taken in by an educational charity for noble girls in St. Petersburg as a scholar, St. Catherine's School. However, the young girl's frail health and financial difficulties prevented her from completing the course. In 1877 she was discharged and completed her education at home.

During this period, the spirit of the English poet JW Rochester (1647-1680), taking advantage of the young woman's mediumistic gifts, materialized, and proposed that she dedicate herself body and soul to the service of the Good and write under his direction. After this contact with the person who became her spiritual guide, Vera was cured of chronic tuberculosis, a serious illness at the time, without medical interference.

At the age of 18, he began to work in psychography. In 1880, on a trip to France, he successfully participated in a mediumistic séance. At that time, his contemporaries were surprised by his productivity, despite his poor health. His séances were attended at that time by famous European mediums, as well as by Prince Nicholas, the future Tsar Nicholas II of Russia.

In 1886, in Paris, her first work was made public, the historical novel "Episode of the life of Tiberius", published in French, (as well as her first works), in which the tendency for mystical themes was already noticeable. It is believed that the medium was influenced by the Spiritist Doctrine of Allan Kardec, the Theosophy of Helena Blavatsky, and the Occultism of Papus.

During this period of temporary residence in Paris, Vera psychographed a series of historical novels, such as "The Pharaoh Mernephtah", "The Abbey of the Benedictines", "The Romance of a Queen", "The Iron Chancellor of Ancient Egypt", "Herculaneum", "The Sign of Victory", "The Night of Saint Bartholomew", among others, which attracted public attention not only for the captivating themes, but also for the exciting plots. For the novel "The Iron Chancellor of Ancient Egypt," the French Academy of Sciences awarded him the title of "Officer of the French Academy," and in 1907, the Russian Academy of Sciences awarded him the "Honorable Mention" for the novel "Czech Luminaries."

About the Spiritual Author

John Wilmot, Earl of Rochester was born on April 1 or 10, 1647 (there is no record of the exact date). The son of Henry Wilmot and Anne (widow of Sir. Francis Henry Lee), Rochester resembled his father in physique and temperament, domineering and proud. Henry Wilmot had received the title of Earl because of his efforts to raise money in Germany to help King Charles I regain the throne after he was forced to leave England.

When his father died, Rochester was 11 years old and inherited the title of Earl, little inheritance, and honors.

Young J.W. Rochester grew up in Ditchley among drunkenness, theatrical intrigues, artificial friendships with professional poets, lust, brothels in Whetstone Park and the friendship of the king, whom he despised.

He had a vast culture, for the time: he mastered Latin and Greek, knew the classics, French and Italian, was the author of satirical poetry, highly appreciated in his time.

In 1661, at the age of 14, he left Wadham College, Oxford, with the degree of Master of Arts. He then left for the continent (France and Italy) and became an interesting figure: tall, slim, attractive, intelligent, charming, brilliant, subtle, educated, and modest, ideal characteristics to conquer the frivolous society of his time.

When he was not yet 20 years old, in January 1667, he married Elizabeth Mallet. Ten months later, drinking began to affect his character. He had four sons with Elizabeth and a daughter, in 1677, with the actress Elizabeth Barry.

Living the most different experiences, from fighting the Dutch navy on the high seas to being involved in crimes of death, Rochester's life followed paths of madness, sexual abuse, alcoholics, and charlatanism, in a period in which he acted as a "physician."

When Rochester was 30 years old, he writes to a former fellow adventurer that he was nearly blind, lame, and with little chance of ever seeing London again.

Quickly recovering, Rochester returns to London. Shortly thereafter, in agony, he set out on his last adventure: he called the curate Gilbert Burnet and dictated his recollections to him. In his last reflections, Rochester acknowledged having lived a wicked life, the end of which came slowly and painfully to him because of the venereal diseases that dominated him.

Earl of Rochester died on July 26, 1680. In the state of spirit, Rochester received the mission to work for the propagation of Spiritualism. After 200 years, through the medium Vera Kryzhanovskaia, the automatism that characterized her made her hand trace words with dizzying speed and total unconsciousness of ideas. The narratives that were dictated to her denote a wide knowledge of ancestral life and customs and provide in their details such a local stamp and historical truth that the reader finds it hard not to recognize their authenticity. Rochester proves to dictate his historical-literary production, testifying that life unfolds to infinity in his indelible marks of spiritual memory, towards the light and the way of God. It seems impossible for a historian, however erudite, to study, simultaneously and in depth, times and environments as different as the Assyrian, Egyptian, Greek and Roman civilizations; as well as customs as dissimilar as those of the France of Louis XI to those of the Renaissance.

The subject matter of Rochester's work begins in Pharaonic Egypt, passes through Greco-Roman antiquity and the Middle Ages, and continues into the 19th century. In his novels, reality navigates in a fantastic current, in which the imaginary surpasses the limits of verisimilitude, making natural phenomena that oral tradition has taken care to perpetuate as supernatural.

Rochester's referential is full of content about customs, laws, ancestral mysteries and unfathomable facts of History, under a novelistic layer, where social and psychological aspects pass through the sensitive filter of his great imagination. Rochester's genre classification is hampered by his expansion into several categories: gothic horror with romance, family sagas, adventure and forays into the fantastic.

The number of editions of Rochester's works, spread over countless countries, is so large that it is not possible to have an idea of their magnitude, especially considering that, according to researchers, many of these works are unknown to the general public.

Several lovers of Rochester's novels carried out (and perhaps do carry out) searches in libraries in various countries, especially in Russia, to locate still unknown works. This can be seen in the prefaces transcribed in several works. Many of these works are finally available in English thanks to the ***World Spiritist Institute.***

CHAPTER I

The sun was setting, shining its purple rays over the vast plain flanked by the dark walls of forest and the arborescent mountains. Dense , tall scrub was groing all over the countryside, here and there, groups of trees with huge trunks and exuberant foliage could be seen, which formed an almost impenetrable canopy.

Animals of enormous size and strange appearance could be seen running stretched out placidly warming themselves in the sun. Their long and flexible bodies, ended in a tail, like a dragon's; two pairs of short and thick feet were used for locomotion, and huge wings, as powerful as an eagle's, which allowed them to take flight, and their narrow heads with big eyes, suggesting intelligence, resembled those of achenes. They were totally black animals, like the wings of a raven, or even an auriferous reddish-purple with a greenish tinge.

Not far from that unusual herd, under the dense foliage, a large group of men of colossal stature was gathered. Their only clothing was animal skins that covered their reddish- blue hips. Their black hair, wiry and disheveled, fell over their shoulders; their faces with their coarse features and protunding jaws, were immature. , They were armed with thick, gnarled sticks and small stone axes tucked behind their belt: they wielded a long-coiled rope, one end on which was tied to a stone. Huddled around tree stumps or on the grass, they were talking; their guttural voices could be heard from afar . They were, apparently, shepherds.

Suddenly, one of the men stood up and pointed to a group of women, recognizable by their long hair and large breasts; they had just come out of the forest and were striding towards the men. Like them, their clothing consisted of a single garment, a kind of loincloth made of braided sugar cane leaves. Inside their rustic baskets and straw towels, they brought lunch to the shepherds. It consisted of various kinds of fruits, roots and raw fish inside birchbark containers, there was a yellowish liquid with an aromatic smell.

After depositing the food at the men's feet, the women prostrated themselves in deference before them, then quickly stood up and began to say something, causing quite a stir among the shepherds.

The man in the cave is calling us. Why is that? — surprised one of the men, visibly upset.

Have the others also been called? — one of them asked.

The messenger told us that some messengers have left for the valleys and forests. But the meetingin the Valley of the Salted Rock, is only for the elders and some special guests. — One of the women assured us. After eating quickly , everyone set off.

After a long walk, the crowd came out in a wide meadow bordered by colossal trees; their trunks were hollow inside and served as homes for the aborigenes.

The unique burrows were carpeted inside with animal skins, right there you could see household utensils made from tree bark and food supplies . While the women took care of the house, the children, completely naked, ran around happily in the open air. There were at least a hundred of these tree houses.

Among the residents, the excitement was visible. Gathered in small groups, they were discussed something loudly; the newcomers immediately joined in the conversation.

Then, from the crowd, about fifty men and women came forward and headed down the trails towards the forest.

After walking for a long time, they found themselves in a wide valley surrounded on its flanks by forests and sharp mountains, furrowed by a multitude of fissures.

In the center of the valley, a colossal cubic rock stood on a mound, and on top of it rested another cone-shaped stone, resembling a small obelisk. All around that cone of black basalt, polished and shiny, resinous branches were piled up.

The place was crowded with people. Men and women, forming a compact block, huddled together at the foot of the mound; the reddish, smoky light of the torches cast purplish glows over this strange gathering.

Suddenly, the crowd stirred and squeezed together to form a passageway and a whisper could be heard rolling through:

The man in the cave...! The man in the cave...!

Through the passageway formed between the crowd, a rather strange looking man was arriving. He was huge in stature and as thin as a skeleton. His oblong, bony face , with his tick lips , flat nose thin and low forehead ;was livid and reverberated a blue hue, as if the blood flowing under his skin was the same color. His eyes sat deep in the orbits and were incredibly bulging; however, the most surprising thing about this man was the existence of a third eye, located at the back of his neck, while his head was practically devoid of hair. He was wearing a tunic made of animal skin, his arms, and legs of disproportionate size were bare.

At his arrival, the crowd fell genuflecting and began to repeatedly beat their foreheads against the earth. Responding to the greeting with a slight inclination of his head, the man went to the mound, climbed the steps, circled the stone seven times, bowed to it, bent down to the ground and prostrated himself in front of it, reciting magical formulas in his guttural voice.

Then he poured a tar-like liquid over the foliage, took two flat stones from a bag tied behind his waist and began to rub them against each other, until they sparked, igniting the branches around the conical stone.

At that moment, a roaring noise was heard, and a tick smoke rose into the air . The three-eyed man began to roar and whirl with extraordinary speed, being imitated by the crowd. Men and women holding hands formed a chain around the rock, whirling in a mad dance amid wild roars, which was probably a kind of singing, since the voices sounded high and low, without any rhythm or melody.

In the meantime, the column of smoke, was densifying, spreading and rising like a curtain in the windless air.

Suddenly, a flame appeared among the clouds of smoke, rising in a fiery column and tinged with all the colors of the rainbow, forming, in the end, a sphinx of colossal proportions.

Both the man in the cave and the whole crowd stopped, got down on their knees and began to gaze ecstatically at the sight. Then the mysterious being began to speak. The powerful voice, which seemed to come from far away, reached all the way to the back rows and sounded like a megaphone.

I have come to tell you, inhabitants of the valleys, mountains and forests, that the time has come for the gods to descend. His coming will dispel the darkness, for it is his desire to mingle with the people, teach them the deep mysteries, show them the riches of the soil and make them discover the wonders of heaven. They will transform you and your generation will be known as the one that had the fortune to see your descent from on heights, to settle here. The gods are coming! So, prepare yourselves, inhabitants of the valleys, mountains and forests, for the great day: eat or drink nothing for the next two days, and, on the third , gather in the valleys, at the foot of the mountains, to see the descent of your future lords and masters . The time has come!

The voice fell silent , the vision became crude and vanished into thin air. For a few minutes, everyone remained paralyzed, stunned by what they had just heard; then the crowd surged like a wild sea. Surrounding the cave man , the natives peppered him with questions. He explained that the enigmatic creature they had just seen had been sent by the gods to announce their descent. Then he instructed them how to fast and to purify themselves by bathing in the rivers, and finally, he ordered them to dress in new and clean clothes. After these instructions, he detailed the places where everyone should gather to watch the and unique spectacle: the descent of the gods from on high - mysterious beings on their mission to transform the world.

The crowd dispersed in haste to pass on the extraordinary news to others.

The two days following that memorable night passed with feverish excitement.

On the appointed day, early in the afternoon, the whole population was on their feet; nervousness was growing by the hour, and anxiety about that extraordinary event seemed to take over not only the people, but all of nature.

The impatience of the wild mob was growing; some of the bravest and more shrewdest young men, having already tamed the winged animals described above, mounted their backs and took to the heights to watch, among the first, the awaited gods.

Finally, a pinkish light poured into the sky, reverberating to golden yellow, and against that radiant background the enigmatic fleet began to appear, descending at dizzying speed from the celestial heights.

From each ship, like suns, streams of blinding light poured down, chords of unheard music reached everyone's ears.

The harmonious sounds, soft and at the same time indescribably powerful, made every fiber of those humans tremble, even the rudest; silent, astonished and trembling, they were dazzled by that extraordinary spectacle.

The music of the spheres provoked yet another very unexpected phenomenon: from the depths of the swamps and rivers, from the mountains and forests, came the most varied species of animals and monsters, large and small, all of which had previously provoked great fear in people, making them flee in terror. However, the terrifying beasts apparently had no intention of causing any harm to humans, bewitched as they were, listening to the magical melody that seemed to envelop all men and animals, calming them down.

Meanwhile, the space fleet drew closer to the Earth. The lights streaming from it became multicolored, and the valleys and mountains were alternately flooded with sapphire blue, emerald green and ruby red; the air became saturated with wonderful, aromatic fluids.

By now, you could clearly see, an open hatch, where tall, slender human beings stood, wearing white robes or wrapped in veils that looked more like silver mist. Their countenances were of heavenly beauty and, indeed, to the primitive beings they seemed divine.

With a serene and thoughtful air, the adepts examined that new land - their future battlefield - and that mass of people, which whom they were summoned to reform, to provide spiritual light and human warmth, to minister the foundations of the Creator's magnitude, the principles of order and guidance for the path of perfection.

Silent as if lulled by melodious waves, the air fleet flew over the valleys and forests and, soaring into the heights, disappeared behind the mountains.

The primitive mob seemed lethargic . A new feeling came over them, a mixture of enchantment, exaltation before that perfect beauty and recognition of their ugliness. It was not a feeling of envy, because for them those beings of otherworldly beauty were gods.

Thus exalted, in a state never before experienced, the impressed savages looked towards the mountain range, behind which the gods were supposed to be. A superstitious fear overwhelmed them when, suddenly, above the pinnacles of the mountains, igneous triangles began to appear and then the colossal image of a winged creature holding a flaming sword appeared. And everyone understood that those places had become sacred and that none of the inhabitants of the valleys, mountains and forests could dare approach that abode of the gods.

On one of the mountains that bordered the area where the fleet of adepts had descended, there was a huge cave formed partly by nature itself, and partly by the human hands. About twenty people had gathered there. Some of the walls of the underground room were adorned with sculptures; a luminous sphere attached to the partition wall, cast a soft bluish light over the room. In a deep depression, resembling a niche, there was a huge block of ruby stone carved in the shape of a triangle, accessed by a few steps. The block, topped by a large cross in solid gold, glowed in phosphoric sparkles, seven finely crafted gold lamps hung from the ceiling above the cross, each of which flickered with a flame of a different color, corresponding to the hue of the rainbow. The multicolored lights reverberated pictorially over the gold and large crystal chalice at the base of the cross; on either side of the chalice rested huge metal-bound books. In a smaller adjoining grotto, also illuminated by a sphere fixed to the wall, there was a table and some stone benches.

Some ardent people stood in front of the niche. After bowing three times to the ground, they sang an imposing and melodious hymn in chorus, , and passed into a small cave next door, where some sat at a table, others paced back and forth. Everyone seemed visibly disturbed and wrapped up in deep thoughts.

They were beautiful men, in the bloom of youth, with varied features, albeit thin and appearing to be ascetics. All of them invariably had an inner light that seemed to filter through their skin, partially illuminating their energetic faces: their gazes showed great intelligence and iron will, even if they gave the impression of being affected by a deep sadness.

They wore the same type of long, dark leather robes with strings and straw sandals.

Finally, an apparently superior man broke the silence.

— Brothers, our work is over, so is our atonement, I hope..." he announced. — The time has come for us to stand before our former masters and judges, to give an account of the colossal mission entrusted to us. It seems appropriate to me to gather the documents that constitute the results of our work and take them to our masters.

— The bell has not rung yet, but I agree with you. We would better be ready! — said one of the men, standing up.

They fetched a huge number of parchments and placed them on the table. They recorded astronomical events, the positions of the constellations and the movement of the planets since time immemorial; others contained the history of the evolution of the planet and the races that inhabited it; others, finally, contained a detailed account of each person's work and the results obtained.

As soon as they had finished packing and tying up the bundles of valuable documents, three loud chimes were clearly heard. Everyone shuddered, some blushed nervously.

— Let us make a last ablution and raise a purifying prayer before presenting ourselves before our judges," said the first one. Silently, one after the other, they approached the fountain which gushed a thin stream of water over the cave walls, forming a pool; they washed their faces and hands in clean water, and then returned to the larger cave, where they said a prayer and sang a hymn. The imposing chant, performed in great jubilation and ardent faith, praised the powers of good and the bliss of purification; while this grandiose praise lasted, the niche was flooded with a wonderful pink light, the chalice flashed in radiant beams and was half filled with a golden liquid.,nd those present, as if transfigured, contemplated that magical spectacle. Jubilant and as if transfigured, those present gazed that magical spectacle. Then, one of them went up the steps, picked up the chalice, took it and passed it to the others so that they could also drink from the enigmatic contents. Then, the one who looked like to be the superior, took the chalice in his hands, another held up the cross, the rest divided up the books and parchments and, each holding a load in one hand and a lit wax candle in the other, they all headed towards the stairway carved into the rock and hidden behind a ledge.

They came out in a wide area surrounded by high mountains; there, amidst lush vegetation, stood a huge building with unique architecture. A large staircase led to a gallery with columns in the shape of tree trunks, where aromatic herbs were burning in huge bowls carved from stone. It was there that they stood in their simple, dark work clothes.

From that height, an astonishing panorama unfolded before them. Not far from the staircase, a path led down flanked by flowering bushes, to a wide meadow, where the adventurers from the dead planet were landing ; one after the another, the aircraft anchored, and their passengers descended from them, who then gathered together.

In groups. One of the groups was made up of people completely covered by long veils; an intense light filtered through the silver cloth, as if it came from incandescent metal, while auriferous halos shone around their heads . A little further on, the wizards were grouped together in their white robes, with flares on their foreheads, denoting their rank, with insignia glowing on their chests. Further on – like radiant visions – were the female wizards;

the Grail knights, resembling a silver beehive; the adepts of lower rank; and, finally, a large number of earthlings who deserved to be transfer to the new planet. The last few looked dizzy, trembling in groups under the guard of the security guards.

The great servants of light, headed by the hierophants, carrying chalices topped by crosses, went to the palace, where they were awaited by the pioneers of the young planet. The latter prostrated themselves at their feet and, rising, joined them. Only the superior magicians, and the Grail Knights entered the immense hall, standing in a semicircle at the back. In the center, in front of the superior magicians, stood the small group of workers of the new world. Immediately, they handed the adepts the cross, the chalice, and the books bound in metal covers.

Then the stentorian voice of one of the men, whose face was covered by a cloak, was heard in the quiet room.

— Glory to you, my children! Hard work has atoned for your sins; may the chains that bind you to the past be broken! May the former purged return, already purified, to the bosom of the servants of the light, and may their spiritual resurrection be celebrated.

Coruscating flashes of lightning shot out from the superior magicians, covering the workers with a fiery film, as if they were being burned. And when the reddish haze cleared, an incredible transfiguration took place. Instead of the old leather garments, the workers of the new planet were wearing white robes; their incredible beauty countenance now exuded a jubilant joy, and on their foreheads appeared the first torch of the magicians' crown.

The newcomers from Earth surrounded, embraced and congratulated us. There were old friends among them, and the joy of the reunion was great.

The transfigured , however, did not forget their role as hosts and tried to accommodate the visitors on the new planet. Firstly, they took the superior magicians to a specially prepared place, while the other travelers were invited to a huge hall, where a large table with a trivial banquet awaited them: milk, honey, fruit, and bread.

Ebramar also found an old companion among the purged and made him sit down with him at the table.

— I am very glad that your trials are over, Udea. We are very grateful to you and your friends for this wonderful palace you have prepared for us as a shelter, and it is so comfortable. — Ebramar confessed.

Udea, a handsome young man with serious features and large, dark, thoughtful eyes, sighed.

— We had plenty of time to build it. And even so, it is not enough to accommodate everyone, although we have adapted many caves where the lesser magicians can be installed. As for comfort, it is the minimum acceptable, as is the meal. We have no food resources and could only offer you what we had. Every block of stone in this building has been a light of hope for us, that you would come here, and we would return to our fellow human beings; that you would bring us the relics of the past, living memories of the dead Earth, once our cradle.

— Oh, Ebramar! What a terrible nightmare this life has been from the moment I found myself on this savage planet, populated by inferior beings incapable of understanding me. Certainly, I had unfortunate friends, but the atmosphere was unbearable. And the knowledge that we ourselves were to blame for this harsh fate ... Regret and remorse overwhelmed our souls! For we had been deprived of everything; we had only our knowledge, and our only amusement was the enormous work ahead of us. It was hard. Sometimes I thought I could not stand it; how hard it was. And, unfortunately, I was immortal...!

Udea's voice sounded of lived suffering; Ebramar squeezed his hand tightly.

— Chase away the bad memories, all the more so because they are inopportune! The gradeur of a job well done and the brightness of a well-deserved reward will make you forget the bitterness of the past. The golden torch on your forehead, symbol of the immortal wizard's crown you have regained, has erased all your mistakes and sufferings. It will illuminate your clear future, and then... We will walk together.

Udea's eyes shone with love and deep recognition.

— You are right, Ebramar! I hope to walk, without any more scares, the path of perfection, under your tutelage and leadership. I want to thank you, my friend, for everything you have done for me. You never abandoned me, and, in the most difficult moments, the warm emanation of your love came from the distant Earth to console me, support me and lessen the sufferings of the purged !

Ebramar smiled and nodded

— You cannot praise what was a pleasure for me. And now, I repeat, expel those memories! We will have plenty of time to talk. Well, the meal is over, come on, I want you to meet some friends of mine!

They approached a small group chatting by the window, and Ebramar introduced Nata and his other disciples to them.

— Here are two valiant workers of science: Supramati and Dakhir. I was very pleased to guide them on the path of development. And this is Narayana, my "prodigal son", who has finally returned to his paternal home; it is true that he has caused me a lot of trouble, but he has also brought me much joy. I present to you the most cheerful and humane of the magicians, and I am sure that we will still see him conquering and founding some great kingdom, with a legendary name that will remain in popular memory infinitely.

They all burst out laughing and, after chatting jovially, everyone went to take care of their lodging.

In order to have an idea of the circumstances that led to the events described above , and to explain the presence on the new planet of the members of the Brotherhood of the Immortals , some explanation is necessary.

Despite the rigid discipline and hard work demanded of the members of the secret brotherhood, the adepts remain ordinary men, and none of them, despite the knowledge they have acquired, can completely master the weaknesses that lurk in the depths of their souls. Such beings are sometimes subject to unbridled passions, as a result of which they commit acts so unworthy of an adept, that their expulsion from the community becomes inevitable.

However, simply excluding them presents a danger, because they possess great powers, the abuse of which may bring many evils; moreover, because they have been initiated into the great mysteries of science, they can influence the very course of events, by prematurely spreading their knowledge among a crowd that is intellectually developed to apply it, but still too ignorant to refrain from using it for evil. But how do you get rid of these dangerous people? Taking the lives of those who are saturated with primal matter is not an easy task. For this reason, transgressors are offered two options: either voluntary death, which is very painful, through the decomposition of the living body, or to go, as an illuminator, to another planet, where the legislators will stay in the future, where the level of progress is very low. There they can work with a deadline set by the masters, or until the masters go there.

Atonement is hard, but it purifies the outcast, repairs their old mistakes and, at the same time, serves as an ascension

The sentenced who opt for atonement through hard work are left by the High Council in a lethargic state, and the enlightened ones then take them to a distant planet: the field of the future work of the great hierophants of the extinct worlds.

The purged are equipped with the most indispensable things: magical instruments, supplies for any eventuality and a library specially composed not only of scientific works, but also of those that can contribute to mental relaxation. At the request of their friends, the exiled can also take some luxury objects and, finally, everything that is indispensable for the performance of religious services, in order to attract the pure fluids, which are necessary for the balance of atmospheric currents and the control of chaotic forces.

CHAPTER II

From that very day on, a feverish activity began on the new planet. While some disciples of the great magicians worked to complete the installation of their masters' laboratories, adjust the research equipment, among other tasks, others supervised the unpacking and storage of the most valuable manuscripts, containing the history and scientific works of the extinct planet. All those treasures from the past were kept in underground rooms, specially prepared by the purged adepts.

The earthlings were gloomy. Segregated from their homes, customs and earthly possessions, they looked like a dizzy herd, clinging to each other in fright; their appearance inspired pity. Their protectors realized in time the low morale of the weak spirits, and immediately took energetic measures to lift them out of their torpor and despair. Aware of the best remedy, the magicians initially divided them into groups and ordered each one to take care of its own facilities, in specially prepared caves, or to help the adepts with less complex tasks.

The more active and intellectually developed earthlings soon adapted and came to the conclusion that the situation was not as bad as it seemed at first. The place was a true paradise on earth due to its stunning beauty, its indescribable wealth of exuberant fauna and pleasant climate. Thus, the most energetic earthlings were able to influence the others, who were less active and less mentally developed; soon, all that small army began feverishly to build temporary homes and sorting out the huge inventory, brought by the space fleet.

Not even three weeks had passed, and the first work had already been completed. The magicians' laboratories were working in perfect order; their disciples were toiling away, passing on orders from the Master's to the magicians of immediately lower rank .

A meeting was then scheduled to discuss and analyze some special and secret measures that would define the fate and formation of the future races. — Brothers! Our greatest commitment is to the people we have brought , who will form the nucleus of the new races and civilizations," declared one of the hierophants presiding over the meeting.

— For the time being, they are armed only with the faith by which they were saved, but that is little in the view of the work to be done. It will be no easy task to establish a relationship with the savage peoples, to enlighten them to instill in them the first notions of arts and crafts, to develop the vulgar mind and to fix new principles to curb their cruel and savage customs. Even earthlings, in view of the sufferings endured by their civilization, which reached its apogee, but consigned the rigid but just laws of their ancestors to the grave, have much to learn about true justice and goodness. To train the embryonic races from their own representatives, we need schools and time. We do not lack the latter. We will begin with the construction of the city that will house the schools of initiation and, for the construction of the divine city, the respective tasks were distributed according to the abilities of each one, and the meeting was adjourned. The small group of friends converged on the terrace. Narayana invited everyone, including Udea, to the terrace, next to the room he occupied; with Udea he found a sincere friendship. Throughout the trip to the new planet, Narayana had remained taciturn, it had been too painful for him to leave Earth; but that day, the cheerful magician returned to his usual good humor.

A table full of magnificently prepared fruit and vegetable dishes awaited his guests on the terrace. They did not mince their words and paid due honor to the f meal. Ebramar smilingly asked if Narayana himself was not responsible for those delicacies, the work of a great chef.

— God forbid I get my hands dirty with that! — joked Narayana, full of satisfaction. — I brought a cook and a servant with me, and as you can see, the result is not bad at all.

To the surprise of Supramati and the other visitors -except Ebramar, who was laughing behind his beard-, he added with good-naturedly that Narayana had not lost his administrative skills. Narayana then added in a jovial tone:

— Listen, my friends, how it happened! On the last day, when our old Earth was groaning to no end, I was about to board my aircraft to go to the agreed meeting place. I have to confess that my mood was as dark as my surroundings . Suddenly, two men, mad with fear, threw themselves at my feet, grabbed my clothes and begged to let them go, swearing eternal gratitude.

I was about to give them a hard time, when, surprised, I recognized them as the servants of the rich man Solomon, who I had nicknamed the "new Lucullus". I even knew one of them: he was a cook like no other. I soon realized that, wherever we were going, a servant like that would be indispensable. Just imagining that I would have to eat some root vegetable ragout, perhaps prepared by a bogeyman or some other monster, gave me the creeps; the idea of cooking, myself, did not excite me.

Likewise, having a servant with one or three eyes ... A servant like that either saw too much or too little... I did not like that either. So their appearance came in handy; as for the cargo... The poor things did not weigh much.

— Do you believe in God? — I asked in an angry tone.

— How could I not believe in God's punishment in the face of the terrible effects of his wrath? -They burst into tears.

— And in Jesus Christ, our Lord, do you believe? — I continued by asking.

They persevered and, still clinging to each other like ticks, they swore on the cross that their only hope was the Savior's mercy.

So, I quickly took the flask with the primal essence out of my pocket and made them both take a sip, settling them in the aircraft beforehand.

— Since they are smart boys, they soon became familiar with what is around, and the cook presented me with a list of edibles products, some of which you have just tasted. As for the servant, he is very helpful and extremely religious. I am very happy, friends, to be able to offer you something edible.

And now, dear Udea, I would like to thank you and your friends for arranging a beautiful shelter for the unfortunate space navigators.

In a jiffy, he blew a few kisses at Udea, who was sitting next to him, to the delight of those present and his new friend, who had not laughed so much for a long time. Even the other wizards, who had been serious about the events that had taken place , relaxed and laughed a lot.

As they got up from the table, Ebramar put his hand on Narayana's shoulder and said affectionately.

— "My 'prodigal son', you really are the 'earthliest' of magicians! Despite the time and years you have lived, despite your level of knowledge and perfection, you have retained the youthful joy of life. Preserve this heavenly gift and pass it on to all those around you, because joy supports you and your work and makes any task less arduous.

Narayana's dark eyes shone with satisfaction and gratitude.

— Thank you, my dear master, I will always try to be like that, even after I win my seventh torch, which will not be soon.

Now I have a pleasant task ahead of me, that will occupy me for a long time: building the palace. I hope it will be one of the most beautiful in the city.

— I do not think your desire to build an enchanted castle is difficult – Udea observed. — All the metals here on the planet are still in a semi-liquid state or, at worst, very malleable. We have crystals of incredible hues nearby, which can generally satisfy all tastes and requirements, and your nose will certainly come in handy.

— Thank you, Udea. You will show me the source of these resources later. And you, Ebramar. When will you start building your house? It is an undertaking that cannot be postponed and is so pleasant!

— I don't deny that building one's own house is a very rewarding experience, but I think that other work is more urgent," the wizard objected, shaking his head.

—Do not forget that we are not here to have fun, but to fulfill a great mission: to benefit the planet. Of those we have brought with us, we will train kings, priests, collaborators in future governments, artists, common and specialized workers. It will not be easy to train this workforce, so that each one can scrupulously fulfills their role as enlighteners of the barbarian and savage tribes around us. Therefore, I consider it my top priority to build schools and temples of initiation, and only then to begin the constitution of nations.

Narayana scratched behind his ear.

— You are the very embodiment of detachment, Ebramar. Was it not decided today that we would first start building the city first? Where will we live then?

— Calm down, impatient soul! You always forget that haste is the enemy of perfection. Everything will be done in time, because we can simplify the work to a minimum. Or have you forgotten that we have powers and tools that will cut granite like wax, turn any obstacle into ashes and lift weights equivalent to pyramids with a bale of straw? With these powers we will carry blocks, and with them, we will erect the walls of palaces and schools, we will carve underground temples in the mountains, adorning them with majestic sculptures, we will excavate caves and galleries. And in the distant centuries to come, pygmy men will gaze in bewilderment at these subterranean cities and cyclopean works, wondering with perplexity "what human hands, what generations of giants, were able to excavate, in time immemorial, to dig, carve and cut out of the rock massifs such artistic wonders of extra-human proportions?"

Our poor little broken Earth also had similar architectural monuments; but men of science, in their absurd ignorance, did not know which era to relate them to. Yes, the monuments were erected by giants, but giants of knowledge at the dawn of civilization!

— Of course, master, as always you are right! — added Narayana. — So, the most majestic, the most beautiful and the most luxurious of the kingdoms we have founded will be mine, Ebramar.

Ebramar smiled and looked affectionately at Narayana.

— I thank you for your impetuous exaltation, even if I do not have the slightest desire to reign; I will serve our common cause, as a priest, teacher and enlightener , in the great temple of our future city: the "City of the Gods", as it will be remembered in the popular memory, where the celestial visitors descended and gave rise to the divine generations that governed the peoples of the "golden century". There, as popular beliefs, vaguely stored in memory, say, was the earthly palace, where the tree of the knowledge of good and evil flourished.

In the following days, the work continued unceasingly. Some of the adepts got busy dividing the earthlings into teams of workers, according to their skills and knowledge, to build the city of the magicians. At the same time, the higher- level adepts drew up the plans for the upper city and the underground city , where the temples of the mysterious "sacraments" would be located, where ancient documents and treasures would be kept, along with the monuments of the dead Earth. The magicians also distributed the women into brigades and assigned them tasks for the future establishment of colonies and schools.

All work was restricted to the mountainous region, where the refugees from the extinct planet came down, among the inhabitants of the forests and valleys, the excitement continued. News of the coming of the gods continued to circulate, and those who had not taken part in that extraordinary event were anxiously checking in with the fortunate witnesses.

Everyone glanced curiously towards the mountains, behind which the air fleet had disappeared; however, no one dared to approach the place, out of superstitious fear. Sometimes the curious would catch a glimpse of some strange signs amidst fiery beams on the peaks, or, from time to time, an unusual rider would appear riding a winged dragon and soon would disappear into the distance. Then they would say, "Look, one of the gods has gone out for his daily ride!".

A new meaning of life was dawning on the savage and apathetic peoples; their heavy and obtuse minds were not in position to understand the reason for the adventurers' arrival. Who were they and where did they come from?

Getting no answer to their questions, some of the more lively ones went in search of the three-eyed man. The latter had little to add, and merely repeated that the gods had come to bring new knowledge and benefits to the people who inhabited the forests and valleys.

The three-eyed men were representatives of the almost extinct genus of primitive giants. During the slow evolution of the human race, their physical appearance changed: their gigantic stature diminished, the third eye began to weaken and finally disappeared completely, leaving the only trace of its existence the pineal gland, which even formal science admits is the remnant of the missing eye.

However, nature erases everything that has been generated slowly and gradually. I Isolated individuals of the species of the three-eyed giants still existed among the regeneration peoples; however, their very rarity surrounded them with a mystical aura, and they were considered to be superior beings.

In the meantime, an unexpected event that had never happened before , shook the population, pushing aside all other interests. In one of the tribes that inhabited in the hollow trees, a child had a sore throat and died the next day in horrible pain; the mother and some members of the family died later of the same disease, and the contagion spread with incredible speed, reaching tribes and tribes, and making numerous victims.

A mad panic seized those simple and primitive beings, who were unaware of any method of ending the epidemic, and whose very ignorance led to the spread of contagion. Desperate, they nothing left but to go to the three-eyed giants, or as they called them: "cavemen", for help and advice. One of them had the following idea:

Let's do like we did that time, when they announced the arrival of the gods. Remember the giants helped us? Let's call them to scare away the death that surrounds them.

At night, a huge crowd gathered around the cubic stone with a basaltic cone on top. Life the first time, they lit resinous branches, danced and go down on their knees; but as that vision of that time had not reappeared, Ipaksa (the threeeyed man) ordered them all to shout, as loud as they could, so that the gods would hear their cries. Howls and inhuman screams hang out across the valley, like a raging hurricane. Suddenly, oh happiness! — A flash of lightning illuminated the mountains, shrouded in the darkness of night; It meant that the gods had heard them! Fears and hopes stirred in the scattered crowd; but, as soon as the sun had risen over the horizon, a winged dragon began to descend on the houses of the village – if those holes in the trees could be called that — riding a woman in white robes.

A silver veil enveloped her like mist; two golden flames adorned her golden diadem, girding her beautiful hair. She carried, in her hand, an oddly shaped casket with marvelous ornaments. A bluish aura surrounded her head, and a phosphoric light radiated from her hands and clothes. Like a radiant vision, she went to visit the homes affected by the disease; the frightened people hid or even fled from her; but, seeing how the illuminated maiden bent down meekly and humbly over the sick, taking out brightly colored vials from the box anointing some people's throats and others' chests, while dripping a liquid into the mouths of the dying or placing her hands on their heads, everyone calmed down.

So, with great interest, she visited all the houses and, in all of them the results of the medication were miraculous: the hoarseness disappeared, breathing became clear and strength was restored. When she left the last house and the winged dragon took the unknown benefactress away, the aborigines fell to their knees and then, perhaps for the first time in their primitive souls, a feeling of adoration stirred . From that day on, the epidemic began to subside rapidly and, some time later, simply ceased to exist; a few torrential rains cleared the air.

Little by little, news came that the beneficent goddess had been to all the regions affected by the contagion, and that no one she had touched had died of the disease. In the villages, the strangest rumors spread. Those cured by the goddess claimed that her hands were like a baby's, resembling the petals of fragrant flowers; that a life-giving warmth poured from between her fingers;

that she walked without touching the ground and that there was fire in her jars.

Among the earthlings who quickly adapted to the new planet and strove to be useful to the community was a young scientist, the astronomer Andrei Kalitin, converted by Dakhir during his stay in Russia and taken to the new planet.

Accustomed to serious mental work, he was able to recognize the incredible luck that had saved him from the terrible catastrophe that annihilated the earthly world, so his gratitude to his savior knew no bounds.

Like the others, he had woken up when he arrived at his destination, and at first, he was overwhelmed by the fact that he was in a strange world; but after the first impressions , he tearfully expressed his gratitude to Dakhir, , begging him to continue to be his protector and master and to accept him as a disciple.

— Now I understand how ignorant I was, but I have wiped from my mind everything that I had conceived before. I look forward to working under your guidance, and I will be an obedient and diligent student, he added.

— So, it is decided, my young friend! — said Dakhir, smiling warmly and shaking his hand, "As of today, you are my disciple. However, I do not consider your previous knowledge useless; we will only re-evaluate it to separate the false and the misunderstood.

That same day, Dakhir set up his new disciple near his house and, although he was overburdened with work, as he was responsible for analyzing and classifying the documents gathered by the former purged, he always found an hour to study with him. Dakhir would point out Kalitin's mistakes or give him a more correct interpretation of scientific issues. Sometimes he took him on his business trips, giving him the opportunity to get to know his new home better.

The construction of the first temple had been entrusted to Narayana; Supramati, whose soul had awakened the passion of the ancient sculptor , readily accepted the task of decorating it . In view of the desire of the higher magicians to complete that first sanctuary as soon as possible, the work was aided by a mysterious power that only the higher magicians knew how to control.

Once, having something to discuss with Supramati, Dakhir invited Kalitin to accompany him to the city under construction.

The path to the sanctuary crossed galleries cleverly concealed behind artistic props; a soft, bluish light illuminated the passages to the enormous hall, of dizzying height, where the two magicians worked.

Dressed in a linen blouse, Narayana worked at the back of the room; Supramati, near the entrance. Amused, they did not notice the arrival of Dakhir and his disciple, who stopped in silence. Dakhir, who did not want to disturb his friends, hoping that they would notice his presence, began to examine the surroundings, where he had been many times before.

Kalitin stared dumbfounded at the wizards, not understanding what they were doing. In his outstretched hand, Supramati held a metallic staff, shiny like polished steel, which he moved up and down, either stretching it or shortening it. From the tip of the stick, sparks would shoot upwards and disappear into thin air; each movement of the stick was accompanied by a slight sound vibration with incredible modulations. Another phenomenon intrigued Kalitin even more; without the slightest contact with the rock wall , a human figure of colossal dimensions was being cut out of it. It seemed that the artist was simply retouching his work from a distance, sometimes accentuating the depth or expression of the face, sometimes finishing off the details of the clothing or hair.

Narayana's work seemed even more surprising. Nothing could be seen in his hands; only, from time to time, a metallic light flickered through his fingers, spilling out in sparkling streams. At the same time, by an invisible force, huge blocks of granite came off the wall at the bottom of the cave and, instead of falling to the ground, melted into the air without leaving a trace.

Kalitin was stunned to see this and let out a deaf scream. The two adepts interrupted their work.

— I am sorry if my disciple has disturbed you; it is just that he is completely dumbfounded," explained Dakhir, embracing his friends.

— Yes, really, for someone who is not initiated, our work is capable of provoking such an exclamation of astonishment – observed Narayana, laughing.

Noticing Kalitin's avid interest with which Kalitin looked at his hand. Narayana held it out to him and showed him a strange object in his palm. It was a ring with sparkling hands, yet Kalitin could not define it in the midst of so much turmoil .

His thoughts swirled around him, and he seemed to hear nothing around him; Narayana's loud laugh and a light touch from Dakhir's hand brought him back to reality. He apologized awkwardly but could not refrain from making a request: that he explained to him how the device worked.

— In the evening, at the time of our talk, I will explain everything you are seeing here; for now, be patient, as this is the main virtue of those who seek knowledge,' said Dakhir, saying goodbye to his friends and leaving the cave.

Never before had Kalitin waited so anxiously for night to arrive . He was studious enough to understand that the adepts draw on the powerful forces of nature, but what were those forces? – He could not discern them and tried futilely to compare them to one he knew.

Entering Dakhir's office, he noted with satisfaction that on the magician's table were two instruments identical to those of Narayana and Supramati. Dakhir began the lecture by explaining the composition of the atmosphere and added:

— The strange force that has aroused so much curiosity in you is nothing more than the vibratory force of the ether; its management contains the arcane meaning of all physical forces. As I have already told you, sound is the most terrifying of the occult forces. Sound aggregates and disintegrates; sound, like aroma, is in reality an incredibly tenuous substance drawn out of bodies with the help of a thrust or beat. Sounds, produced in a certain volume and combination, in such way as to generate certain ethereal chords, penetrate everything they can. The same principle explains the power of music, which can irritate as well as lead to a state of ecstasy, or calm, that is to say: it acts on the spiritual state and can provide the appropriate force to magical formulas. The formulas, like the melody, are made up of special vibrations, according to atheir intended purpose .

To give you some idea of the tenuity of the etheric current, it is enough to tell you that its density, compared to that of the atmosphere, is like that of hydrogen, compared to platinum, or that of a gas and the heaviest of metals.

All bodies, animals, plants, vegetables and minerals, were basically formed from this diluted ether; it means that all the diversity of species, in which the forces of matter manifest themselves , have a common origin, and are mutually dependent , being able to transform from one into another. Those who use the ethereal vibration can manipulate any matter.

— Allow me, master, to ask you one more question," said Kalitin, a little indecisive.

— As I understood, the vibratory force used by our friends, has the ability to break down and aggregate the atoms of matter;

however, I witnessed something even more phenomenal. It seemed that it was not a current of some force, but the hand of an artist sculpting.

— However, it is as simple as the action of any other natural force. The ore, like other materials, is made up of isolated particles in continuous movement, which are subjected to the forces acting on them Heat, for example, has the fastest and most visible effect, but the current of ether, controlled by the conscious will is even more powerful and subtle. The internal movement of the rock or metal mass allows it to submit to the mental force of the skillful craftsman who manipulates it. When this manipulation is combined with the powerful force of the etheric current, matter submits to its will, as if it were a simple visible material force. In short: matter is temporarily animated by the spirit that penetrates it, subjugating it to its will.

— Thank you for your explanation. I still cannot understand the mechanism by which the blocks are detached from the wall. I have just seen a huge block detach itself from the rock and disappear immediately without a trace.

— The force of the ethereal current, when it cuts a block out from the rock that the craftsman needs . It breaks down the atoms, dissolving the molecules.

— But then, by God, what are they transformed into by this miraculous force?

— In ether, a protoplasm common to all," answered Dakhir, smiling. I must say that the application of the vibratory force of the ether is infinitely varied. It can fulminate like lightning, cure various kinds of diseases, benefit a physical organism, restoring its depleted strength, or , just as easily, bring back to life a dead person whose astral body has not yet definitively separated, because the acoustic vibration combines elements in a kind of ozone, which is impossible to produce by common chemistry, which nevertheless has extraordinary life-giving properties. I will now show you some of the instruments we have been working with. We obviously have many others, but we will talk about them later. Take the stick! Donot be afraid, it is not activated!

Kalitin picked up the metal stick with superstitious reverence and examined it. It seemed hollow inside, had a handle with many locks, control buttons and springs, and was fitted with a telescopic movement mechanism.

Dakhir explained that, by operating the buttons, it was possible to adjust the power or direction of the force and, depending on how it was used, the instrument served as an extractor. Kalitin then went on to examine another device. As already mentioned, it was a kind of hollow hoop. Attached to a hook, inside it, were eighteen resonators. On top of the hoop there were, in decreasing size, several needles or vibrating rods, arranged in circles on three external resonators, connected to each other by metal filaments.

In the center was another hollow hoop, a kind of drum, with two rows of circular tubes, not even visible to the naked eye, and arranged like the pipes in an organ. Right in the center of the second ring was a rotating disk, and in the notton of the device was a small sphere, hollow inside, from which the power conductors came out.

— When the device is activated, the disk spins at an astonishing speed; the power of this motor is practically unlimited. Now I'm going to activate it, and all I have to do is press this button with my fingernail. Like that! — said Dakhir. — Now I'll show you how it works. See that little dead animal on the chair by the door? Bring it closer, we will break it down into tiny, invisible elements.

Kalitin examined the animal he had placed in the middle of the room from a distance. Suddenly, a fiery beam sparked from inside the device and hit the animal, which was literally projected upwards, disappearing without a trace, as if it had never existed.

Dakhir placed three filaments on the microscope slide and, when Kalitin looked curiously at the object magnified a thousand of times, the magician added:

— Do you remember that device with which you could see the state of decomposition of our dying Earth? Yes, it was also charged with ethereal vibratory force.

If I wanted to roll up with the energized filament around anything, even weighing tons, it could be suspended in the air without any difficulty, and transported, for example, to another end of the garden. What is more... The spaceships that brought us here were also equipped with these devices. Properly polarized, they could carry enormous weights, reach high altitudes and incredible speeds, in any direction.

— Oh my God! How interesting ! I do not think you will ever tell me how to control this power," Kalitin complained.

— You're right, son! It is not enough to work hard and study, you will also have to discipline your soul and demonstrate total control over yourself.

— OH! Will I survive that long? — Kalitin sighed.

— A mischievous smile appeared on Dakhir's face.

— Do not worry, you will have plenty of time! I want to make a confession . At our first meeting, I gave you a liquid to drink. You drank it thinking it was poison and waited to die, but then you survived. It was the primal essence, the elixir of long life, and whoever drank it on our ill-fated Earth would have a long planetary life. Here, in our new home, we are mortal again, like those we brought with us. Although with the conditions for us all to survive a few more millennia . The reason for this is simple: because of the arduous mission ahead of us, a short existence would be meaningless. The adepts we are educating will be our successors and future guardians of our mysteries. So, as you can see, you have plenty of time; nothing, no enemy of the common mortals, not even old age or weakening of strength, can prevent you from realizing this great and blissful destiny.

Livid as a corpse and trembling like a green stick, Kalitin listened to him. His mind refused to comprehend this new and astonishing revelation; only after a long conversation with his protector did Kalitin regain his relative serenity.

His melancholy, however, lasted for some days. Such a long existence ahead of him frightened him; little by little, however, his strong spirit overcame this weakness, and he firmly decided to make himself worthy of that extraordinary destiny forged by the Heavenly Father. Following Dakhir's instructions, he undertook not to reveal anything to anyone about what he had come to know.

After regaining his spiritual equilibrium, the ethereal force, whose properties intrigued Kalitin, once again became the subject of his reflections. One evening, talking to Dakhir, he brought up the subject again.

— Tell me, master, it seems that this marvelous force has always been kept under a veil of secrecy by the magicians. Its existence was never suspected on Earth, otherwise I would have heard of it and what it was capable of. I can only imagine what kind of advances it could bring to industry, science, and the arts.

— You are right. Your idea was known, at least in part. Do you know enough about the past of our ancient home, Earth? Then you must have heard about a continent called Atlantis, sucked into the ocean.

— Of course I have heard, I have even studied it .

— Well! The Atlanteans knew the ethereal force and used it. We have an Atlantean among us, his name is Tlavat. He was from a school of Egyptian hierophants; I will introduce him to you later. But let's get back to the subject. The Atlanteans called this ethereal force Mach-ma, and its terrible astral power contributed greatly to the extinction of the continent itself.

Hindu books also speak of a vibratory force; thus, in Ashtar Vidya, it is said that a machine charged with this force, placed in a "flying ship" and directed against an army, could turn it, with all its elephants, into a pile of ashes, like a bundle of straw.

In another ancient Hindu book, the Vishnu Purana, the same ethereal force is mentioned in an allegorical way that is understandable to the profane : the "gaze of Kapila", a sage who turnedKing Sagar's six hundred thousand children into ashes with a single look.

— I understand that the knowledge of the Atlanteans perished along with their continent; however, there were survivors of the catastrophe. How could such an important secret be lost forever?

Dakhir shook his head.

— Experience showed that possession of this secret could bring to untold catastrophes and greater caution become necessary. The use of this dangerous force, shrouded in a triple veil of mystery, was kept in the form of undecipherable symbols and was entrusted only to higher initiates. However, strange as it may seem, in the second half of the 19th century it was discovered by a man, who also found a method, through ingenious devices, to use some of its properties, but this led to nothing.

— Who was this man, and what were the causes of the failure that led this phenomenal discovery to be forgotten? — Kalitin asked excitedly. — The 19th century has gone down in history as a time of high culture and great scientific discoveries, which paved the way for the great progress of mankind," said Kalitin.

— You have asked me many questions, which I will try to answer as far as possible. His name was John Worrel Kelly; his life full of sacrifices was a succession of the most tragic episodes of a genius. Everything that envy, petty resentment, slander, disdain, and scorn can conjure up was placed in Kelly's way. It was a characteristic trait of the time in which he lived; there was no "scientist" capable of understanding his colossal work and, within that society, no industrialist, literary man or representative of the clergy, enlightened and altruistic , capable of helping materially the poor inventor, who found himself on the trail of one of the greatest mysteries of nature. They tried to poison him, he was persecuted, called a cheat and a charlatan; the peddlers, eager to profit from his discoveries, but frustrated in their intentions, threatened him with imprisonment. Finally, driven to despair , he destroyed most of his devices and his discovery fell apart.

But this is revolting! — Kalitin was outraged.

— The issue is not as simple as it seems. It is still not possible to say that Kelly's discovery could bring any benefit to mankind by becoming the property of the masses. That was a bad time, the 19th century, which you describe as highly cultured! There is no doubt that science experienced remarkable successes, there were many discoveries, including Kelly's, but the period was marked by the flourishing of the worst human vices: wild selfishness, the ruthless pursuit of pleasures and the rejection of divinity, which plunged the world into a deep materialism, the consequence of which was the paralysis of all sublime feelings. It was precisely in the 19th century that the paradox was born, the worst of all that humanity could have known: the pseudo-humanitarian thesis that justified the most heinous crimes, covering them up under the veil of madness, neurosis, degeneracy and so on . A real incitement to cruelty was practiced, whether through vivisections, political murders, abject weapons of extermination such as explosive bullets, etc. It was from the 19th century onwards that atheism gained momentum, moral decadence began, and unbridled cynicism , which led to the breakdown of society, generated fluidic epidemics of madness, suicides, stupid murders, evoking from chaos the gloomy forces that led the planet to its anticipated destruction. So, imagine Kelly's discovery at the disposal of those "individuals"; anarchists, violent psychopaths, and so on , the "Cains" of the human race. Had they been able to harness ethereal force , they would have annihilated millions of people, in their bloodthirsty fantasy, pulverizing the continent into atoms and perpetuating countless hecatombs. This could not be allowed. The Divine Servants, who watch over the destinies of the world, could not allow malicious and perverted mankind to have at their disposal a force which, in their filthy hands, would be capable of becoming truly diabolical. Kelly's discovery took place many millennia before his time and was therefore doomed to oblivion, mainly due to the lack of knowledge that it is in man himself that the controlling principle of the etheric vibratory force resides. Kelly could not even imagine being one of those rare persons, with special psychic abilities; and he could not pass on to others what were attributes of his own nature. As evidence of this, it is known that Kelly's instruments did not work when operated by others. This alone was an obstacle to his discovery succeeding. The enlightened know that behind the visible phenomena of nature are rational beings, called "forces" or "laws" by humans, who operate the latter, which, in

turn, submit to higher-level beings, considered by the enlightened to be the force and the law.

Just for the reader's benefit, I'm attaching an appendix at the end of the book with information collected on this character - JOHN KELLY. - Typist's note. This conversation impressed Kalitin even more than the previous one. His mind began to have a new vision of the Universe, of its laws, of the Divine and Inscrutable Being, from Whom everything emanated. Every time a new horizon opened up before his mind, his faith was ignited even more, and then he prayed fervently and simply, thanking the Higher Being, the merciful Father of all that exists, for the graces He bestowed on him.

Due to the various resources and special expedients available to carry out the work, the construction of the underground temple was coming to an end, and the magicians were preparing to consecrate it with the first office. For the solemnity, initiates of all degrees gathered at the site. The earthlings were led into an adjoining room. They could not stand the atmosphere of the sanctuary, which was saturated with strong aromas.

A pale, softly bluish light poured into the temple; the iridescent outlines of Kabbalistic signs and hieroglyphs dotted the walls like a phosphoric lattice.

The temple ended in a semicircle; with seven steps leading up to an empty platform for the altar.

In the dark depths of the rock, a circle of multicolored flames was burning; in the center of it, a disk two meters in diameter was shooting out shimmering beams. Around that kind of star, the mysterious and terrifying title of the ineffable and inscrutable Being, around whom the universe is founded and revolves, was engraved in fiery hieroglyphics.

Concentrated and austere, the initiates stood in a semicircle in front of the niche; on one side, the magicians; on the other, the sorceresses; all in white linen robes. First, they said a fervent and silent prayer while genuflecting, and then a majestic chant sounded in a crescendo.

The beautiful melody, sometimes abrupt, sometimes soft, grew louder and louder until its grandeur seemed to shake the whole mountain, even to its base. Gusts of wind swept through the temple; then there was a deafening roar, as if the thunder rolled through the rooms and underground galleries; fiery lightning zigzagged through the air.

Suddenly, with hisses and bangs, a fiery mass rose from the vaults and hit the raised platform at the back of the temple.

When the flame was died down, behind the dissipating smoke, a block of stone was exposed, the same one that had served as an altar next to the last source of primal substance on Earth . Moved by the wizards, the valuable symbol – a sacred reminder of the destroyed world – would once again serve as an altar for the first sanctuary, built by the refugees from Earth in the new world.

Three of the older hierophants, adorned with the shimmering crowns of magicians, placed a large crystal chalice with a crucifix on top, on that mystical altar. Inside the chalice bubbled flaming primal matter, harvested from one of the Nine Fountains of the new world.

From the pyre carved into the rock, in front of the chalice, a flame that would never go out reverberated all the colors of the rainbow.

At the end of the first office, the initiates took an oath: to faithfully fulfill the task entrusted to them, to give all their strength and love to the new land, their final home. At the end of the ceremony, the hymn of thanksgiving was sung, the crowd slowly dispersed, and the phosphoric signs were extinguished, except for the circle with the name of the Ineffable One.

CHAPTER III

The construction of the city of the magicians was proceeding at a good pace. The adept builders were top-notch, all the more so because they had incredible resources at their disposal, since most of the metal and other materials were still in a malleable state, which significantly simplified their use in sculptures. And the fairy-tale city, home of the legendary "earthly paradise", turned out to be a miracle of harmonious beauty and refined art.

In the middle of vast gardens colored by a multitude of flowers and enlivened by fountains, the palaces of the magicians stood, true works of art, both inside and out.

Our old friends settled near each other; their palaces were something extraordinary.

Ebramar's residence was in the center and around it, connected by long colonnades, in a perfect rectangle, were the palaces of Supramati, Dakhir and Narayana and Udea; all of which were of different colors.

Ebramar's palace and the adjoining galleries, imitating four spires, were as white as snow. Supramati's palace seemed to be made of gold; Dakhir's, ruby red; Narayana's, sapphire blue, and Udea's, emerald green.

However, those buildings were not only intended to meet the humble needs of the magicians, they were to provide shelter for a great number of disciples and family members under the tutelage of the great adepts. As soon as the city was officially inaugurated, the organization of family groups was promoted, as well as the beginning of classes in the initiation schools and in the establishments for the teaching of trades, agriculture, and the art of governing the uncultured hordes of aborigines.

The earthlings could not wait for the great festivities for the inauguration of the city to begin; the release of marriages was a source of great anxiety for many. Not everyone accepted the chastity imposed during the years of construction. The fair sex, isolated from men, was under the special surveillance of the initiates, undergoing an education to prepare them for the role of wives and housewives, in very different conditions from those they were used to on Earth.

Generally speaking, the education of that diverse mass of earthlings was difficult and complex, as it was made up of people from different categories, both ethnically and in terms of character, social position and intellectual development. They were believers in God and well-meaning enough, but, despite these virtues, they were people of their time, full of erroneous ideals and vicious culture, too refined and perverted.

Regardless of this, the essence administered produced a strange and miraculous healing in their bodies; their dull, malnourished bodies, with shaken nerves, acquired vigor and life pulsed impetuously, in other words, they became active artisans, fit to build future civilizations and be the ancestors of the most civilized races.

One fine afternoon, after lunch, our old friends were gathered on one of the terraces of the Ebramar's palace, specially built by the purged for the refugees from Earth. They were talking about various catastrophes and cataclysms that would be used in the future as a way of reaching out to the local population. Later, they would be rescued, and the foundation stone would be laid for the knowledge of God and the holding of religious cults, albeit incipient.

Gradually, the conversation took a different turn. The subject of future festivities came up and, above all, the marriage of the magicians only the higher-level initiates remained unmarried). The ceremonies would take place in the underground temple, where the mysterious cubic stone was located, after which the adepts and their wives would be settled in their new homes. The blessing of the act of union of the adepts of lower degrees had been scheduled for the following days.

Udea was not taking part of the last part of the conversation. Looking sad and pensive, he leaned against the railing and, from the expression on his pale, handsome face and his dreamy eyes, seemed to be far away with his thought.

Narayana, who was watching him, slapped him hard on the shoulder with his hand, and he, shuddering, stood up and was so disconcerted that everybody present laughed.

– What are you thinking, incorrigible hermit? Do you not like the subject? Is there anything better in the world than women? That goes for a magician as well as an ordinary mortal. Look , he is counting his fingers and does not give a damn about the conversation! Wake up, my friend, and live life! What are you missing? The trials are over, the past has been erased, a cloudless future looms before us, and the first spark of the wizard's crown shines on your brow. Of course, all this is nice, but a home with all the comforts, a beautiful housewife who loves you, pampers you and makes sure you are well-fed, all this is important and easy to get. Do not forget that!

The incorrigible Narayana's speech caused another burst of laughter, this time accompanied by Udea, who soon realized that having Narayana as a friend, he was in no danger of forgetting the true meaning of life.

When the laughter stopped, Ebramar said jovially :

— Despite the unusual suggestion, I must admit, my friend, that Narayana is right; it will be wise of you to find a life partner. You are dwelling on the past, your difficult times at work, banished on this planet. You have to shake off the dust; love comforts and is the best balm for an ailing soul.

— Just order me... — sighed Udea.

— How can I order things like that?

— Why not? You are my best friend, a tireless protector, who managed to bring me here, to this lost planet. You have supported me, alleviated my sufferings, consoled the banished in the worst moments of his banishment. Who could advise me better? So, I repeat: if you think it's necessary, look for a magician who wants to be my wife.

— It won't be difficult! I bet that many of them secretly long for a party like Udea. It will be difficult to choose," Narayana butted in.

— If you know the intimate desires of our girls so well, then help him in this delicate matter," Ebramar observed mockingly. — With your permission, Udea, I can only suggest who I consider most worthy; but it is you who will have the last word in choosing the companion who will treat the wounds of the past.

— You know, master, if you had a daughter, I would have suspected that you are trying to arrange an advantageous marriage with our mysterious brother of few words. — Narayana joked, laughing and looking mischievously into Ebramar's eyes.

— It is a pity that Ebramar does not have a daughter; I would have married her, certain that everything that comes from our incomparable friend brings good luck," Udea retorted.

—— You're right! That's why I liked you straight away. Seeing your appreciation for Ebramar," Narayana exclaimed in a rush. And the characteristic rapture shone in his big black eyes . —

Look at that! All those gathered here are his spiritual children, a creation, so to speak, of a master who has no parallel. His affection, erudition, and tireless patience have made us what we are now. We must, then, as a family, close ranks around him, united in love and gratitude.

With his eyes watering, Narayana took Ebramar's hand and kissed it. Ebramar quickly pulled it away.

— Stop that, you panderer, and stop singing undeserved praise to me! How can we give credit to a father who strives for his children? This kind of love, a disguised for selfishness and vanity, does not deserve any praise. But I see, Narayana, what you are getting at with your subtle speech. You are curious to know Udea's story, the circumstances that led to the hard trials he endured with such brilliance.

You read my heart like an open book, oh, the best and most perceptive of spiritual fathers! — Narayana laughed. — My curiosity is not frivolous; it is the fruit of sincere affection and the certainty that he needs to open up to his brothers and friends. And to complete it, my friend, I swear, despite my curiosity, to refrain from listening to anything that might cause you any pain, because I know how painful memories are, even for the perfect heart of a magician," Narayana added, squeezing Udea's hand.

Udea stood up, and his dark eyes cast an affectionate look at Narayana.

— You are right, brother, I have no reason to hide the past! My crime justifies the severe punishment of banishment, and so who else but you can I entrust the story of my decadence and atonement?

Glory be to the Ineffable One, whose wisdom and mercy turned a criminal into a useful being, allowing him to evolve and benefit from the gifts of the heavenly Father.

It is true that the sacrifices have been enormous, but only in this way is it possible to tap into the spiritual riches hidden in the recesses of the human being, develop his short-sighted and ignorant intellect, provide him with conscious willpower and arm him with powers over the elements of nature. It is precisely in the furnace of trials, in the alternating battle of defeats and victories, that a new being is formed who begins to intuition of his Creator, and to venerate His immeasurable wisdom and to try to fulfill His will judiciously. Before I go on to tell you about my vicissitudes, I would like to say that the greatest misfortune of mankind, the worst trial for men, which unleashes in them the most harmful instincts, drives them to the precipice and delays their progress towards perfection for a long time, is injustice.

— I agree with you. However, the first notion of justice, innate to man, is not based on his commitment to justice in relation to others, but what he thinks is a prerogative that can be demanded of others in relation to his person," said Ebramar, sighing.

— This is a consequence of their weakness and imperfection. Every being, created by God, carries in their soul a clear notion of the immutable principle of Divine Justice, and, if this principle is disrespected, the victim of the injustice rebels and in their heart begins to foam the bile of hostility, of cruelty, desire for revenge or retaliation. His worst passions flow from the disturbed core of man, and turn him into a demon. It is different for beings evolved in higher spheres, aware of the Law of Karma, which can collapse on them in similar situations; they resist in silence; but what about those who are in the lower steps of ascension? A simple-minded human being nurtures an unshakable faith in their rights, suggested by the incorruptible voice of instinct; moral degradation begins from the moment they become aware that the law of justice does not prevent the stronger from oppressing the weaker. The root of all revolutions and follies is injustice. It is the origin of the decadence of peoples, which inevitably leads to the unleashing of laws, identical to those that govern the Universe.

It is enough to violate the chemical or cosmic laws and soon disintegration ensues which is an imbalance, a destructuring of the elements, in other words: order is only possible through obstinate effort. The elements must be in harmony, balance is only achieved if each atom performs its predetermined function. Injustice, then, is a dissonant principle that breaks harmony, ruins entire nations and populates the world with demonic beings.

Forgive me, brothers, for this digression, the fruit of bitter memories. It was precisely injustice that was the reason for my crimes and sufferings," Udea justified, barely containing his emotions.

I was born as the heir to a powerful king called Pulastia . Nature had been generous with me, but I had an explosive temper, I was extremely arrogant, rebellious, and overly ambitious. I adored my mother, a humble and beautiful woman; to her, I owe all the seeds of good sown in my soul. She was not happy in her marriage. Irascible, perverted and rude, bordering on cruelty, the king did not value my mother , a person of irreproachable morals, enchanting beauty and a rare intelligence. I was her only son and, naturally, she loved me with all the strength in her soul.

With my father, on the other hand, I did not have a friendly relationship. He did not love me and made a point of showing it . Any mischief was cruelly punished; sometimes, in his bad moods, I simply ended up being A scapegoat Such injustices and many other things later gave way in my soul to a spiteful, almost hostile feeling towards him.

My father had a younger bastard son, the fruit of a relationship with my mother's maid . I cannot say what tricks Suami, as he was called, used to win my father's heart,, as he was hideous, gloomy, false, and bad-natured . He hated me, envying me the position of successor to the throne, and always managed to concoct a series of villainies, the consequences of which were harsh punishments for me. Furthermore, if, on the one hand, Suami envied me the position of successor , my father hated the popularity I had among the people, due to the philanthropic acts with my less fortunate future subjects, when I tried to alleviate the evils caused by the injustices and illegalities of the king, for whom there was no law but his will or whims. Imbued with the values of justice, passed down from my mother from a very early age, I tried to be as fair as possible, because I thought that was the main virtue of a king.

The heavy atmosphere at court, created by my father's deaf hostility and Suami's disguised hatred, aggravated my irritation. To stay out of troubles, I devoted myself passionately to hunting and studying of the occult sciences, taught in our temple. It was only later I realized that this was nothing more than a mere abecedary of the remarkable science; however, the fractions of knowledge I gained aroused in me an enormous interest in the subject and I eagerly sought to attain the mysterious powers whose strenght I vaguely sensed. When I turned twenty , my advisor began to urge the king to marry me and my father, begrudgingly, ordered negotiations to begin with the neighboring house.

On that occasion, I distracted myself by hunting in the mountains of one of our far-flung provinces. Brave and agile, I knew no fear and liked to venture into dangerous endeavors. That day, luck did not smile on me. My shotgun did not hit the hunted animal mortally, but it lunged after me, , biting my shoulder and tearing my arm apart with its claws. I lost a lot of blood and fainted. When I woke up, I was very weak; I went out into the forest and ended up getting lost at dusk. It was a real miracle that I was not devoured by predators; the eminence of danger gave me the strength to continue. It was dawn when I saw a large inhabited house, surrounded in the valley by mountains. I crawled to it with the last of my strength.

In a shelter lost among the mountains lived a small community of women dedicated to the veneration of a goddess whose cult resembled that of Vesta. All of them had taken vows of chastity, kept the sacred fire for the goddess and dedicated the rest of their time to prayers and occult sciences. In a nearby cave lived an old sage who was responsible for the virgins' studies. I was well received and treated; no one even asked me who I was. The wise old man turned out to be a wonderful doctor, and my wounds soon healed. Most of the women in the community were old, except for some very beautiful young women. I fell madly in love with one of them , Vaikhari, a stunning beautiful girl, and despite her shyness, I decided to marry her immediately. As I hurried home , I announced my decision to marry Vaikhari to my father, vehemently discarding another suitor.

At first, he ridiculed me; but, after hearing a ecstatic description of the girl's beauty, he pondered and announced his decision to travel with me to the community to ask Vaikhari to agree to be my wife. I was very happy and so we set off in the company of a large retinue, protected by a strong detachment of the army.

We camped in the vicinity of the community; one of my father's advisors was sent with the marriage proposal. Later, the old doctor-priest himself came to the king to tell him that the young priestess had taken vows to serve the divinity and should remain at the temple. However, my father was not a man to submit to the decisions of others; he promptly demanded a personal response from Vaikhari. She came dejected and apprehensive, begging the king not to force her to break the oath to the goddess; but he retorted that refusal could mean the destruction of the temple with all its buildings, and also the beheading of its inhabitants.

Vaikhari ran frightened to the temple to beg the goddess to release her from the oath and save her sisters. Later it was said that as the priestess was bringing an offering to the altar of the goddess and making the smoke, raising her prayers to the divinity, a white dove appeared from the flames, landed on the virgin's shoulder and then took flight; at the same time, the iron ring, which was carried on her finger as a sign of initiation, opened and fell to the ground, as if an acceptance of the goddess' release.

Vaikhari then followed us into the city; I was overjoyed, without suspecting that both my death and my mother's were already sealed in the inhuman heart of my father, who had fallen madly in love with my fiancée.

My kind mother accepted Vaikhari as a beloved daughter. Preparations for my wedding were in full swing, when, on the eve of the ceremony, I received a major blow: my mother was found dead in her bed. She had been bitten by a snake that had lurked, they said, in the flowers brought to decorate her chambers. I became desperate. The wedding was postponed for three months because of the mourning. Those were difficult times, but I became even more attached to Vaikhari, who shared my pain, comforted me and, apparently, began to feel love for me. My father was gloomy, thoughtful, spoke to me little and distracted himself by hunting alone, and sometimes invited me to accompany him. Suami, however, would not let of me or my fiancée. I knew he was spying on us, and his insistence made me furious.

Mourning was coming to an end and I had to accompany my father on a hunt; he was more taciturn than usual and opted for more secluded paths, steeper and more dangerous trails.

- I was following him silently when I spotted a wild goat standing on the cliff. I pointed the animal out to my father and approached the edge of the trail, stretching out my bow, but at that same moment I felt a sharp blow on my back, I staggered, lost my balance and fell... After that, I don't remember anything else... When I came to my senses, I saw that I was in a gorge surrounded by cliffs; the land around me was covered in dense moss, which had probably cushioned the force of my fall. My clothes were torn by the rocks, my body was covered in bruised, and my back hurt terribly. It is difficult to describe my state of mind at the moment I realized that my own father had tried to kill me. At that moment, I thought that his act was intended to ensure Suami's succession, and a terrible hatred for both of them germinated in my heart. I was alive, but the instinct of self-preservation made me try to save myself. I felt that the dagger was still stuck in my back, but I did not want to take it out, so as not to exhaust my strength with more blood loss. Crawling around a small clearing, I discovered a trail that went up in zigzags . I will not try to describe the effort and sacrifice I climbed it; sometimes I faltered, but then I climbed again. Finally, I managed to reach a larger area and with great joy I glimpsed a spring, gushing out of the rocks. I was thirsty and quenched my thirst with cold, crystal-clear water; however, my strength left me and I lost consciousness again.

When I opened my eyes, I found myself in a cave, dimly lit by a torch attached to the wall. I was lying on a bed of moss and leaves, lined with a woolen scarf; an old man kneeling beside me was rubbing my temples with a life-giving aromatic essence, I felt relatively well. My wound was bandaged, it did not hurt much, but my whole body was burning, and my head felt like it was going to explode. Only then did I discover that my life had hung by a thread for a few weeks. When the danger passed, my weakness was such and my strength was so depleted that I could not lift a finger. Recovery was desperately slow.

The good old man, called Pavaka, continued to look after me like a devoted father. Often, and for a long time, I watched him with curiosity, because despite the gray hair and beard, his bronzed face had no wrinkles, and his eyes burned as if he were in the splendor of youth.

Of course, I was worried about my own fate. I imagined the surprise that my appearance would cause, because they would surely considered me dead. I intended to reach a village near the capital, gather the residents, and tell them the whole truth. I was counting on the people to answer my call, dethrone my father and bring justice. In addition to my thirst for revenge, my desire to find Vaikhari devoured me. However, my strength and health were not returning, I coughed blood and at the same time felt a terrible sharp pain in my back and chest.

One day, while taking a short walk with Pavaka's help, and returning to the cave totally weakened, I asked my savior when I would finally recover, as I could not wait to leave.

Pavaka shook his head, gave me something refreshing to drink and said:

— My friend, you are a man, and I think I must tell you the whole truth. You will never recover, because your internal organs have been affected and, if your disease profresses as it is , you have no more than two or three days to live.

Noticing my shock that the revelation had caused me and that blood was flowing to my lips, he added, squeezing my hand:

— Do not despair! There is a way to cure you, to restore your former health, to give you a long life; however, this can only be achieved through many sacrifices.

— What sacrifices? I will do anything, as long as you cure me.

— First of all, you must give up everything in this world.

— I cannot do that, revered Pavaka. I am the successor of a great kingdom and a fiancé in love, whose chosen one probably mourns me like a dead man. Giving her up is harder than life itself.

Pavaka look at me with a sad and pitying look.

— As for that, my son, give up hope! It has been a few weeks since Vaikhari was betrothed to Pulastia and…

I did not hear the end of the sentence. I felt as if I had been hit on the head with a hammer ; at the same time, I felt as if a f fiery saber had been driven into my chest and I saw myself plummeting down a cliff ... Until I lost consciousness.

It was only after two weeks that I opened my eyes, weak and shattered, but fully conscious, remembering everything that had happened. A hurricane was raging in my soul; Pavaka, however, did not allow me to give free rein to my anger, giving me tranquilizers that made me sleep almost uninterruptedly, and so my strength began to return.

Once, feeling a little more vigorous than usual, I took the old man's hand and said :

— I have a great request for you, Pavaka. You are a wise man; give me a medicine that will give me strength just for a few weeks. I do not want to survive. I want to revenge on the monster who ruined my life, deprived me of everything I cherished; he murdered my mother, I am convinced of that, and took possession of my fiancée.

- I wanted to tell him the whole story, but I saw that Pavaka already knew everything; to my words he reacted unfavorably, shaking his head.

— I agree that your father is a monster; revenge, however, is pointless nonsense, believe me! I have no conditions for your request; I can either restore your health and give you a long life, or let you die here. But think well before you decide! Suppose I accept your request, and you manage to get to the capital, dethrone and kill your father, what would you get out of it? A brief reign of a few months, poisoned by remorse and suffering of death, not to mention the fact that it would be impossible for you to possess the woman you love? If, on the other hand, you spontaneously master your vain greed , renounce fleeting power and the woman separated from you by an abyss, you will consolidate a life of hundreds of years, immortal youth and beauty, and the doors of the temple of knowledge will open before you. I can see from your aura that you have a powerful and energetic mind, a sign that you will be able to attain knowledge that will arm you with practically unlimited powers. What is the point of ruling over a rude and ungrateful mob if you can command the elements of nature, rule over armies of servile creatures who will carry out your every command?

Pavaka withdrew, telling me to think about it and make a decision on my own ; but my energetic temperament helped me to overcome my indecision quickly. For the first time after being wounded, I coldly assessed my situation. My physical state was proof that the earthly body was beginning to decay, and death, I must admit, frightened me greatly. However, the offer of an enigmatic future was attractive to me. What could I regret in the world if Vaikhari was irretrievably lost? When Pavaka returned, I told him my intention to renounce earthly possessions to become an adept and devote myself entirely to science.

I did not pay much attention at that moment to the enigmatic smile that appeared on the old man's face. He only replied that my wish would be fulfilled; as soon as I took the oath, he would give me the healing medicine.

After helping me to my feet, he opened a door at the back of the cave that moved on invisible hinges, hidden behind a rock, and led me to a spacious grotto whose existence I had not suspected. A faint bluish light illuminated the room; at the bottom, at the height of some steps carved in the rock, there was a table covered with a tablecloth, woven with gold threads.

On that kind of altar, there were two seven-armed candlesticks, in the center of which there was a chalice crowned by a golden cross and a metal box, sparkling with precious stones. In the two side tripods, the essentials were smoked. Next to the entrance there was a pond, into which a mineral spring flowed.

Pavaka ordered me to undress and then dive into the water, which I did with great effort. He then rubbed my body with an aromatic essence and dressed me in a long white robe.

I felt very refreshed, even though I was very weak. Pavaka held me and led me to the altar; I knelt down on the first step. Then, opening the metal chest, he took out a flask, a partially filled crystal chalice and a golden spoon. He poured a few drops from the flask into the chalice; the liquid seemed to fizz, and a red vapor rose, mixing with fiery rays. Then Pavaka ordered me to swear an oath, and I did so, repeating his words with difficulty, for I was still weak; then he ordered me to take the chalice.

Shaking in waves of heat, I lost consciousness, and a dream, or lethargy, lasted a long time, because as it turned out later, during that time I had been on a long journey; when I woke up, I found myself in one of the distant Himalayan palaces where adepts undergo their first initiation.

Pavaka told me the truth. There was not a trace of my disillusioning illness left ; I was as strong and healthy as ever and I immediately began my studies. I worked tirelessly ; the masters were amazed at my successes. I bravely endured the trials that increased my knowledge, disciplined my willpower and made me master my weaknesses. I was thrilled by the mysteries I had achieved and intoxicated by the powers I had acquired. Time, however, passed imperceptibly.

After completing difficult tasks in science, which I did brilliantly, I was awarded the first torch of the magician's crown; later, after a short rest, my masters announced that the time had come for me to begin the ordeal that corresponded to my degree, which consisted of going as a prophet to a distant country to preach the principles of good and raise the morality of its inhabitants, who were steeped in vices.

The chief magician asked me the usual questions: if I felt strong enough to endure the sacrifices and humiliations, repaying evil with good, offenses and ingratitude with love; and eventually to seal the truth of the doctrine preached with my own blood, under no circumstances revealing my origin and my powers. Without hesitation, I answered that I accepted the test and that I hoped to fulfill it worthily.

I did not realize the presumption of my answer; I was blind to my weaknesses, imagining myself invulnerable from my position .

Udea was silent for a moment and ran his hand over his pale forehead; a bitter smile of disgust froze on his lips.

— I was frivolous," he continued, strutting. — Despite my knowledge, I d was anaware of how complex and difficult it was to govern, using the authority of the forces of good, in the face of the stubborn and rebellious human crowd. Surrounded by the calm and harmonious atmosphere of my studies, I completely forgot about the forces of resistance, hatred, and vice that inhabit the human heart; I forgot that it was easier to tame a bunch of wild animals than a crowd of degenerate bipeds, greedy for pleasure, cruel and vain of being "people", believing they had taken a great step that distinguished them from animals; while preserving all their animal instincts, they have only freed themselves from the reins that nature created for lower beings. With their presumption, hypocrisy, ingratitude, ambition and cold cruelty, human beings surpass all animals. Blinded by conceit, I did not realize the danger that lurked whitin me; because of my vanity, I considered myself capable of taming others and myself.

The masters seemed disappointed with me, but Ebramar looked at me sadly and whispered:

— Brother, ask for a postponement, fortify yourself with prayers and prepare yourself for your sublime mission. Do not underestimate the danger that surrounds you! The inevitability of an elightened person's contact with the mob, with the consequent absorption of their contagious emanations, demands a difficult battle. Give yourself some time before engaging with the people if you are not sure of victory.

Oh, if only I had followed the wise advice! But, no! Thinking that it was the result of excessive zeal, I did not want to wait any longer, aiming to climb the hierarchical ladder quickly, and I left...

One night, one of the higher magicians took me to a distant country, where I work, and put me up in a cave:

"You are going to live here in isolation; a few hours away, on foot, you will find a village with a large number of sick and obsessed people. Your mission is to treat them, to attract general attention and take advantage of the situation to start preaching."

At dawn, I set off The surroundings seemed familiar, but I paid no attention , absorbed in my thoughts, and soon I reached the valley, where, surrounded by gardens, a huge city spread out. As soon as I had walked a few streets, I was perplexed.

Before me stood the great temple, which I knew so well, and which was the main sanctuary of my homeland. So many times, I had climbed those steps, accompanying my father to some religious ceremony. It was there that I should have reigned, yet they sent me to dogmatize my own people. Stunned and overcome with emotion, my eyes watered; everything in me trembled, thousand of memories flooded back .

But I didn't have much time to indulge in the memories. From a nearby house a man and a woman came running out , all in rags, with disheveled hair, foaming at the mouth, their faces disfigured by convulsion; they were howling like madmen and were so disgusting. Behind them, a group of people were running in pursuit, trying to grab them. The sight instantly reminded me of my mission and the masters' instructions.

Putting my memories aside, I raised my hand and both obssessives stood still in their places. I approached them, made some passes, pronounced abjurations that expelled the demons of the unfortunates and managed to free them.

A crowd then formed around them, and seeing that the formerly possessed had come to t heir senses, some people approached me and told me, trembling with superstitious fear, that the city was suffering from a violent general dementia. The terrible evil forgave no one; old or young - everyone. Anyone suffering from delirium would try to strangle the first person who came along; they would perpetrate all kinds of indecencies in the public streets and, some time later, they died in terrible pain . The worst thing was that the disease was contagious, and often those who helped or grabbed the insane became victims of the same disease . To reduce the incidence of the epidemic, the king had all those who showed signs of insanity arrested and sent to a camp outside the city, surrounded by guards.

I ordered them to take me to that place and I confess that I had a lot of work to do to expel the armies of maggots and other demonic spirits; but after a few hours I managed to control the situation.

After that victory over the darkness, I gave a lecture, explaining that the cause of that evil was the people's crimes and depravity . Finally, I announced that I could be found in the cave in the desert valley, where there was a spring, and that all the sick should be taken there.

I returned to my room in a terrible state of mind. Memories came flooding back like an avalanche; the past came to life as if it had happened the day before and took hold of me. I did everything I could to fulfill my duties. I healed the sick and preached to ever-increasing crowds, but I avoided going to the city for fear of the impression it would make on me.

Thus, the days went by in exhausting work, while the nights were a real martyrdom, as the past loomed ever larger. I already knew at the time that around three centuries had passed since the day I disappeared , but that our clan still ruled there. I also knew that Vaikhari had died giving birth to a daughter, who later married the neighboring king; Pulastia had passed away very old, leaving the throne to Suami. As for me, they thought I had perished by falling into the abyss.

The current young king was called Pulastia, just like my father. They said he was also cruel and explosive. He was about to marry a stunning beautiful princess, a relative of his.

When I heard about the bride's official visit to the capital, I wanted to see the two bethrothed, who had taken my rightful place t.

The whole city was decked out as if for a party. Despite my popularity, the people's attention was focused on other things that day; so, the only distinction I had was the chance to sit in the front row, very close to the royal palace.

Soon the procession appeared. The king's face was familiar to me, but the sight of the bride, covered in jewels and sitting in the carriage, had a devastating effect on me, so much so that I let out a deafening scream. She was a living portrait of Vaikhari.

My cry was heard by the king, who turned his head in my direction in surprise and looked at me with disdain. Our gazes met and at that moment I recognized his eyes. To the enlightened gaze of a magician, the mystery of the past had been unveiled: before me was my old father reincarnated...

A minute later, the procession disappeared inside the palace; I hurried to mingle with the crowd and returned to the cave.

The night that followed that day was a nightmare. In a few hours, the serene harmony of the magician collapsed; from the unknown depths of my being came impetuous gusts of the passions that I thought had been mastered and forgotten; with astonishing speed, the ancient man swelled up in me, swallowing and sinking the adept; in my heart germinated the irresistible desire to occupy the throne of the ancestors. To rule the people who loved me. In the same way, my passion for Vaikhari was rekindled. The past centuries did not count; I was living in the present, resurrected, and my soul was in a real hurricane at the thought of the man who had killed my mother, being the living incarnation of Vaikhari. As if I could not be happy! I was more beautiful and powerful than my rival, whose only advantages were title and wealth. I was overcome by the uncontrolable urge to exchange my rough leather garments for the purple clothing and imperial jewels, to win the heart of the beautiful bride.

Numbed by impure feelings, I did not notice Sarmiel's pulsating servants around me, although I did not stop paying attention to their suggestions either.

"— The consummation of your will is an inalienable right! The encounter with the murderer who forgot his paternal duty is a work of the law of karma, which will strike the criminal down with the hand of his own victim! Who will stop him from becoming a monarch later on, so that he can do even more good, sow faith in the Divinity, heal and polish his people? Imagine the fascinating advantage of being a king and not a wandering beggar among this rabble!".

- In my imagination, the advantages of glory and love loomed large. Sweating profusely, my heart pounding with tempestuous passions, I still put up some resistance to temptation; I did not summon the masters and protectors, for fear that they would forbid me to use my powers. And nothing stopped my madness; I remained the complete master of my actions and hidden powers.

The last scruples quickly dissipated, and when the first rays of the sun illuminated the sky, my plan was already in place; the invisible forces that would perpetrate my intentions were already at work. I was no longer in a position to fight against the malevolent emanations of the passions that had arisen in my soul, I was a terrifying sorcerer, a great sage; I lacked the spiritual essence of a true prophet, who sacrifices his life for the truth he proclaims.

At dawn, Pulastia, fell ill. Her whole body was writhing in pain and covered in abscesses and sores; as the normal remedies did not help, I was called. My fame had reached the palace, and I was the object of the princess's curiosity; in addition, her younger sister had suffered from epilepsy since childhood, and also wanted to see me.

For the journey to the palace, I dressed in a long white tunic, with a simple silver sash, and a muslin turban on my head. I knew I looked beautiful, and through the princess' eyes, I felt that I had enslaved her heart.

I treated the ilnesses of the queen's sister and Pulastia; I severely warned the latter for his crimes and injustices, which were known to all. I announced that these acts were precisely the causes of his illness and that, in order to be definitively cured, he should remit his guilt with penances and isolate himself for thirty days in the temple. Out of the city.

Furious, but frightened, Pulastia obeyed; while I, barely disguising my malicious glee, watched him leave the palace, where he would never return.

The way to the throne was clear. Without hesitation, I set out to win the sympathy of the people, whom I come to rescue from morality and convert them to God. To this end, I perpetrated a series of catastrophes.

I began with an epidemic, which was soon eradicated; I applauded a hurricane, appearing before the terrified crowd in flames and lightning. Finally, I evoked a terrible deluge, whose waters flooded the capital and its surroundings; that's when Pulastia drowned. During this last cataclysm, I appeared above the raging waves, surrounded by a flaming halo, commanding armies of elemental spirits and pronouncing formulas against the waters, which soon returned to their beds, obeying my will.

The people considered me a benefactor-god and offered me the crown and, as a wife, the bride of the deceased king. I accepted. The wedding and coronation took place with unprecedent pomp. The young wife adored me, the people worshiped me and I, intoxicated with love and power, was proud and happy.

Thanks to my magical knowledge, a fabulous fertility boosted the country, provoking the envy and hostility of the neighbors. Instead of using my knowledge to calm and benefit the neighboring peoples, I decided to punish them for their insolence and envy. Oh, how far I went down the way of evil!

A devastating war broke out. One of the kings, who was hostile to me, was captured and, sentenced to death by me; his country was annexed to my kingdom. However, I was less fortunate with another adversary, and my army suffered so many losses that total defeat became inevitable. I personally took part in the fighting and fought furiously. Inebriated with blood and fury, I decided to summon my magical powers to help me, and began to revive soldiers, heal the wounded, and materialize the dead with maggots and demonic spirits. And these unusual armies brought victory. Like a devastating hurricane, I swept through the conquered country with my army, which I announced would be annexed to mine, and, along with a huge booty, I took the imprisoned king with me.

After that victory, won thanks to the help of evil, I took a liking to black magic; I also feared retaliation from the masters for deviating from their precepts. Sarmiel, who watched over my decline, took advantage of my insanity by helping me learn evil, through his servants. I finally had a meeting with him, and an agreement was made whereby the Prince of Darkness undertook to assist me in all my endeavors, and to provide me with the lugubrious armies of his servants; while I, for my part, undertook the obligation not to put into practice the "foolish" instructions of the magicians, in order to avoid recruiting souls to supply the armies of evil.

In vain my wife begged me to pardon the captured king and give up a new war; I would not listen to her. I became insolent due to impunity, and was intoxicated with my hidden power, with the honors bestowed upon me, with the superb conscience of having increased the territory of my kingdom, and finally with the gratitude of the people, proclaiming me a genius for my great deeds, with practically no human losses.

My second son was born and I decided to mark this happy event and, at the same time, the glorious end of the last war, with a great feast in the palace and other popular celebrations. On the day of these festivities, all the important personalities gathered: courtiers, civilians and military personnel; food was served and gifts were distributed in the palace squares and cortyards.

During the banquet, the sky was suddenly covered in black clouds and thunderstorms drowned out the music. The guests had already drunk too much, and I overdid it with strong wine. The storm, which was disturbing our fun, possessed me; I got up with the intention of performing a sconjuration against the storm and showing everyone my power over the elements. Just then, a bolt of lightning struck and set the room on fire. I felt a sharp pain in my chest, the flames engulfed me, and an agitated wind swept me up , whirling me around like a dry leaf. Finally, I felt as if a hammer had hit me on the head and I lost consciousness…

CHAPTER IV

When I regained consciousness, I found myself in a semi-dark place; I was so weak that I could not move or think. Gradually, my head began to work, my eyes became accustomed to the surroundings and I realized that I was lying on a bed of moss in a small underground room, covered in a wool blanket. There were no windows or doors, only a faint greenish light filtered down from the ceiling. On one side of the wall there was a stone tank with a spring trickling ou of it on the other side there was a bench and table, on which lay a clay mug and a cup , and next to it a piece of bread.

I was in a dungeon, but where? For what reason? However, the disordered thoughts did not give me an answer and I fell asleep exhausted. Waking up was horrible. My memories came back, and then I realized that the masters had put an end to my crimes and abuses by striking me with a thunderbolt and locking me in the dungeon.

No matter how much of a scoundrel I had been, I was a member of the brotherhood and should be judged. A cold sweat covered my forehead.

I cannot say how long that mad despair lasted, but the evil miasma emanating from the soul tickened and filled the room with a fetid smell; my body was covered in ulcers and sores. The bodily sufferings were so dreadful that they overwighed those of the spirit.

Finally, after some time rolling around with terrible pain in my lair, Ebramar came to my aid for the first time; and his kind voice whispered in my ear, "Pray. Udea. Repent, purify yourself with humility, otherwise you will not be able to appear before your judges. Any kind of penance is better than this inactivity that gives you disconnected thoughts and excites your passions".

The stream of light he gave me made me feel surprisingly better; just knowing that I still had a friend who had not abandoned me, and whose affection made him look for me out in the dungeon, turned my soul around.

With my eyes burning and my heart pounding, I saw a stream of light concentrated on a radiant crucifix, consecrating the stone reservoir. The sacramental symbol of eternity and atonement illuminated the dungeon with a soft bluish light; its rays emanated life-giving aromas and warmth. I still had a sense of the undefeated power of this symbol, known to the enlightened as the Seal of the Sublime, and I suddenly had an irresistible urge to seek shelter under the shadow of the cross to re-establish my former purity; I crept to the repository. In the midst of a feverish nervousness, tears finally gushed from my eyes; beating my forehead on the floor, I murmured a prayer.

From that day on, I prayed uninterruptedly; every day I bathed in the reservoir, and every time, a sticky, fetid substance came out of my body. Little by little the pain went away and the heaviness in my body eased; it became easier and easier to concentrate on my prayers. The outbursts of regret for having allowed myself to indulge in the pernicious dazzle of passions became more frequent.

One day, as I was wailing and praying , begging the merciful Creator for forgiveness, I heard the distant ringing of bells; my heart froze. Immediately, I realized that it was the hour of my trial A minute later, I felt suspended in the air, soaring gently toward the vaults. There, where I had seen a greenish light, it turned out that there was an opening, enough for me to pass through; once I had passed through, I found myself in a long, vaulted corridor; at the back there was a door, which I went to as if pulled by an invisible force, and the opening closed.

The door opened silently and before me stood the gallery of one of our temples; the bells tinkled monotonously as if at a funeral; I was standing next two well-known adepts; dejected, with tears in their eyes, they took off my ragged robes, dressed me in a black robe with a white sash , placed a lighted red candle in my hand and, through a long, dark corridor, led me to the door and then left

With a heavy heart and anguish in my soul, I stood at the threshold. I was exactly in that room of the temple, known as the tribunal At the back, in a semicircle, my masters, the wizards, and the hierophants presided; since I was a wizard, decorated with the first torch, I could only be judge by wizards of higher rank , so the remaining part of the temple was empty. The looks on everyone's faces were full of sadness; overcome by a feeling of shame and despair, my knees trembled, the candle fell, and, covering my face with my hands, I began to cry bitter tears.

Never so clearly, as in that minute, did I recognize my mistake and the depth of my fall.

— Get up, unfortunate man! Our hearts bleed at the sight of your headless brow, reduced to ashes, already adorned with the glow of knowledge," said one of the grand-magicians. — To everyone's misfortune, Udea, we cannot let you live with us. Your crimes, being a magician, are terrible; moreover, you possess knowledge too powerful to be able to blend in with the crowd, and your abuses of power have unfortunately proved it.

— I have no more knowledge. I am more ignorant and blind than a mere mortal," I stammered resignedly.

— We had to deprive you of the ability to do evil until your fate is determined. However, we do not want your immense work to come to nothing. Despite of your mistakes and decadence, we love you and would like you to walk the path of repentance and purification, submitting voluntarily to our decision. Ordinary human beings see in the sentence of the judges nothing more than a revenge for disobedience to establish laws, whereas, in reality, it is a form of reparation.

— I submit to the sentence! — I said.

— Then listen to what we have decided. You will go to a totally different world, where we will meet after the destruction of this planet. On that earth there will be a lot of work and the level of humanity there is close to that of an animal. The knowledge, that gives you your powers, can only be used for good, because it will be impossible for you to seduce an inferior humanity that is incapable of understanding you. However, your commitment, will be to enlighten these people; by fulfilling this mission of hard work you will atone for the past and be rehabilitated . We do not hide that your ordeal will be very hard and the work colossal; so, we offer you another option.

You have irretrievably lost the right and the possibility os staying in this world, due to your immortality and the possession of terrible knowledge. So, if the purge seems too severe and difficult , you could die a slow and painful death. In this case, you will take a portion that will decompose the body, cell by cell, slowly absorbing the primal matter, leaving your astral body exposed. At the end of this destructive process , you will go into space to be reborn, but already as a mortal; then, gradually, through countless reincarnations, you will be able to regain some of your current knowledge. Now, the choice is yours!

I was terrified of the idea of leaving Earth for a distant and unknown world; moreover, I did not fully understand the true meaning of the sentence. To order forced labor, and the most arduous. The other option, which threatened me with the loss of the knowledge I had acquired and banishment from the brotherhood, to which I was proud to belong, seemed to me the darkest imaginable. So I accepted, without hesitation, to atone for my guilt and regain everyone's trust through hard work.

The magicians celebrated my decision and showed great affability, perhaps, out of pity for someone condemned to death. They gave me some time to rest and recover my strength; I took advantage of Ebramar's company, who, with solidarity and influence, refreshed my mood, comforted and encouraged me.

Finally, the day of departure arrived, and I went to receive the solemn blessing for my day's work. As I knelt before the chief magician, he blessed me, anointing my forehead with oil and sprinkling me with holy water; and from the eyes of the great hierophant, a sparkling ray shot out and struck my forehead.

An indescribable sensation overwhelmed me then. My brain seemed to be free of something cold and heavy; I understood at that moment that I was recovering my knowledge and this, I knew, it was even clearer and more powerful than before. I felt enormous happiness and the prospect of atonement was no longer anguishing; in a burst of faith, I vowed to work tirelessly and to be a submissive instrument of the Creator's will.

I said goodbye to the brother magicians and the adepts; the great hierophant gave me a warm liquid in the chalice, and I drank it. Ebramar helped me to lie down on the bed and I fell asleep, lulled by powerful sounds; it seemed that harmonic waves were nestling me in space; soon afterwards I lost consciousness…

I woke up in a small cave; a pale bluish light poured into the room like steam. I felt a strong pressure in my head, my legs and arms went numb, and I had no idea where I was. Rising to my feet, I examined everything around me and only then did my memory return and my heart beat faster . Curious and disoriented, I took a close look at my new home with its belongings left behind , miserable remnants of the bright past.

At the back of the cave, I saw an altar with a seven-armed candlestick , a chalice topped by a golden crucifix, a magic aurifulgid cross – a gift from the hierophant on the solemnity of initiation – and a book with a metal binding. On one of the walls, on top of the shelves, there were parchments, manuscripts and books, , a veritable library that allowed – as I discovered later – the continuation of my studies.

In the center, I noticed a large stone table and a stool made of the same material; on the table there was a lamp, of a type that is still unknown. There were also two large boxes with utensils and belongings necessary for toileting, as well as superfluous offal, which Ebramar had kindly provided me with. In the chest next to the table, there was everything that could be useful for magical actions, : tripods, instruments, incense, herbs and various potions.

The adjoining cave had a deep reservoir that received crystal clear water from a mine in the rock and, next to it, a stone bench and a bed of moss, covered by thick blanket. Two large chests held the costumes: dark leather and wool - for work -; linen -for religious ceremonies-. Right there I found a hooded cloak and sandals made of leather and woven straw. On a small table next to the bed was my crystal harp and a large parchment with the seal of the chief hierophant. After unrolling it, I read a message that read roughly as follows: "You find yourself, my son, in a wild and desolate place, but full of natural riches, the exploitation of which is within the reach of your powers and knowledge. Use them and you will generate the desired abundance. Knowledge will make you master of the elements; in the library at your disposal, you will find all you need to increase your strength and broaden your knowledge.

"Study, but do not rush, because haste is synonymous with imperfection. By working, you will not notice the time passing, and you will not know boredom: a scourge of the lazy and root of all crimes. Those who work devour time. You know that for thought, there is no distance, so, your call for advice or support will reach our hearts and ears." Next came instructions on the diary I should keep to record my work and the development of the planet

Despite the great hierophant's words of consolation , I felt discouraged and weak. To distract myself, I went out to explore the surroundings. I had barely taken a few steps. I froze in horror. My shelter was nothing more than an artificially excavated cave , or the work of nature itself, inside an enormous dark and bare rock that stood alone in the middle of the plain. In the distance, as far as the eye could see, stretched a marshy region, from which steamy clouds rose; in some places geysers projected pebbles high into the air.

The air was heavy and dense, saturated with sulphuric evaporation; a curtain of gray mist covered the sky, letting in only the pale daylight , which cast a lilac haze over the horizon.

I had already undergone a fertilization test in a deserted and sterile place, but that had been child's play compared to what I would have to do. My heart squeezed painfully.

In that swampy desert, where you could not even see a moss , I was alone with the mission of facing a disgusting nature in the midst of an irritating semi-darkness, breathing air that almost made me lose my senses. I ran back to the cave and dropped to the ground.

My head was spinning, my heart was racing, and my breathing was panting. I thought I was dying, but then I remembered my immortality and became more desolate.

The task entrusted to me seemed beyond my strength; to live there would be sheer endless agony, since dying was impossible.

It was difficult. It was the worst moment of my life. Suddenly, in a soothing whisper, I heard the ineffable voice of Ebramar:

"— Cheer up, Udea! Pray and you will find strength for everything."

I shuddered and stood up. Then I was alone; there was a being who cared about the banished. And the faithful friend was right; before beginning the gigantic work, it was necessary to purify myself and strengthen myself in prayer.

I shook off the stupor, put on the white robe, and began to pray and chant magical hymns under the sound of the crystal harp. Caught up in the ecstasis of prayer, I felt the sounds of the instrument become more powerful; the air trembled and oscillated and my cave was filled with light; a purple essence poured from above into the chalice, emanating steam. I took the essence, and the mysterious liquid spread in an fiery stream throughout my being, giving me miraculous strength. Never had I felt so vigorous, never had my brain worked so easily , and never had my knowledge been so clear.

I left the cave again, but this time the gloomy picture of nature suggested neither fear nor disgust; I only saw a field of work. Wasting no time, I set to work. First, I evoked the fluidic colossi of nature; the rational forces of fire and air, water and earth; and these workers, subjugated to my will and wisdom, joined me like four clear rays and became my helpers and servants.

The chaos of the enraged elements often roared around me again, but aware of my power over the armies of astral workers, my fear disappeared, and the excitment reached such a level that I did not feel the slightest bit tired.

On the day when my first efforts were successful, when the noxious evaporation dispersed and a little corner of blue sky and the king star appeared, an ardent prayer of thanks to the Ineffable Being, Creator of all those wonders, gushed from my heart.

The tendency of primitive peoples to deify the sun is natural and understandable; they sense that it is from the sun that the source of life emanates.

It was with this powerful collaborator that I continued my work. Under the effect of its flaming rays, the earth breathed; the swamps disappeared; the traces of the earth's aura, which contained the constituent substances of visible forms, quickly materialized, and the ground was covered with exuberant vegetation.

Admiring the incredible landscape, the fruit of my work and knowledge, I was overflowing with satisfaction at having done my job. But I was alone, always alone... Sometimes, my soul, anguished by the longing for my homeland, yearned to hear human voices and the to rest my tired mind. In those moments, I always counted on Ebramar's friendship and a blessed forgetfulness closed my eyes. Then I would see my friend; his warm, translucent hand would rest on my forehead; his eyes look at me with affection and I would feel my being impregnated with a life-giving warmth, different to that provided by the energy of nature. I felt the current of love spreading through my being. It is not by chance that love generates happiness, because it is a peculiar substance whose power affects even the enlightened .

Once, during an apparition, Ebramar said to me:

"— Put on your cloak, Udea, and pick up your staff and your harp; then keep going until you find what you want so badly."

He smiled, squeezed my hand and... I opened my eyes.

After saying an ardent prayer, I took the aforementioned objects and left the cave, the place of my torture and hard work. The road seemed endless; I first crossed the lands that were my spiritual possessions, then I crossed unknown plains with luxuriant vegetation and gigantic, unusual animals. The beasts, however, ran away frightened when they smelled a strange odor, typical of initiates.

Finally, I reached a wide river. The access to the other side was downhill; the opposite bank – a rocky slope – rose in terraces framed by dark forest.

The cries of birds and the noisy flapping of wings caught my attention. Then, I saw a huge white phoenix; on its long tail and wings, its winged plumage was mixed with turquoise feathers, its head, denoting intelligence, was adorned with a golden tuft.

I gasped with joy as I recognized the mystical bird, the winged messenger of the magicians. The bird flew along the bank; I followed it until I came across a gigantic tree lying across the river and forming a bridge. That took me to the opposite bank.

My winged guide waited for me and ran off inthe direction of the forest, sometimes turning his little head to make sure I was following . As we entered the forest, I was pleased to see that we were following a passable path, that snaked between the trunks of the centuries-old giants; their huge branches intertwined to create an enormous canopy, through which a greenish half-light filtered through.

After an hour's walk, we came out into a wide clearing; suddenly I could not hold back a cry of exclamation; before me loomed a portentous sphinx, had it not been reddish. But from the whiteness of the snow, I would say that it was identical to the Earth. On the top of the Klafta that covered its head, an emerald light shone down; at its feet, in an open position, was a flat, tall block of rock with cabalistic signs and inlays. A brilliant light filtered out from inside. In the meantime, my splendid winged guide let out a joyf, fluttered his wings and flew away, while I stood still in indecision

Suddenly, a tall man , in a long white suit appeared in the doorway, with an insignia shining on his chest; his head was also adorned with Klafta. It is difficult to express the feeling of happiness I felt when I saw him. Unable to utter a single syllable, as a spasm caught in my throat, I threw myself at the stranger's feet. He hastened to lift me up again with his strong arm and said to me in a deep and harmonious voice:

— Udea, my son, do you not recognize me?

Without stopping trembling , I stared at him and then I recognized in him one of the great hierophants, Narada, for whom I felt a great appreciation because of his wisdom and inexhaustible kindness.

"— Master!" I exclaimed, kissing his hand."

"— How did you get here?".

"— Come on, let's talk!" — He said, leading me down the corridor illuminated by phosphoric spheres.

We entered a small room decorated with many comfort objects , which I had not seen for a long time. He made me sit down and said:

—" Did you askme how I ended up here? Have you forgotten that many of our brothers and sisters, on attaining higher knowledge, have voluntarily retired to this place to guide and support those who came here banished to atone for their guilt? Some of them, for various reasons, had to return to Earth; so I was one of those who wanted to replace them here".

The joy of finally meeting a human being again, and even more so a master, with whom I could talk, moved me so much that my eyes watered. Narada put his hand on my head and said in a participatory tone:

"— Calm down, my son! I see that the worst part of your atonement is over; now you can rest and, later , I will show you many interesting things that are already beautifying our new home."

I lifted my head; the magician's gaze revived and calmed me; such was the understanding of human weaknesses manifested by those impenetrable eyes, combined with the condescension of infinite love.

"Master, are there many purged brothers here like me? — I asked, calmer now.

"Yes, about a hundred. They are scattered all over the huge continent; later I will introduce them to you so that you can work together, but before that you need to rest. Come on, I want to show you our temporary facilities".

Narada occupied three rooms. One was the library, the second was a well-equipped laboratory with various instruments, and the third was his bedroom, which also served as his workplace. The next room was assigned to me, and soon I was sound asleep in a comfortable bed.

The days that followed were indescribably pleasant; I rested physically, while the meetings with the master were an inspiration for the soul.

Several times in our conversations we touched on the subject of the Earth and the master gave me the pleasant satisfaction of seeing Ebramar and exchanging a few words with him. Once, while examining some new instruments in the laboratory and asking how they worked, I remembered having heard before that the masters communicated with other planets; so, I took the opportunity to ask Narada if he had any contact with our old Earth. Narada smiled and said:

— You cannot get used to considering this place of banishment as your new home. That is a mistake of your part, because both this world and that one, are pearls in the crown of the Creator, where He has lavished His Gifts. Yes, I communicate with my brothers and sisters and, since this satisfies you, I will show you the apparatus I normally use, but we will have to wait for nightfall.

As night fell, Narada took me to one of the neighboring buildings. It was a very tall stone tower, and we went up a spiral staircase. There, on a kind of base, was an instrument in the shape of a telescope – later invented on Earth – . At the end of the long tube was a movable disk, internally covered with a gelatinous substance, variegated by thin, phosphorescent lines.

"— With this apparatus, we can see what is happening on our old Earth. The enlightened notables , however, from all the worlds of our system, use more sophisticated apparatus."

— And which of the planets is the most interest; which is the most evolved? The level of Earth leaves much to be desired, although the world we are on is already populated by savages! — I observed.

— Do not talk like that! Why so much disdain for this poor world? You know from experience that where you came from, not everything is all virtue and harmony; the people who live there are quite debauched. The most evolved of the planets in our system is the sun; it is forbidden to the lower races and there is no death there.

— What I mean is that the beings who inhabit the sun have reached such a state of perfection that they are able to pass on to the higher systems without physical death. A sun always presents itself as the last level of each system and, as strange as it may seem to na unversed person, the sun is inhabited, even though no man-made instrument would be able to show what is behind the fiery curtain of the king star.

But, let us get back to our subject of communication with Ebramar. Sit in your chair and bring your eye closer to this opening.

I settled in while Narada pressed a button; suddenly, the disk began spinning with impressive speed. At first, I could make out nothing but fiery scratches. After a while, the frequency of the rotation slowed down and a huge dark mass seemed to approach. Soon the outlines of a large continent appeared; the objects became sharper and sharper, and I could already make out mountains, valleys, etc. The impression I had was that I was sitting by the window and that local panoramic pictures were passing by me. Suddenly, my heart beat intensely, the place was familiar to me: Ebramar's palace appeared, surrounded by gardens and, on the avenue leading to the terrace, I glimpsed the wizard himself with a scroll in his hand. He also seemed to look at me, greet and smile. Seeing my friend again and the places where I had spent so many happy days, I was so moved that my head was dizzy. I straightened up and the images from the device stopped.

Narada put his hand on my head and, a minute later, I had calmed down.

— Are you using etheric vibration to focus on objects? — I asked.

— Yes. You know how sensitive this substance is; by learning the laws of its control, you can achieve surprising results. Thought is nothing more than a more perfected form of the same miraculous and sensitive substance. Where is the limit of the power of thought? What is the place it cannot reach? What distance, what space, does it not travel faster than light, oblivious to any obstacle? If it is done well , it can leave its mark . Let's do a little experiment . Let's go down to the laboratory!

Once in the laboratory, Narada picked up a disk, the surface of which was covered with a layer of a gray, gelatinous substance. At the edge, a small spiral , as thin as a strand of hair, was attached to it, the tip of which ended in a tiny needle, which glowed white when the master touched the bottom of the spiral with his hand.

— Now concentrate hard to see my thought, which will fly like a messenger to Ebramar, so that he can print some words on this disk.

He concentrated; a translucent sphere seemed to form on his forehead, reflecting the image of Narada himself, and from the sphere flashed a fiery ray that disappeared into space, leaving a phosphoric trail. A second later, a second clear focus appeared and, in front of it, like a shadow, hovered Ebramar's head; a beam of light hit the oscillating disk, and the needle drew in phosphoric t letters: "At your request, cordial greetings to you and Udea."

Leaning over the record, I heard Ebramar's voice perfectly, whispering the same words, and I was wafted by the scent of his favorite perfume.

One morning, Narada said to me:

– Now that you are rested, your body and soul are refreshed, it is time to star work again. "Tomorrow we will go out together: a special mission awaits you among your new brothers".

The next day, as planned, the friends gathered at Ebramar's house; Udea then continued his narrative, which had been interrupted the day before. Before dawn, Narada came to fetch me and told me that, without delay, we should set off on the journey he had talked about the day before. The place we were walking through became more and more mountainous; we entered a rocky crevice that, to my surprise, widened after a few steps and, at the bottom of that sort of corridor, there was a narrow circular staircase that led us to an underground channel, illuminated by a soft pale blue light. Near the bank we found a boat tied up; we got on board, I took the oars, Narada sat at the helm and we set off.

I need to tell you about the Colony, where we are going – said Narada. Its population is not large enough or sufficiently evolved to receive the first foundations of the enlightenment from the mentors that will be brought by great initiates from the dead planet. I will leave you as the head of these aborigines; with them, you will have to reveal all your administrative skills, provide them with benefits through your medical and scientific knowledge, to make yourself respected and feared. Later on, your work and the progress you have made will be evaluated; however, I am very sure that your future descendants will not belittle their father. By the evolution of their physical appearance and mental capacity, you will have the opportunity to keep up with the successes , as they are mortal, whereas time does not exist for you. This means that you do not need to hurry.

I must confess that when Narada said this, I broke out in a cold sweat. To physically unite with those semi-barbarians, seeking to improve the race, seemed to me the height of invention in relation to myself and, at the very least, a punishment that was too harsh. Narada read my indignant thoughts and warned me in a stern, disapproving tone:

— Beware, Udea, of the germs of pride, rebellion and selfishness, that poison your soul! Curb these clumsy spoils of the past! The sacrifices of those who worked here before were far worse. They were also evolved beings, initiated, accustomed to refined beauty, but despite everything, they managed to establish relationships with the savages, seeking to lay the foundations for the improvement of the race, bringing it closer to what we see today. Settlements similar to the one you will find are scattered all over the immense continent.

I answered nothing; using willpower, I stifled my previous irritation; and then we docked. Through a staircase carved into the rock, we crossed a series of caves, connected as in a single environment, illuminated by spheres of concentrated electricity. In the first and largest of the caves, a spring flowed from a wall, pouring a stream of water into a large tank; a few stone benches could be seen here and there. The adjoining cave served as a sanctuary and workroom; it was properly equipped for religious ceremonies, studies and magical activities. The third cave, finally, turned out to be a bedroom, provided with a comfort I had long since become unaccustomed to. Next to the bed was an upholstered chair and, on the table, I saw the chalice that had belonged to me in the time of my fleeting greatness. Next to the wall were two cupboards and some metal chests, whose contents, Narada asked me to inventory immediately. In one of the cupboards I found clothes for me; in the other, food supplies: wine, honey, powdered concentrate, etc. The contents of the chests intrigued me at first. One of them was literally clogged with ornaments so grotesque that I salmed the lid with disdain; in the other, there were many multicolored fabrics, and in the third, various objects that I did not want to examine too much.

— Every morning - Narada told me – you will find more substantial food in the first cave. Try to eat well, because the contact with t he lower beings will absorb a lot of astral force. Do not starve yourself; eat as much as you want! Later on, I will send you an helper and, if you need me , you can contact me through this device, that allows you to communicate with whoever is in my laboratory. And now, let's go! I want to show you your settlers. We returned to the first cave, where he showed me an opening in the rock, which turned out to be a real window – narrow one, to tell the truth – but through which we could see a meadow, flanked by a wooded hill and a lake.

The panorama literally stretched out at my feet; in the meadow I could see a crowd of men, women and children, surrounded by a flock of the most diverse animals. Sitting in small groups in the shade of the trees, all naked, they were eating voraciously something I could not make out. Surprised, I observed that their appearance was not hideous; perhaps they were too tall and stocky, but their countenances had nothing animalistic about them, and many even showed intelligence. At my surprised expression, Narada explained :

— This is the result of millions of years of work by countless enlighteners who came before you. The continent we are on is the fourth on this planet, it is also the fourth human race that we are perfecting here; but on the planet there are, of course, the reminiscenses of other races, doomed to extinction over time. Each of them hadspecial mentors in turn, according to the level of evolution. From semi-fluid giants – as the first form of the solidified astral cliché -. They were veiled and transfigured by the enlightening spirits; passing through the crawling invertebrate humanity, which multiplied like vegetables – by germination – and, later, became bisexual, already a more improved race on the physical and mental plane. The human race, as you can see, has come a long way. The current population is already prepared to receive the civilization that will bring the great mentors and welcome the first kings of the divine dynasty. It is up to you and others to prepare the way for them by launching the promoters of future development, such as the arts, sciences and laws, both divine and human.

After giving me several advices and instructions, Narada left, promising to send me a helper as soon as I felt the need.

I was alone again, but I no longer needed to get used to the solitude; so I began, first, to study the place and, later, the people entrusted to me.

When I analyzed the first question, I discovered that a volcanic eruption was about to occur in the area; the people of the valley were in inevitable danger from the flooding of the lake. A survey of the surrounding area showed that on the other side of the mountain there were higher and therefore safer valleys; these could be reached by trails, that I began to clear vigorously to make access more confortable.

My observations on the population showed that the natives lived in totally savage conditions; they did not form families, nor did they know how to make fire, taking advantage of the ignition produced by eventual lightning, whose flames they maintained despite fearing them.

Having made my preparations and taken advice from Narada, I thought the time had come to appear before my pupils, whose poor and vulgar language I had already mastered.

One night I went down to the camp, where part of the tribe was sleeping under the open sky. Seeking to give my people a greater enchantment, I evoked some thunder and enveloped myself in radiant light. Some of the aborigines, who were sleeping more lightly, woke up and saw, stunned with awe, a man in white surrounded by radiant lights. I made an emotional speech, saying that I had been sent by the gods, the fathers of their ancestors.

— I will return to save you from imminent danger and later I will come to teach you how to soften the wrath of the gods. Do not dare disobey me! — I threatened and disappeared.

The next day, the villagers only commented on the appearance of the messenger of the gods, their ancestors; a young disciple of Narada came to help me in the endeavor to help the population.

It would be too long to describe each stage of the preventive actions that would culminate in the success of my initiative. Underground tremors, a localized flood and some terrible weather would soon be confirmed. I made myself appear with my companion, and those who had already seen me recognized me and submitted to my orders. As soon as the last inhabitants had left the valley sentenced to death with the rest of the animals, a devastating earthquake struck; the ground sank, the hillsides surrounding the valley collapsed and it became a huge lake.

My authority was solidified, I had enough prestige to initiate enlightenment actions.

After settling the villagers in the caves, I gathered the elders together and explained that, to appease the wrath of the ancestral gods, who governed the storms, the lives and health of men and animals, it was necessary to evoke them, pray and work hard. The gods, tireless workers, could not stand idleness, especially from their descendants. It was also necessary to erect an altar in honor to these protective gods and thank them for their salvation.

I ordered them to bring blocks of stones which, stacked according to my instructions, formed a large altar, on which resinous branches and flowers were placed. Once lit, the people fell genuflecting and, with wild and disconnected cries, poured out their gratitude to the invisible force that governed the destinies of all.

From that day on, with the help of Nami -that was my assistant's name - we began to teach them how to make fire, milk cattle, harvest honey and make bread from seeds crushed between two stones. Using grass and sugar cane leaves, we taught the women how to weave mats, baskets, and loincloths to cover their hips. When the population had assimilated the first working techniques, I moved on to the next stage.

In one of the large caves, I built a pedestal on which I erected a statue, explaining that it was the representation of a god who appears to mortals by day in the form of the sun, spreading life and warmth, and at night watches over those who, when they die, descend into the kingdom of darkness.

I then thought that the time had come to institute ceremonies that could deeply shake the minds of those savages; they would remain in their virgin and pure souls, more sensitive to receiving any impression. To do this, I chose some young men, dressed them in loincloths and told them that, in accordance with divine orders, they had been chosen for special services. With the trumpets I provided them, they were supposed to call out to the people at dawn and dusk and accompany them in their songs. At these gatherings, I would lead the services, smoke aromatic herbs before the statue and chant prayers relevant to the occasion.

People gathered in crowds, sang genuflected, brought flowers and fruit as offerings, fascinated by the statue adorned with a jeweled necklace, whose head was covered by a metal crown. The six young men who watched over that first shrine, proud of their role, carried out their duties zealously.

At that time, a new opportunity arose to solidify my popularity and increase the faith of my settlers.

The flood drove out a huge number of monstrous animals – survivors of almost extinct species – that were sheltering nearby They fled the cataclysm and took refuge in high places. The beasts caused enormous devastation among the livestock; they often devoured human beings, and the population did not know how to defend themselves against these terrible predators. In response to the complaints and requests for help, I first ordered everyone to pray together to ask for help from the Great God and the ancestral gods.

Accompanied by some braver natives, I went down into the valley where most of those beasts were taking refuge and, with the help of the etheric vibratory force, I turned them into ashes.

A superstitious dread gripped the population; my prestige, as a superior being and messenger of the gods assured me, in fact, unlimited authority. This was doubly useful, because among the people – although savage, but already quite evolved – rebels began to emerge who were disgusted with my transformations and the obligation to work. The fear I instilled, however, moderated the discontented.

Once the first religious office had been instituted, it was necessary to solemnly mark the three great events in the life of a human being, namely birth, marriage, and death; and to make their rituals sacred and attractive, always producing a deep emotion. Thus, these events should be joyful and accompanied by various festivities, capable of promoting a kind of magic circle around the religious ritual. Even though faith may wane, the intoxicating sumptuousness of the rituals would ensure their continuity, which is very important and even indispensable from the point of view of the occult, and powerful due to the magical force of the movements, dates, etc. It was necessary to establish, as solidly as possible, those customs and rituals, which could be passed down from generation to generation, from father to son; they would promote the manifestation of the mysterious forces of good, and would bind humans at least through the expression of the external form, even if they could not intuit their arcane meaning.

Before introducing the marriage ritual, it was necessary for my "subjects" to be called by their names - a practice that did not exist - then I refined their rudimentary language and prepared them for starting families. That is how I began the project.

After gathering the people of the valley one day, I announced that the Great God had ordered, through me, that each man of the tribe should choose a wife, to whom he would be united by a ritual, witnessed by the divinity, mistress of life and death, of the health of men and animals, of storms and deluges. I also added that only those who were thus united in this way, and their children, would enter the abode of the gods after death, where they would eternally enjoy all blessings, peace and joy.

This announcement caused a huge stir; however, no one dared to object and, under my and Nami's supervision, the necessary preparations were made for the formation of the families .

Each couple, by divine determination, would be obliged to occupy a separate room; for this purpose, caves were adapted and huts erected. My partner and I distributed the most necessary utensils: earthenware, wooden dishes , fabrics and so on.

These preparations served the purpose of teaching the technical fundamentals of crafts, since it was their competence to produce manufactured goods, a divine gift At the same time, primitive speech was enriched with a large number of new words. Finally, from the adolescents of both sexes, who were too young for marriage, we formed choirs, who would perform singing and smoking incense to mark the first day of the sacrament of marriage with the greatest possible solemnity. Finally, the great day arrived, and the bride and groom, in their colorful loincloths , necklaces and diadems on their heads, walked in double file to the cave; all the villagers were in new clothes, adorned with rudimentary knick-knacks and trinkets that we had distributed.

In front of the statue, they smoked with incense ; I celebrated the ceremony myself. I gave the bride and groom strong wine from the golden chalice – never tasted before – and before each couple I pronounced the sconjurations of conjuration that foreshadowed divine wrath on the spouse who dared to connect with anyone other than the one granted to them before the countenance of God, the heavenly lord.

The impact of the ritual on my savage subjects was enormous; under the effect of the mystical breath, whose power they sensed, their vigorous bodies trembled with superstitious fear.

Later, I instituted religious ceremonies to mark birth and death.

Some time later, my assistant and I left our cave, which was forbidden to all inhabitants, and moved to the valley, where we built two small houses to live in, which, despite their poor and rudimentary appearance, were real palaces for the natives. I chose a young , pretty and intelligent girl as my wife. She did not inspire me with love, of course, and her intellectual limitations prevented her from being a true companion in my life; however, she was humble, fearful, and obedient, and so our life was bearable. Nami also married, and we both had many children, who later married. Our clan stood out significantly from other populations for its beauty, bodily flexibility and intellectual development.

Over the course of many years, I dedicated myself to the spiritual and intellectual improvement of my settlers; I taught them how to work the land, how to cultivate the vineyard, how to worship God; in order to perform the offices of the temple and maintain the eternal fire, I formed a community of virgins, who submitted themselves to a special regime, spiritualizing the body. Both my children and Nami's, who were more intellectually advanced, became priests and doctors; the former I taught how to perform religious rites and revealed some magical formulas; the latter I initiated t into the art of preparing various kinds of medicine, diagnosing the most common diseases, including the treatment of fever, tuberculosis, toothache, ulcers, wounds, hemorrhages, with their sympathy formulas, etc. All this "knowledge" had to remain hidden, and only to be revealed under na oath of silence to the most worthy of the descendant generation. As noble and rudimentary as this knowledge was , it gave the representative of the divinity due consideration.

I also took care of defense against wild animals and restless neighbors. Under my guidance, the first weapons were made, when I trained how to use them and, at the same time, recruited groups of warriors.

I was already a great-grandfather when I received word that my masters were coming to inspect my work. I waited for them without any fear, aware thta I would not be embarassed by the work I had done.

The physical and intellectual appearance of the people improved drastically; order prevailed; activities were buzzing; the beauty and gracefulness of the forms of that handful of human beings were very close of the species that would be brought by initiates from the extinct planet, making miscigenation possible. The masters were delighted and allowed me to leave the settlement, which was a source of great joy, as I was very tired.

So I gathered the people together and announced that the gods were calling me back and that the time had come for my death, which would be incognito so that no one would look for my remains. As my proxy, I appointed one of my grandsons, an educated , energetic and very intelligent young man. I made the people swear allegiance to the new lord and that, when he died, he would choose a new successor.

In a pompous ceremony, I transferred the helmet, shield and sword to him, symbols that should forever remain forever with the leader of the people, obliged to submit to him. After giving the last instructions to my successor and bidding farewell to the people, embittered by my withdrawal, for I was well-liked, I retired to the mountain and disappeared; some time later, Nami did the same.

I am sure you would share my emotion when I set off towards the sphinx, as if relieved of a great weight. A long, long time has passed since the day I set off by boat through the underground canal. And how quickly it passed! People who work do not feel it! Narada received me cheerfully congratulated me on the ordeal well endured and asked me if I did not have some wish with which he could reward me.

Only then did I realized the physical and mental exhaustion caused by a century of inhuman work.

— Well then. I am not given the gift of death," I said, "but if it is possible, give me complete rest, a dreamless sleep, so that my soul may rest without thinking or worrying about anything. I crave rest so much and I am so tired, that a state of complete oblivion would be an immense grace.

— I understand, my son, and your desire for spiritual and carnal rest is legitimate. Go to your cell, I will bring you your reward! — ordered Narada.

- A young disciple of the magician came to my room, suggested me to take a bath, then dressed me in a long linen robe and took me to a room, that smelled wonderful . In a niche in the wall, a comfortable, soft bed awaited me; I lay down and the disciple covered me with a blanket.

Just then, Narada arrived, carrying a cup of lukewarm liquid; I drank it delightedly. He put his hand on my forehead and immediately I heard wonderful music. The calm melody lulled me gently, and it seemed as if I were floating in the air, swaying in the clouds of blue heavenly space, saturated with dizzying aromas . Finally, I lost my senses...

I could not tell you how long I was asleep, but I think my sleep was long. When I woke up, I felt quite refreshed in body and soul.

It was then that Narada introduced me to other purged people, and among other activities, we started building this palace.

The hardest things were behind us; I and my colleagues no longer felt so alone, and the work was not so hard either. But there is nothing more to say, because nothing special has happened; finally, your arrival has dispelled the last shadow of the past and given us back everything we had lost.

Udea fell silent, gazing thoughtfully into the distance; the others were also immersed in their thought. The silence was broken by Ebramar, who stood up, shook his friend's hand and said in a participatory tone:

— Your story soothed your soul, the brothers mentally shared your work and rejoiced in your victory. Raiseyour head now, Udea, forget the past and look courageously to the future; it holds many clear joys and dignified work, so necessary in our strange life.

— You are right, faithful friend! Be my guide in this new phase of my existence. I promise you obedience and good will, to the best of my ability," replied Udea cheerfully.

After a lively conversation, the friends split up

CHAPTER V

On the pinnacle of a high rock, towering over the mountains and valleys that surrounded the city of the Magicians, sat a man, gazing somberly and thoughtfully at the marvelous and imposing panorama flooded in gold and purple by the rising sun.

He was a young man, tall, slim and well-built ; his expressive and remarkably handsome face, exuded intelligence and determination. The thinker's wide forehead was framed by dense black hair with strange strands ; in his large, dark, velvety eyes there was an expression that betrayed the tempestuous passions in his soul.

His gaze fell on the distant valleys and forests, and his hands clenched in anger . He was seized by an irresistible and mad desire to go into those unknown wildernesses, his new world, full of mysteries and wonders never seen before; access to it, however, was forbidden.

The lonely dreamer sighed heavily, stood up and looked around the city of the Magicians, surrounded by high walls along its entire length. The lush vegetation embraced the numerous palaces, the tall astronomical towers and the colossal buildings of the temples and schools. The young man's gaze drifted indifferently across that magical picture and stopped at the temporary dwelling of the wizards, built by the purged.

From that height, the immense building was clearly visible, and the observer's keen eyes searched for and finally found Dakhir's palace, whose silver wing; in one of the garden's boulevards, he distinguished two tiny female figures in white, heading towards the building. His face flushed and, as soon as the white figures disappeared into the shadows of the trees, he started down the narrow path. His countenance became heavy, his eyebrows clenched, and his chest breathed slowly, apparently dueto a strong emotion.

The young man was called Abrasack, he was under Narayana's protection and was his favorite disciple. And now we will say a few words about his past and the event that led to his friendship with that eccentric, but brilliant personality that preserved so much of "human" in him, despite the weight of the centuries and the vicissitudes of his extraordinary existence.

At about the time when the catastrophes described in " Divine Wrath" were unfolding on the dying Earth, Narayana on one of his adventures around the world, happened to be in one of the countries undergoing a revolution.

There, a republican government had been in place since ancient times and, as is characteristic of the time, there was total freedom of manners. However, a few years earlier the government regime had been overthrown by a young man, a descendant of the dynasty that had ruled previously, who, very ingeniously and using his energy, managed to gather supporters and emerged victorious against a weak and debauched system, re-establishing the monarchy and usurping the crown.

Thanks to his shrewd intelligence, cunning and iron will, the young king managed to hold on to power for many years; his enemies, however, took notice and, since they were in the majority, finally triumphed. With all their bitterness that is so common to foolish and low souls, the victors sentenced the dethroned monarch to be hanged with all the royal decorations.

Narayana's aircraft was passing over the execution site at the moment; the strange procession caught his attention, although the superb posture of the condemned man and his unwavering courage in the face of the vexatious and poignant condemnation produced a feeling of sympathy in the magician.

As he quickly familiarized himself with the circumstances of the event, he became indignant at the cruelty and mockery of the despicable mob. Instantly the decision to save the unfortunate man matured in him, and as soon as the procession reached the great square, where the gallows stood, the plan of rescue was put into execution.

The weather that day was foggy, threatening rain, but then everything went completely dark, lightning flashed and a hailstorm hit him on his head; the people panicked. Taking advantage of the commotion, Narayana made his way through the crowd and managed to reach the condemned man, standing impassively, and, squeezing his hand tightly, whispered in his ear:

— Take off those ridiculous rags and follow me quickly! I will save you.

With fearlessness and great presence of mind, the young king threw off his cloak and raiment and, , like a snake, set off at a rapid pace, sneaking through the crowd after his savior, until they stopped at the aircraft.

Narayana took the young monarch to the Himalayan palace. The young man's gratitude, his obedience, and application made him even more available to the protector. And the more he talked to Abrasack, the more he became fascinated by his rare abilities, his ease of learning things, his energy and willpower, for which there seemed to be no obstacle. So, when Abrasack begged Narayana to take him as a disciple, the magician agreed without hesitation; he was so fascinated by his disciple, that he even got angry when Supramati once made the following remark to him:

— If you have studied Abrasack's personality, you will have realized that he is not worthy of being an adept and receiving arcane knowledge. Listen to my advice: reveal the mysteries to him in sparingly.

— I do not understand why you dislike this extraordinary young man. You, Dakhir and even Ebramar do not seem to trust him.

What do you have to fear, summits of knowledge that you are? What does it matter how little I can tell him? — Narayana retorted, annoyed. Because of his impetuous temperament, mixed with courage, weakness and grandiose impulses, Narayana valued and was fascinated by the same attributes as the others.

— With what you have given him to know, it is enough for him to overreact; the day will come when you will regret your overconfidence. Well . Do as you wish," concluded Supramati with his usual impassivity.

But Narayana was fiery man, and Abrasack was able to win his confidence. The disciple's lively spirit , his iron will, the speed with which he assimilated the most complex questions, enchanted the master; and with his characteristic rashness , Narayana taught him many dangerous mysteries.

One day Narayana could not contain himself and boasted to Ebramar of the disciple's achievements, of his wealth of knowledge, which had never been exorbitated .

The magician gave him an enigmatic look .

— It is true! His mind soars, while his heart stagnates. He assimilates the mechanics of the great creative machine well, but he does not understand its divine wisdom. Beware, Narayana, you are creating an artificial magician, full of pride and greed. Like Prometheus, he can steal the sacred fire and set the world on fire; he is not humble in spirit, as a true magician should be, and he never addresses the celestial forces. It is true that he sacrifices everything to achieve his goal; but I fear that his goal is not to ascend to the light.

As the final catastrophe approached, Dakhir advised Narayana to leave Abrasack on Earth, but the magician was indignant at such cruelty.

— I am convinced that one day you will still need his head; a wise and active man is worth more than the group of idiots you are leading, he assured him angrily.

Later, seeing Abrasack's despair when the sun stopped shining and the end was imminent, Narayana was tempted to give him the elixir of long life. Abrasack was happy and proud to no longer be a mortal, and to know that even in the new world he would be assured of long centuries of life.

At first, after arriving on the new planet, various scientific tasks and household chores occupied his mind, but gradually his enthusiasm for science waned, and his rebellious spirit was filled with other intentions.

He was initially smug and curious. Despite his wealth of knowledge and power over the elements, he had never had the opportunity to test them. And the divine city, with all its serene harmony and stern discipline, became tedious to him; the ban on leaving it seemed like an insidious arbitrariness, while his work in the city, without a stimulus of danger and a practical objective, was absurd and boring.

Yet another circumstance inflamed his insane thoughts. When he met Dakhir's daughter Urjane in the new land, an impetuous and burning passion took over his being. Like a seductive apparition, she hovered in his imagination, day and night, the image of the girl who had bewitched his heart.

Light and translucent, she seemed to be woven of air and light; in her blue eyes was reflected heavenly purity...In Abrasack's unsubmissive soul, there was a mad desire to possess Urjane, even though he knew his love was not reciprocated . The daughter of the three-limbed wizard was surely destined for some higher initiate, perhaps Udea, who knows, or one of Supramati's sons. Dakhir's coldness toward him was proof in itself of the unfeasibility of such a love. Ppossessing the young woman by force would be sheer madness. However, Abrasack was not one to stand still in the face of obstacles; on the contrary, they exacerbated his stubbordness even more.

During their rare encounters, when they had the opportunity to exchange a few words, Urjane showed him total indifference – she hardly noticed him – but this fact only inflamed his stubborn passion even more.

His intention to seize Urjane at any cost was growing, but before he could perpetuate the kidnapping, he had to find a refuge for his prey, and an army to defend himself. Planning all his actions required him to leave the city of wizards; so, he decided to flee.

As the ambitious project began to instigate his mind, he realized that different spectral beings were gathering around him, a reflection of his disconnected desires that boiled like incandescent lava. They were faithful companions, dangerous henchmen who shared his daring intentions: his own offspring in moments of extreme excitement, when unbridled thought generates fomenters of rebellion and disruption.

It is no coincidence that the summits of wisdom, divine messengers, always infused and prescribed discipline and vigilance over thoughts: the brain – an enigmatic and dynamic machine – not only generates stupid or innocuous thoughts, but sometimes produces living forms equipped with dangerous forces.

It would be very strange – and rightly so – if criminal thoughts, a living manifestation of astral forms, could go unnoticed by the great magicians. Undoubtedly, this would be impossible, and the great initiates were well aware of Abrasack's plans. Indeed, his intended escape, with his daring actions, prompted a meeting of the hierophants, with the participation of Supramati and Dakhir.

Dakhir, the first to discover the rebel's intentions and the one who was watching his every move, explained Abrasack's plans and the main reason that induced him to perpetrate the adventure: his passion for Urjane. He then asked the chief hierophant if it would not be the will of the High Council to prevent the kidnapping of his daughter, or if the events would take a different course.

— I have already discussed future events with the brothers, and we have decided not to put any obstacle in the way of the man destined to take the people to the highest level of evolution. An action generates a reaction, the shock that this man will provoke is inevitable and useful for the peoples, shivering in idleness.

It is a pity, my son, that the sweaty and radiant child has generated such an impure passion in this young man; but your conception of life is lofty, and you understand the full extent of the greatness and predestination of your daughter's trial. As far as Narayana is concerned, who through his stubbornness and carelessness lured a dangerous young man into our midst , setting him up to defy us, it is he himself who will have to confront the insurgent, and let that be a lesson to him. We will make sure that he does not suspect the ingratitude of his favorite, until it suits us.

In fact, absorbed in other thoughts, Narayana, who had little to do with Abrasack, suspected nothing. For some time now, he had been working feverishly on the decoration and furnishing of his new palace, a tedious work of art. Nothing seemed beautiful enough for the person he would like to inhabit the abode; Narayana's fickle heart surrendered to a deep and ardent love.

He had known his beloved girl practically since the day she was born; before his eyes that enchanted flower called Urjane was growing and blossoming, and he had not even noticed when the bonds of friendship gave way to love. And what an old friendship it was! No one was so capable of amusing the girl, surprising her with the most unexpected gifts or entertaining her with tales as Uncle Narayana. Dakhir and Edith had noticed the change in their affections for some time, but they did not make it difficult for them to get closer Edith liked Narayana; and since he had received his first torch as a magician, Narayana's heart had undergone a great change for the better t. Certainly, he had subdued his earthly weaknesses and was evolving, while his best attributes of character were being further enhanced.

The conversation about the union of the magicians allowed Narayana to discover his true feelings for Urjane, even though the idea of marrying her was a source of inner struggle. For the first time in his life, he felt like an old man in relation to that child; recalling his rebellious past, he feared that Dakhir - and not without grounds – would treat him with suspicion and would not want him as a son-in-law. Even the capricious and intractable temperament of an old man lurks under a magician's torch, deaf to the arguments of reason, whatever they may be. However, an unexpected and decisive explanation happened between him and Urjane.

During a tour of the divine city, when he was showing her his palace, and they were chatting animatedly in the garden, Narayana, in response to Urjane's comment about the beauty of the palace, said:

— Yes, it is not bad for now. But the real enchanted palace will be built in my future capital. You know that one of the kingdoms in which the first divine dynasties will rule is destined for me. I will have to build a capital, of course, and I will call it "Urjane", as I have promised you before. The palace that I will inhabit with my consort will be a true marvel. I even have a project.

Urjane suddenly blushed and lowered her eyes; then, without her expecting it , she let it slip:

— And who will be the queen, Uncle Narayana?

Narayana's black eyes shone, he bent and took Urjane's hand.

— Would you like to be the queen in the city of your name? — he asked, half-joking , half serious , staring into her worried little eyes. — But then, I would not like to be called "Uncle Narayana".

— Yes, as long as my parents let me be your queen. Now, you must promise not to love any other woman, because I know your reputation as an airhead," Urjane replied firmly .

Narayana burst out laughing.

— Apparently, Madame Eva has been here, because in all worlds, women are the same! As for the bad fame that goes around about me being an incorrigible slob, it is all rubbish. It is just that, being a born artist, I have never stopped admiring feminine beauty; moreover, I have never had the opportunity to love and admire someone like my little Urjane. I solemnly swear that I will be faithful to you. Tomorrow morning, I will ask your parents for your hand.

The next day, in the morning, Dakhir and Edith were on the terrace of the house. The lush green of the trees protected them from the sun's rays; aromatic shrubs, planted in large pots and scattered around , formed haunting corners. Edith was working at a table in one of them..

On the table were two large flat crystal vases; one with gold, the other with silver; the metals were as malleable as wax. Picking up one metal or the other, Edith's slender fingers fashioned a basket of fruit, a fantastic work of art. She had been working on making decorations and utensils for their new palace in the divine city, where they would soon be moving .

That day Edith was very distracted and sometimes her hands rested idly on her knees, while her thoughtful gaze lingered on the exuberant picture of nature.

Dakhir, dressed in a white wizard's robe, was standing on the terrace parapet. At that moment, his handsome countenance was also clouded and his thoughtful gaze wandered far away. Letting out a deep sigh, he wiped his hand across his forehead, as if chasing away dull thoughts, and approached the table.

— Narayana is coming to propose to our daughter. You know: they had a decisive conversation yesterday," he remarked.

— Yes, she loves him, and that is understandable . He is a charming man and knows how to win women's hearts – said Edith.

— It's true. He is a master at it. I am convinced that, this time, he nurtures a deep love for our Urjane, and this feeling is the most solid of all those that have ever inhabited his heart. He has changed for the better since his last initiation," Dakhir considered, and his face creased in a wry smile. — Had it not been for this unfortunate Abrasack, brought about by him, Urjane's happiness would not have been so brief; and is the poor thing up to the task of enduring the cruel trials that await her?

— You know, Dakhir, how dangerous it is, even for a pure and balanced soul, to be surrounded by diabolical beings with their low instincts and the influence of unbridled passions! And she will be right in this hell ," remarked Edith, raising her watery eyes to her husband.

— It seems that Urjane is already aware of the storm, Edith continued, because she has been complaining of bad omens and the sensation of being invaded by black fluids as heavy as lead.

— It is true, a tough battle waits Urjane ; but she is the daughter of wizards and will not fail in her destiny. What merit is there in being good, pure and magnanimously , where there is no challenge of temptation and adversity to habits. Where there is nothing to excite the vile instincts that lurk in the ignoble dephts of the human soul? Only by fighting can you know your strenght, while the events to come are already mapped out in the book of destiny. Ascetics have abandoned the world, seeking silence and isolation in forests or deserts, which make it easier for them to concentrate. Urjane will preserve the radiant purity of her soul in the midst of the storms; I am quite sure that she will return triumphant," assured Dakhir, squeezing his wife's hand tightly. — Well, here comes Narayana!

On the lake, he pointed to a boat, propelled by an oarsman; standing in it was Narayana, dressed as a Grail Knight. The sun's rays reverberated off his metal helmet and silver tunic, and his tall, slender figure stood proudly against the azure background.

— What a beauty! He was born to destroy women's hearts," Edith laughed.

Narayana jumped nimbly onto the dock steps and walked quickly towards them. As he arrived, he stopped and said with a half forced, half mischievous smile.

In front of the parents who are not ordinary mortals, I could avoid the need to announce my request. Its content is known to you, and I also know that it will not be denied; however, I would like to hear from you that I am not an unwanted son-in-law.

Dakhir shook tightly the outstretched hand and greeted him.

- Welcome Narayana! We have nothing against the chosen one of Urjane's heart. We are sure that you will love our daughter faithfully and that she will be happy with you.

— So, our old Narayana, the wind-headed , has become a Narayana serious man," Edith added.

— You are right, my dear mother-in-law, my virtues will still amaze the world. But where is the enslaver of my heart, who made me come to my senses?

— You will find her near the bird nursery; and now, while you are talking, I will set the table to invite our friends to toast to the health of the bride and groom. How is that for na idea, Narayana? — Edith asked, in a breeze tone.

— I think it is great, thank you! It will be as if we were still in our wretched dead land. Oh, it had to end just now, when I am getting married! What a pity! Good or bad, she is always sweet – concluded Narayana with a sigh – Well, see you later! I am off to find my beauty.

After placing his helmet and sword on a chair, he climbed down from the terrace and quickly disappeared into one of the garden's dark avenues.

Stepping out onto a lawn, in the center of which a fountain was spraying its waters, and next to which was a bower covered with climbing plants, in the midst of dense vegetation, he saw Urjane, sitting on the bench. A basket was resting on her side, and in her hands she held a pot of seeds, which she threw out in handfuls. All around her, over her lap, shoulders and on the ground, flocks of birds with multicolored plumage were flocking and snacking on their food. At the same time, she stroked a beautiful turquoise bird with a silver tuft, perched on the edge of the pot. Urjane was all charm, dressed in a wide white robe, girded with a silver belt. When she saw Narayana, she blushed, put down the pot and stood up.

— Do I need you to try to guess why I have come? — Narayana asked, giving her a bewitching look and an irresistible smile. Urjane raised her clear blue eyes.

— Would I be Dakhir's true daughter if I could not hear the voice of your heart, even if your lips were sealed? You know, feel and see my passion for the "prodigal son" of magicians. I love you, and I am not ashamed to say so. I am ready to share your life with you, your work, your success, or misfortune, and to follow you towards the perfect light, when the plan outlined by our masters will be fulfilled, she said.

— I will always try to reciprocate your love," he assured her, serious and moved by her words, and wrapped his arms around her.

At that instant, a harmonic vibration was heard; they were powerful and sweet chords that made every fiber of the body tremble.

— It is music of the spheres, expressing the consent of the higher magicians to our union, blessing it – Narayana rejoiced. — There is Ebramar's gift," he added, pointing to a large white bird with a golden tuft, which was landing from above, holding in its beak a crown of phosphorescent white flowers in its beak, which it then placed on Urjane's head.

The bride and groom knew that this was one of the magical birds used by the great initiates, so they both stroked and kissed the winged emissary's silky little head. Letting out a joyful cry , the bird flapped its wings and flew away.

While the couple talked, Edith called some of Dakhir's young disciples from among the earthlings to help her prepare the banquet and distribute invitations to their friends.

The preparations were already finishing when the guests began to arrive. Ebramar arrived last, while simultaneously, through the opposite door, Narayana and Urjane entered.

Narayana gazed happyly and gratefully at the circle of friends. His entire spiritual family was gathered there: Ebramar and Nara, Supramati and Olga with the children, Dakhir and Edith, Udea, Nivara, among others. Ebramar was the first to embrace and bless the bride and groom. But when Narayana approached Nara and his gaze met the breezy smile of his former consort, he gave her a noisy kiss on her cheek and whispered in her ear:

— I will try to be a more faithful husband to her.

— We hope so. It has been quite a sacrifice to work for your perfection. And now you will have to justify our efforts," she replied good-naturedly.

As they passed into the living room, Ebramar observed:

— Before we sit at the table, let us say a prayer of thanks to the Ineffable Being, who has given us so many gifts.

Everyone was silent and reverent, and soon a chant echoed, the like of which had never been heard by any ordinary mortal being so wonderful was its interpretation, impregnated with faith, love, and gratitude.

After the prayer, a lively lunch began, with cheerful conversation. Only Narayana was thoughtful. When Nivara expressed his delight at the diversity and richness of the products on the planet, and added that, in the midst of such abundance, one could even forget that one was in another world, Narayana suddenly interfered:

— You are right, Nivara, when you say that our new home provides us with so many good things; it would be ungrateful of us not to love it and not feel good here. Let us toast, however, to the memory of the dead Earth, where we made the most difficult passage of our lives. It is not our poor wet nurse's fault that ungrateful humanity has preyed on it and taken advantage of it, destroyed and sucked out all its sap, allowing the chaotic forces that brought it to an premature end to fall upon it. I believe that in everyone's heart we should reserve a space for it, because we owe her, with no doubt, all our memories of imperfection, of happy and bad moments, of misadventures lived, of love and hate of victories and failures, in other words, of all the challenges our fickle soul has faced -he picked up the chalice and stood up.

— Let us toast to you Earth, our beloved cradle; let us raise friends, a prayer, friends, and weep!

Following his example, everyone stood up and the eyes of many welled up with tears. Narayana's speech brought back thousands of memories; many cherished shadows rose from the drain of the past and the hearts of those people torn from humanity were stirred.

— Gratitude is the noblest of virtues and a human duty. Let us sing, then, a requiem for our beloved cradle, and may it be reached by the feelings of gratitude overflowing from our hearts ; may they warm and comfort those who atone there, on the dead Earth, for their insane uprising against the Creator and His unbreakable law - Ebramar said .

This time the song of the magicians poured forth in a storm of sound, ravishing the soul, and from all beings streams of fire and radiant light poured forth, densifying into the shape of an glowing sphere, which, like a comet, crackling and blazing with sparks, rushed through space towards the distant Earth, shrouded in black clouds and devoid of light and heat: the terrifying dungeon of the repudiated.

The news of Narayana and Urjane's nuptials spread quickly among the inhabitants of the divine city and among the earthlings; for Abrasack, in particular, it came as a shock and initially left him totally shocked. By fate's design, the adored woman would belong to his savior, benefactor and master, from whom he would kidnap her away. At first, he was ashamed and felt some remorse; but the praiseworthy impulse soon vanished like smoke when he met the bride and groom, together with the other disciples, on the occasion of the greeting visit.

At the sight of Urjane, his soul raged in a storm; Narayana, blind and distracted, did not notice. As for the bride, she did not even look at him in the midst of the crowd of other disciples, and he, later, simply disappeared. Returning home, he unleashed all his despair and fury; all the nefarious instincts he had nurtured boiled up in his soul, suffocating his remorse, gratitude, and scruples. When, a few hours later, he stood up, pale as a corpse, but calm, his eyes sparkling with hatred, and in the implacable folds of his lips clenched, an unshakable determination could be read.

Determined to flee as quickly as possible, he began to feverishly prepare for his departure. On Earth, he was already regarded an excellent horseman and, in the new world, he had even tamed a winged dragon; a magnificent all-black animal, that obeyed him like a dog and understood his every gesture or word. It was on it that Abrasack used to take his airplane rides, within the allowed limits; but that was too little to face the wizards. To this end, he had been gradually stealing from Narayana those magical objects that might later be useful to him, but that also did not take up too much space.

In order to carry out the escape, Abrasack wanted to take advantage of the moment of excitement that would be caused by the final preparations for the consecration of the city and the solemnities of the wedding.

One night, he placed his secretly acquired treasure in a large elongated box; at the bottom he placed the flask with the primal matter of the extinct planet, since he had not been able to store that essence of origin in the new world. Obviously, that essence was no longer effective for planetary life, but it was undoubtedly a powerful tool against various diseases and ensured a fairly long existence. Then he hid in the box some parchments with ancient texts of magic formulas, and in a chiseled box, he placed some amulets and some very powerful magic rings that he had managed to steal from Narayana's magnificent collection. Inside metallic spheres, the size of a walnut, were several meshes, incredibly thin and light, like a feather, impregnated with mysterious essences, and which possessed no less incredible powers; one of them made the wearer invisible to the eyes of ordinary mortals; the other provided invulnerability to the actions of the elements and extinguished the gravity of the atmosphere. The third, finally, emitted a moonlight-like light and aroma, which annihilated the most harmful miasmas, wherever it was , in total darkness or in the depths of the earth. Along with other gadgets, Abrasack hid a sphere the size of a duck's egg, which, when heated, became transparent and predicted the future .

Finally, he placed seven flutes of different sizes and materials in the box. The sounds of one pacified wild beasts; another calmed storms; there was one whose sounds could, in battle, excite the combatants to total ecstasy. Such instruments were already known in remote antiquity and were at the disposal of the pharaohs; their secret of handling was lost later.

All that paraphernalia, as well as other objects, provided they were used with skill, offered great power, and Abrasack, with the cunning that was peculiar to him, knew how to carefully choose everything that could surround him with a halo of mystery and subdue the savage tribes with the terror of his power, instilling in them the conviction that he was a god, descended from heaven.

— With these resources, I can conquer the world, defeat the magicians and prove to you, Urjane, that I am more than Narayana! — Abrasack muttered, locking the box.

Then he hung the lyre around his neck, lifted the box and hurried off towards the top of the cliff, where his winged friend was waiting for him, with some bags he had brought. Tying all his precious cargo firmly to the animal's back, he mounted it and set off in the direction of the distant forests and plains that seduced them with their impenetrable mysteries, extending beyond the limits imposed. He was going to conquer the unknown world, alone, armed only with his magical knowledge, unparalleled courage and uncontrolled passion.

At the top of a huge astronomical tower in the divine city stood Dakhir and Ebramar; the optical instrument was oriented towards the isolated escarpment where Abrasack's black dragon had landed.

— Now he is tying the box containing Narayana's belongings to the dragon's back," Dakhir remarked dismissively .

— Let everything run naturally, according to the plan outlined in the astral cliché. The time has come for events to unfold that will promote passions, guide brains and produce inventors. Let the blind instrument of destiny take its course! His provocative ambition, when it collides with Narayana's obstinate resistance, will bring about a clash of the spiritual forces of these two powerful temperaments, causing an enormous upheaval, so necessary for future progress.

— In any case, I will keep na eye him, and I will arm Urjane for the fight," said Dakhir, leaving the tower with Ebramar.

Abrasack's escape caused a huge stir and surprised the entire Earthling colony, giving rise to endless gossip. Everyone imagined that the wizards would start the chase and punish the insubmissive one exemplarily; but, as nothing happened, and the adepts treated the event with total indifference, the Earthlings concluded that the punishment had been postponed, but that it would be very severe; on the other hand, the hustle and bustle of the preparations for the festivities to be held made the residents forget about the fugitive, hated for his grooming and lack of sociability.

Narayana was very resentful of his pupil's ingratitude bnd ruthlessness; when he realized how many magical objects that had been stolen from him, he was embarassed and regretted not having listened to the advice of his friends, who had warned him not to trust Abrasack. He had not even imagined the daring intentions, that were being plotted against his happiness in the mind of the cunning fugitive.

Anger and wounded pride prevented him from broaching the subject with Dakhir and Supramati; who also kept silent. however, he told Ebramar how he had been stripped of his possessions, and complained about the vile ingratitude of that man, whose benefactor he had been.

The great magician listened to him, and pondered seriously:

— What can be done, my son? Neglect always leads to painful consequences.

Then, with great solemnity, the city was consecrated, and the adepts settled in their new homes. The weddings were celebrated with no less pomp.

The ceremonies of the magicians were held in the underground temple, while those of the lower degree adepts were held in the large temple in the city; this was followed by the legitimations of the Earthlings brought in. The ritual of the latter was even more sumptuous, to give greater grandeur to the act, which is perhaps the most important of a man's life, the bulwark of the family, the cell of society, from which noble feelings are cultivated; loyalty, patience and mutual tolerance, love, self-abnegation for children, fidelity and mutual support in the trials of life.

Once the solemnities were over, normal life resumed its course, and the Magician began their other work in their new home.

The main task was to protect the sources of primal matter. There were seven in all; some of which were still covered by the waters of the ocean and required care, so attention was paid to those on dry land.

Despite the millions of years dedicated to studying the countless properties of this mysterious force – the vital essence of the Universe – its astonishing powers were not sufficiently known and, in the new land, the hierophants came across certain compositions that differed from the old ones. Thus, there was a need for new scientific research, and a large number of wizards, already graced with two shades of knowledge, volunteered to devote themselves to science and to solitary and prolonged meditation in underground caves, as soon as they were suitable for habitation.

The opening of different schools of initiation began with no less commitment. After due selection among the Earthlings, some of them were found to be suitable for higher initiation, others were assigned to lower-level schools where administrative officials, craftsmen, farmers, and artists were trained. The magicians, depending on their tastes and aptitudes, were assigned to manage and teach in these establishments; the female schools were left in the hands of the magician women.

Busy with the difficult and complex task of classifying and putting in order the documents gathered by the purged, Dakhir was freed from teaching in schools; the same happened with Supramati, who set about organizing a library for the ancient treasures of science and literature brought back from the extinct planet. Although they did not teach in schools, they both had their own favorite disciples, initiates in science and spiritual improvement.

Little by little, Kalitin became Dakhir's beloved pupil, he grew fond of the young scientist because of the application, penance, and humility with which he gave up his old "science" in search of genuine knowledge. Dakhir often took him on his excursions and, every evening, gave him a couple of hours to talk, which for the disciple were the best moments of the day.

Already on Earth, Kalitin had a passion for botany, and now he was forming his own herbarium of the new world, classifying unknown plants by species. At Dakhir's request, Udea, who had already had the opportunity to study the flora of the planet, assisted Kalitin and guided his work.

Once, on his return from a botanical excursion, Kalitin stopped by Udea's house in the afternoon and showed him a very strange plant he had found. It was a bundle of dark red , thin and flexible branches, with tiny eyes and a huge root with a lighter, almost orange hue. The root had an uncanny resemblance to the human body. The pseudo-feet and pseudo-hands ended up of long, thin shoots; the little head, magnificently formed, seemed to have a real face, equipped with a nose, mouth, forehead and three depressions, with three eyes, arranged like the eyes of a cave man— I found this unusual plant by chance," Kalitin began, "in the mountain valley you showed me to do my research. It was growing in the shade of the rocks. I tried to pull it out, as I had never seen a plant like it before, but I immediately felt a strong burn on my hand and a few twinges, like an electric discharge. This intrigued me, and I decided to extract it out at any costs. I dug into the earth around it and, with great effort, managed to pull out this root. Just imagine, As I pulled it out of the ground, it seemed to shudder and emitted a crackling like a moan . As I examined the plant with understandable curiosity, I remembered that on Earth there was a plant that resembled a human body, although its root was much smaller. It was called Mandrake. In my time it was already extinct, or at least I never came across it, but I saw it in an illustration. The plant was considered mysterious, extraordinary therapeutic properties were attributed to it and many legends were told.

— Legends are never entirely absurd and invariably contain a dose of truth, although time and the imagination take care of adorning and disfiguring them," Udea observed, smiling. — This plant and many others of this species are shrouded in a veil of mystery for the uninitiated; to explain this to you, we must go back to the very distant past.

What you see on this earth, its flora, fauna and humanity, are all the perfected fruits, of millions of years, of work by nature and the intelligences that govern the chaotic elements. Your will brought from the Earth's aura the gigantic and clumsy forms, which the heat of the sun densified and provided with an enormous physical strength. These beings, na incarnation of primitive forces, even if they are rude and ignorant workers, become powerful collaborators if guided by a disciplined mind; then each one, associated with the element from which it originated, works actively to fuse it to the Earth and promote the proper permutation. During long, long centuries of work, these ethereal beings become so impregnated with the heavy currents of the Earth's crust that they are unable to rise into space and, trapped by gravity, end up putting down roots in the earth, partially retaining a certain resemblance to humans, having acquired it from them. For a while, these amphibious beings amke up a special fauna; most of them, however, die out during geological revolutions, while others, under the influence of the sun's heat and the weather, change their appearance, becoming increasingly denser . Some of these beings sink into the earth permanently; others, on the other hand, separate from it, becoming crawlers or climbers, in other words, choosing a new path of ascent.

The light that shines on the forehead of ethereal beings, which normally serves as an organ of vision for beings in a fluidic state, becomes densified and takes on the appearance of one, two or three eyes. It would be too long to describe the different forms of these strange beings. You mentioned Mandrake… For on the dead earth, there was a terrible carnivorous plant that could devour a man or an animal, as long as it reached out with its plant claws.

— How interesting! What unexpected light floods the mysteries of the creation of the world and the evolution of beings! — Kalitin exclaimed thoughtfully and seriously.

— Yes, all of nature is an open book, on whose pages are written all the periods of the evolution of the great terrestrial machine, along with everything that inhabits it, but you need a key to this alphabet. The ignorant person gets confused and lost in the list of laws that seem too complex; when, in fact, they are quite simple and work on the basis of uniform planning. For example, do not the legs and feet of some animals, or even their limbs, resemble roots? This is a clear sign of evolution, but nobody realizes it," Udea concluded.

Such conversations left Kalitin deeply impressed, which gave rise to a desire to broaden his horizons and delve deeper into the fascinating mysteries of creation. Once, during an informal conversation with Dakhir, he expressed his desire to gain knowledge and achieve perfection. The magician told him affectionately:

— Your will, my son, is legitimate and praiseworthy; but there is a time for everything. Do not forget that haste is the enemy of perfection. And go on working. As soon as you are sufficiently prepared, I will give you an isolation test, and if you do it properly, it will be a great step forward.

— Forgive me, master, but I do not understand the meaning of isolation . It certainly helps to concentrate on a prayer; but is it enough to advance my learning, something I could do alone without the assistance of a mentor?

- You are wrong. Isolation, in itself, is a wise and powerful guide. Being alone, with only the elements of nature as companions, the mind undergoes a surprising preparation; the elemental mentors will answer the questions posed by the seeker's brain . Solitude and silence enhance the astral forces. Light needs an atmosphere to propagate, and a candle will burn out in a very stale environment ; likewise, internal light is governed by the same principle . Within the heavy and dense material emanations of the crowd, thought also becomes heavy, and the inner light dims and even goes out; in the deep silence of solitude, however, far from the pungent and disturbing mumurs, it is easier for man to concentrate the powerful force of his thoughts into one, and direct them toward the desired goal.

Kalitin then exclaimed, his eyes shining :

— You told me that I would live a few millennia! Sometimes the thought of this terrifies me and I am afraid of going mad; at other times, like now, I feel incredibly happy to know that I have so much time to study the great and fascinating mysteries. I wanted so much to understand this enigmatic substance, which gives the fragile human body this incredible life-giving force, capable of opposing the law of death almost until eternity. Forgive me, master, if I ask you questions that are impossible to answer.

— No, your search for truth is so legitimate that I will be happy to give you a brief explanation. As for understanding all the properties and methods of use of this mysterious substance, which fills the Universe and constitutes the nucleus for the formation of all planets, and the sap that nourishes worlds and beings, no one has yet achieved this.

This substance, which we call primal matter, is like the breath of the Inscrutable Being Himself, which no one can grasp. This all-encompassing breath – sound, color, light, Rome – comes in the form of mist, possesses an astonishing vibration, transforms itself into liquid fire and then spreads out into large drops, which swirl in space until a gelatinous substance does not accumulates, causing the incredible frequency of the vibration to become heavier and slower. The gelatinous mass – I say "gelatinous" only in terms of comparison, because the tenuousness of matter is impossible to describe – begins to rotate, gradually densifies and fills the astral shape, mentally traced by one of the creators of the planetary system.

The great worker and calculator of space traces with his powerful mind the geometrical figures of the routes through which the large and small planets of the system in formation . The first to form and take their places are the gigantic agglomerations we call suns; their fiery rays keep the primordial substance active and, under their heat, it evaporates and pulverizes, impregnating and animating all the atoms of matter. There, where the sun's heat does not reach the primal substance, it remains inactive, for example, in the huge spaces between the islands of planetary systems.

The sun's heat dries the gelatinous plants, which contain the astral form of everything – rocks, plants, animals – and stimulates the vital activity of primal matter. Take an egg, for example. The shape of the bird is invisibly inserted into its very essence. The heat dries the egg white and the invisible form becomes visible, the atom of primal matter, penetrating through the flame of fertilization and activated by the action of heat, attracts from space the substances it needs for the formation of the body, whose cliché is ready, and... The work is completed: from the egg, which served as a kind of cradle, comes a determined being, capable of developing and multiplying.

In ordinary organisms, the vital essence remains in a certain proportion for a certain lenght of time; after this time, the matter accumulated in the cliché is segregated and reaches what we call death. Absorbed by some organism - be it palnt, animal, or human - in a different proportion, the elixir of long life gives it the capacity to continually renew the cells that make it up, ensures that youthful vigor and strength are maintained; and since primal matter contains all the elements of nature, it (primal essence) makes everyone who is impregnated with it, invulnerable to the effects of elemental forces.

The same applies to us immortals. We never grow old, we can live the planetary life, and we are well adapted to mental work.

But let us get back to ordinary man. Like us, he has a brain – a machine – which absorbs a lot of primal force spread throughout the body, especially if he dedicates himself intensively to mental work. In a limited and lazy person, primal matter lodges in the bones and flesh, increasing their sizes and often their physical strength.

By the way, man can attract the surplus of matter to himself through asceticism, contemplation, self-concentration, and above all, through the vibration of prayer and ecstasy. In these cases, the human machine exerts an attraction and absorbs the intense currents of beneficent force, which pour down on him like a kind of fiery rain; his nervous system shudders, sometimes he feels dizzy, when his body, aura or brain absorbs the life-given droplets, which give him enormous strength and illuminate him with astral light.

This happens not only with initiated beings, but also with mortals and saints, who, enraptured in prayer, become imbued with this truly divine force, because it emanates from the Almighty; they become capable of performing miraculous healing and – by renewing the vital essence - even of raising the dead, provided that the astral self has not definitively separated from the body. But the prayer must be made with faith and intensity, because only in this way it is possible to compose the chemistry that attracts balsamic and healing grace , both for those who pray and for the beneficiaries of the prayer.

Initiates also use chemical formulations to achieve the desired effects. The greater their recognizability, the greater the breadth and complexity of their use of primal substance, and the greater the struggle they wage against the terrible force that opposes primal matter. I am referring to the destructive force, which breaks down everything it touches .

Two forces are competing for the Universe, and one or the other cannot win. The matter that unites the cells, animating them and forcing them to interact, ascends in an auriferous spiral; the disintegrating current, in a downward spiral, umber and heavy, tries to destroy the life-giving current.

The great laws that govern the Universe are as clear and simple as divine wisdom; it is human ignorance that clouds the begnning of everything in darknes. The whole system of the Universe rests on the unshakable foundation of these laws, and the great servants of the Eternal , executors of His Will, work.

The simplest and most accessible part of these laws is known by uninitiated mankind; instead of being guided by them, man abuses them, and this abuse generates inevitable suffering and death," concluded Dakhir, releasing the disciple, who left upset by what he had just heard.

CHAPTER VI

Without even turning back to take a last look at the city of the Magicians – the haven of peace, concord, and science - Abrasack soared into space. Above his head, the starred sky sparkled; at his feet ,the plains and forbidden forests stretched out.

There, mired in ignorance, lived the poor savages; in their souls still slumbered the passions that fate had reserved for them to awaken. Like an evil exterminating genius, he, Abrasack, had put an end to the peace of the peaceful hordes; just to satisfy his vanity, he had precipitated the bloody clashes and thrown the clouds of those ants at each other.

The winged dragon was swiftly cutting through space, and the forbidden borders had long since been left behind; but Abrasack continued his flight, driven by the unconscious desire to get as far away as possible from the wizards he had betrayed. Finally, his dragon began to show signs of fatigue, and Abrasack decided to descend. The sun was rising and he saw that he was in a valley surrounded by high forested mountains. "Dark One" – that was what his dragon was called – landed on a small law, covered in dense undergrowth. Abrasack climbed up and saw the entrance to a cave nearby, behind climbing plants. Entering , he observed that the place was spacious, well ventilated, the ground was carpeted with dense, fluffy moss, and a spring gushed from the wall, t the stream of which ran through the cave and, through a rocky crevice, into the valley.

Not far from the entrance, fruit trees were growing; Abrasack picked some fruit, found it to be of excellent in taste, then took bread, and cheese from a packet.

After finishing his frugal breakfast, feeling very tired, he lay down on the moss, put a cloak under his head and quickly fell asleep.

It was quite late when he woke up. When he realized that the Dark One was grazing peacefully on the grass and had greeted him cheerfully with the flapping of its wings, Abrasack returned to the cave, lay down again and began to reflect. He was now free, the path to adventures and the fulfillment of personal vanity was clear and, up to that moment, there was nothing to indicate that the wizards had set out in pursuit of him… But this could happen, and deep down in his soul an restlessness germinated.

Despite his wealth of knowledge and the magical power he had acquired, he was aware that, compared to the great initiates, he was nothing more than a pygmy. The others had powers that could strike him down, wherever he was; he had already had the opportunity to see those forces at work and he did not know how to control them. Well, what did it matter? He was an immortal! As time passed and nothing that threatened him happened, he imagined that, perhaps, the haughty wizards simply would not deign to pursue him, to punish him. He smilled evilly, "You will pay dearly for this arrogance!".

Blinded by insane passion, not even a feeling of affection or gratitude arose in his soul for the one who had saved him from death, who had enlightened him and armed him with the knowledge he would use to harm him; when he remembered Narayana with Urjane, the blood rushed to his head and his face reddened.

With an effort of will, he mastered the inner storm. He had to act and not dream, and to achieve his goals quickly, he could not waste precious time.

When the setting sun flooded the pristine mountains with purple and gold, his plan was already mature, but he had to wait until night to put it into action.

He was alone and, for his projects to bear fruit, he needed shrewd helpers, capable of understanding and carrying out his orders. But where could he get them? It was not possible among the earthlings he had brought with him le, and even those were inaccessible to him. However, after some reflection, a cunning and intrepid sorcerer's mind came up with a solution to the problem.

Invigorated by a humble meal, he decided to spend the rest of the waning day examining the area and, following the bed of the stream, descended into the valley where he found a large lake, previously hidden by the surrounding rocks. Near the shore, he discovered another cave that was less spacious, but which seemed more suited to his plans. Without wasting any time, he began to prepare himself, bringing the objects he needed.

First, he took a red tablecloth, with Kabbalistic symbols embroidered on it and placed it on a pile of stones. Around it, he placed three red candles, forming a triangle; then he put the aromatic herbs in a frying pan and, finally, he filled a crystal goblet with wine. At the entrance to the cave, he hung a metal bell, reverberating all the colors of the rainbow, and tied a rope to the clapper. All done, he began to wait for the right time, consulting a small clock that he had on a gold chain, a gift from Narayana.

As midnight approached, he took the flask with the primal substance out of the box and poured a few drops into the glass. The wine ignited. When he closed the cup, the contents took the form of liquid fire. Abrasack undressed, hung an enameled red star and a talisman in the shape of a breastplate around his neck and laid the book of incantations open on the stone beside him.

Raising the seven-knot staff over his head, he began to twirl it until a red flame appeared at the end of the staff, with which he lit the candles. Then Abrasack bowed to the four cardinal points and cadenced a chant, ringing the bell at the right intervals. Soon the sky was covered in dark clouds and a fierce storm broke out; thunder rolled, flashes of lightning tore through the sky, the water in the lake seemed to boil and, in its chilling waves, crashing against the rocks, wandering flames danced. But Abrasack's stentorian voice covered up the raging elements; he continued to ring the bell, pronouncing the formulas, and in the dark sky geometric and Kabbalistic symbols were now being drawn.

Suddenly, a greenish light appeared and four strange figures emerged against its backdrop. One was red, like glowing metal, with huge igneous wings; the second, gray, with undulating wings, undefined outlines and a light blue star; the third, greenish, with a dark hue, was churning like the sea and on its head there was a crown resembling the f a wave crast; finally, the fourth, stock, black-haired, as if variegated with red veins, it wore a headband , encrusted with rubies, emeralds, and amethysts, and, in the center of the headband, a bright flame seemed to be burning . At the powerful sorcerer's call came the four elemental genies.

— What do you want, son of Earth? The terrible incantations you pronounce are signs of your power," said a guttural voice, as if from afar .

— Do you ask that the armies of the elemental spirits join you, submit and serve you? So shall it be, for your power is great," said another voice, at Abrasack's request.

The hands of four genies joined with Abrasack's hands; then, misty crowds of elemental spirits appeared, and before the magic staff they swore allegiance and obedience to their new lord.

Amid deafening roars, the genies withdrew, and the turbulent clouds of spirits surrounded Abrasack, waiting for his orders.

— Withdraw, spirits of earth, fire, and water; and you, spirits of the air, listen to my commands.

He read out a long list of names and added:

— Go and find the spirits I have appointed and bring them here!

As if swept away by the wind, the spirits of the air disappeared; Abrasack sat down on the stone and wiped the sweat from his face. An undefined anguish squeezed his heart. Thosehe had called, were his friends, helpers and companions in arms and intrigue in past adventures, who had fought for his throne. It would all have ended in hanging if he had not been saved by Narayana. They were active, energetic, cunning and brave collaborators; just the ones he needed at that moment to help him found a new kingdom and, among other things, to assist him in the dangerous undertaking. Will they come? Based on scientific evidence, he knew that some of them were already disembodied, but the evocation did not seem to be working, for some unknown reason. Resuming the summons, he looked out over the lake, and suddenly an undefined noise was heard, which grew into deafening rumbles.

The water seemed to be boiling, and multicolored flames came leaping up from the waaves . Abrasack cringed and, shuddering, raised his hands, drawing Kabbalistic signs in the air, igniting phosphoric flames. Stirring, already at his side, the flames became crude and took on human aspects; glowing eyes gazed at Abrasack.

— My old friends and companions! I have summoned you to make a proposal: would you like to be incarnated in solid human bodies and enjoy the pleasures of life, instead of wandering through space? Will you agree, in return, to help me conquer and enslave the savage hordes that populate this land and, if necessary, to fight with me?

— Give us life with its pleasures, and we will help you become the most powerful king on this planet," the voices replied enthusiastically in chorus.

— Thank you, friends, it will be your will! But why did not everyone I called come? — Abrasack asked his ghostly servants harshly.

— Sire! Some spirits, who did not come, currently live on the dead Earth and have stayed there; others are among the Earthlings brought by the magicians, but we are forbidden to enter there. - strange, faint, disconnected sounds were heard. A look of furious hatred slid across Abrasack's face, but he restrained himself. Approaching a frying pan, he put in some pieces of charcoal, which glowed instantly, and poured the contents of the bowl over them. Immediately, a thick, blood-red smoke rose up, and a numbing smell wafted over everyone.

In the same way that light attracts insects, the crowd of shadows threw themselves on the smoke and, for a few moments, were covered by it. When the smoke cleared, there were about twenty people standing next to the glowing tripe. Their dense bodies looked like living normals they swiftly approached Abrasack.

— Now, everyone, take a sip from this cup; the divine drink will give you full vigor and a long existence.

They all drank greedily and then fell down, as if from dizziness. The weakness, however, was short-lived; when they all stood up, they were fully alive human beings, full of energy, strength, and courage. Stretching out their hands, they gave thanks for that precious gift.

Abrasack greeted them jovially; one of them even received a long hug.

— We are together again, friends, to work and defeat fate. Could you have foreseen, Jan Igomer, that we would meet in another world, after you were killed alongside me by the rebels?

— Where you are king and our brother, you have become a god who lavishes lives, and you have not even change because of it. You have remained as you were, while I have been through many lives since then," remarked the one now known as Jan Igomer.

— If I have changed nothing on the outside, I now have another name. My name is Abrasack, and I am a fugitive rebel who escaped from the prison-city populated by a bunch of tyrants; by the way, before I begin anything, spacefriends, I will tell you about the curious adventures that brought me here.

— I thank you for your trust, but to finish off your generosity, give us something to eat. I am starving, and I think my brothers feel the same way," remarked one of the beings, tall and fat, with a chunky face, who apparently possessed Herculean strength.

A general laugh covered his speech. After the laughter subsided, Abrasack said:

— Randolfo's appetite remains the same; for now, I can only offer a frugal dinner. That is all I have. Let us go to my temporary home and take all the objects that are here; upstairs, I will order the most substantial things.

Stopping near the entrance of the cave, Abrasack asked his friends to wait, entered the cave and pronounced the appropriate incantations so that the invisible servants would bring the most nutritious dinner possible.

Some time later, there was a noise like the rustling of dry leaves being trampled underfoot, igneous and smokey spheres swirled in the air, then a gray mass appeared surrounded by undefined misty beings, and everything suddenly dissipated. Everyone saw a kind of tablecloth o n the floor, woven from leaves, on which rested bowls, boxes and mugs made of wood, straw, and tree bark; everything was rudimentary and coarsely finished. Inside the bowls were various fruits, some raw fish, honey with broad beans, milk, slightly fermented fruit juice, and finally, – of the most substantial kind – there was a live goat, tightly tied up so that it could not move.

— Ready, friends! For now, let us make do with this modest meal, because there are no restaurants around here that can offer my spirits anything better; we cannot count on the city of the tyrants, where there is more abundance of delicacies and dishes," complained Abrasack, grimacing and fixing na orb on the wall , which he had provided before leaving the cave, and which illuminated everything with bright light.

It was now clear that Abrasack's supporters, summoned from space with the power of primal essence, were handsome, and vigorous men, with intelligent faces and intrepid gazes. Abrasack had made a good choice, and with that help many things could be done.

The man called Randolpo examined the provisions, found them acceptable, and said that, even though the fish and goat were intended for food, he was loath to eat them raw and alive; so, he was willing to prepare a rare dish, provided his master provided a fire.

Abrasack lit some resinous twigs and allowed his friend to do as he pleased; Randolpo and some of his companions left the cave.

An hour later, the friends sat around the steaming hot plate; only Abrasack and Jan declined the invitation to dinner.

When the meal was over, Abrasack suggested to his companions that they go to sleep, because without sleep - a divine gift, of which they had been deprived for a long time - no Earthly human being could lead a normal life. The suggestion was readily accepted, and soon a general snoring announced that the newcomers from the astral world were enjoying the first grace of their new existence.

The next day, in front of the isolated cave lost in the mountains, an unusual meeting was taking place. Surrounding Abrasack, his supporters listened attentively to his plans for war against the wizards and the siege of the divine city.

The huge continent had enough space to house many nations, but to successfully carry out such a bold undertaking, a large armed army; would be needed; peoples would have to be enslaved, cities and villages would have to be formed... and all this required time and work.

— Do you know of any savage tribes around here that we could subdue? Everything seems so deserted and uninhabitable! Maybe they need a means of transportation like your Dark One to accompany you on your expeditions. Walking through these virgin forests is impossible! — remarked one of those present.

— You are absolutely right! I expect to receive some flying horses later this afternoon. I have ordered the Dark One to bring me its co-brothers, and , as you can see, it has already gone to collect them.

— How can you communicate with the Dark One? Is it so intelligent that it can understand human speech? — Jan wondered.

— On the contrary. I am the one who talks in its language," laughed Abrasack, and added, whe he saw his companions surprise: "In the occult sciences there is a mother tongue, whose musical rhythm is adapted to the phonic communication of different species of animals, from an insect to an animal close to man in terms of its physical and mental development. An adept will never reach the highest level of initiation if they have not mastered the art of being understood by an animal; otherwise, how can they tame it, make it obey him and, in a certain way, train it? The whole secret is based on sound rhythmicity. Some reminiscences of this wonderful and useful science have been preserved on the defunct Earth among village sorcerers, gypsies, and so on, who were able to communicate with horses, to charm and balk cats, rats and wolves; likewise, the Hindus knew how to tak to snakes. I am sure you have heard of similar things in times gone by; these cases, however, were rare and isolated.

I have studied this art systematically. The good Narayana disseminated this knowledge to me exhaustively, impressed by my successes and application. If he had known what the consequences of these illustrations would be, he would have been less impressed," and Abrasack let out a loud laugh, accompanied by others.

— I know that around here there is a people, if you can call them that, very numerous and bordering on the animal state. I am thinking of using them, not only as workforce, but also as warriors.

— You know how to find them, because the continent, you say, is huge! — Jan asked again.

— Absolutely! I have a map of the planet here... Why this surprise? Or do you think that the wizards came here with their chicks, completely unaware of the world they were about to encounter? Oh, no! The preparations for the transfer took many centuries. Those sent to the new world studied the three kingdoms, so that the future migrants would find everything ready. All the adepts and disciples had the task of preparing detailed maps of the continent, as well as sketches and samples of fauna, flora and minerals, in other words, they needed to be aware of all the planet's riches. As far as possible, I took advantage of the existing documentation and even managed to copy the most important maps. In this way, I have certain resources, although unfortunately there are gaps in my knowledge, as some magicians have treated me with suspicion, creating certain obstacles .

Perhaps they foresaw the risk they were taking with regard to you; but they acted unthinkingly in allowing you to acquire this amount of knowledge – considered Jam in a mocking tone.

— Fortunately, Narayana did not share those suspicions and, thanks to his negligence, I was able to obtain the most indispensable magical objects – Abrasack concluded in the same tone. After discussing the details of the work to be done, Abrasack raised his cup and pronounced solemnly:

— To the success of our enterprise! Like the ancient conquerors of the dead motherland, we are going to conquer this new world, to found great kingdoms in it. With our blood we shall achieve victory and power; and the color of blood will be our flag; fire will be the trail of our march.

— We swear allegiance to the red flag and to you, Abrasack, our benefactor, leader and commander! — His companions pronounced solemnly and seriously

From that day on, the preparations began. Abrasack's staff set about diligently learning the language of the winged dragons to ensure perfect control over those animals, whose memory has been preserved in folk legends and fairy tales, which have always been true .

As soon as Dark One arranged for a flock of magnificent dragons, wild and suspicious, Abrasack approached one of them, stroked him, talked to it and the animal calmed down. This influenced the rest of the dragons, and the whole flock began to graze peacefully in the valley.

When the adventurers had definitely adapted to their winged horses and tamed them, they decided to set off on an expedition, leaving the cave as their headquarters, where some objects brought from the city of wizards remained.

Leaving the mountainous region behind, the space riders steered their flight towards the valleys where, for thousands and thousands of kilometers, impenetrable virgin forests stretched out.

There lived a people that Abrasack planned to subjugate and as they entered, the space knights dismounted, Abrasack ordered his companions to wait for him, and he resolutely entered the secular forest.

After walking some distance, he stopped in a clearing and brought the small magic flute close to his lips and began to play. The melody was strange; the sounds were sometimes loud, lively and penetrating, as if calling out, sometimes slow and mournful, like a restrained cry.

After quiet a long time , the forest seemed to come back to life; at first there was a distant noise, which soon grew louder; trees were being trampled by the crowd , amidst the shaking of the earth and a guttural voice that resembled animal howls. Repellent and fearsome beings emerged from the woods.

They were big-headed giants with animalistic features; their large bodies were covered with brownish-red fur; their huge, muscular arms were equipped with curved claws. They were leaning on or carrying long, gnarled clubs on their shoulders. They stood motionless, staring at Abrasack with their small, sunken, eager eyes. He stopped playing, and made some strange, disconnected sounds, which seemed to be understandable to the crowd, as they huddled together, making sounds, and examining with curiosity the stranger in white robes. Gradually they began to understand each other. Some of the giants ran back into the woods; others remained listening attentively to Abrasack, sometimes responding with their guttural sounds. Those who had left now returned. One of them carried a creature on his shoulder that resembled them, but was much more robust, with a physiognomy that was also hideous, although it appeared to be more intelligent.

He struck up a conversation with Abrasack and, judging by the aborigine's reactions, it seemed that he liked the interlocutor's words , because from time to time he let out grunts of satisfaction, uncovering huge, sharp teeth, and swinging a club that could easily bring down an elephant.

At the end of the conversation, Abrasack took a metallic chain from a bag around his waist, shining like gold, and carrying a kind of medallion with pendants that tinkled at the slightest movement, and offered it to the chief of the tribe, his future ally.

Overflowing with joy, the aborigine let out a loud grunt, tore off the necklace that adorned his lap and put the toast in place; then, clicking his tongue, he leapt across the lawn, to the roars of the fascinated vassals .

When the outburst of joy subsided, the conversations continued. The terrifying lord of the people of the giants seemed to pass them on to his subordinates, who received them with various grunts and whistles.

They were all pleased, apparently, judging by the fact that some giants followed the visitor out of the forest; no one touched him, not even his companions, who, with a mixture of fear and disgust in their souls, greeted the giant monsters jovially, according to Abrasack's instructions.

Riding swiftly on winged horses, they took flight, causing the savages to feel superstitious dread.

Upon returning to the cave, Abrasack told the others the terms of the agreement he had reached with the aborigines, which would allow them the right to choose an area within the savages' domains, in exchange for assistance in building a city and dwellings for the giants, whom Abrasack pejoratively called " monkeys".

The next day, Abrasack and his friends went to the forest with some giants; examined it and chose the site for the future city.

Part of the vast forest land was mountainous, and there, on a plateau, Abrasack decided to build just the town center.

Following the orders of the tribe's leader, the giants set to work, uprooting the centuries-old trees of the virgin forest with their colossal hands, roots and all; and little by little, the area was cleared, and later leveled.

Abrasack then moved into the forest with his companions, who were already able to explain themselves to the giants. Using the trunks of trees that had been uprooted, the aborigines built their houses, which were very rudimentary, although they looked magnificent to them.

The city was then surrounded with a cyclopean wall of huge blocks of rock; wells were dug, and food depots built.

There was total understanding with the workers , thanks to Abrasack's arrangement to serve them a strong drink, made from fruits - abundant in the region -, which everyone enjoyed. Other tribes, skillfully imitating the colonized giants, also founded villages in various parts of the region. In this way, the large population of " monkeys" – as Abrasack called them – grew by leaps and bounds, boosted by the use of magical devices.

For example, he would appear out of nowhere among the workers, issue orders and then suddenly disappear; sometimes, his house would be seen in flames; however, the fire did not seem to be burning at all. However, the event that deeply marked the savages was the following.

During the work of erecting the city walls, one of the giants showed a certain indolence and even insubordination. Abrasack gave him a severe reprimand, threatening him with the staff the monster, however, got angry, and shaking his clenched fists, strong as anvils, threw himself at Abrasack. Although Abrasack looked like a baby compared to the savage giant, he was not intimidated; staring steadily into the monster's injected eyes, he raised the magic staff in a flash. As if struck by lightning, the savage petrified in the same pose in which he tried to jump, hands up, and only a convulsive wrinkle on his face indicated that he was still alive and felt the force that nailing him to the ground.

His companions were stunned; Abrasack hurried them away, leaving the offender alone, unable to move.

It was not until the next day that he freed the giant, who was then completely tamed; he crawled to Abrasack's feet and licked them clean.

The great magician deigned to forgive him, but not before announcing in a stern tone that if anyone else dared, from that day on, to be insubordinate and raise a hand against him or any of his friends, he would be punished in the same way, and would be paralyzed until he died of starvation.

The buzz about the event spread through all the tribes, causing fear and deference for those unusual beings who could control life and death and, if they so wished, fly and disappear in the heights.

At the foot of the plateau on which the city stood, a wide, flowing river ran through a rocky bed. There, the first boat was carved from a huge tree trunk and, the first raft was assembled from the trunks tied together. It would be impossible to describe the joy of the giants, who were initiated into using those two boats; sailing up and down the river, they transported fruits, nuts and poultry by raft, supplying the city's stores.

The savages became accustomed to work, and Abrasack became convinced that even for primitive men the need to work was innate, as it satiated them and developed their skills.

Without losing sight of his main goal, Abrasack began to recruit an army to besiege the city of the wizards, and he had loyal and active helpers among his companions.

Slowly but steadily, the savages learned to make arrows, bows, maces, rudimentary silica axes and other weapons. Several detachments were organized, and although the colossian soldiers weaponry and military training had not reached perfection, the spirits were high, and the bloody feuds, that frequently took place were testimony to the fact that their fighting spirit had been fully developed.

Like a pebble thrown into the water, which spread out in circles as it falls, so the movement of enlightenment, promoted by Abrasack, was enveloping the remote tribes of the endless forests. Throughout the regions, trees were uprooted and rudimentary houses were built, with flat roofs, much to the aborigines' taste. Everything seemed to be going well; Abrasack, however, was still not satisfied and often his face clouded, his fists clenched furiously The memory of Urjane tormented him and jealousy devoured him. The intention to kidnap her and make her his wife remained unshaken, disturbing him by day and haunting him by night; he was overcome with fury, his haughty head hung desolately as he looked around. Where would he install the magician's daughter, accustomed to refined luxury and artistic works, in all their aspects? By now, she would be living in Narayana's enchanting palace, carved in the shape of a sapphire. There, everything was art, beauty and harmony, from the magnificent gardens full of rare birds, flowers, joy, fountains, to the little pendants that adorned the rooms.

With his innate iron will, he shook off the momentary weakness and despair, deciding that Urjane would have to make do with what he could temporarily offer her; then, when the city of magicians was conquered, he would lay all his treasures at the feet of his beloved woman.

Despite this decision, he tried his best to make his future prisoner's home as beautiful and comfortable as possible.

After a lot of research, he discovered a deposit of various precious minerals, and his muscular servants extracted a huge amount of material; but as soon as he finished the design of the palace and thought about making use of that treasure, he became possessed.

— Sometimes I think I am going crazy. I would give anything to smash one of those damned wizards to pieces or blow up this damned planet. Where you find nothing but monsters, empty astral and a nest of selfish tyrants," he blurted out.

— I don't understand you," Jan surprised himself, throwing away a piece of clay in which he intended to mold a vase. — In addition to your ugly subjects, we have a beautiful colony of earthlings here, not to mention that we ourselves, by taking the graceful magicians you promised us, will generate a caste of warriors, kings, and priests. And how can the astral of this Earth be empty? I have come out of it, and I assure you that I am populated and whole.

— Ah! you don't understand anything! — Abrasack retorted, annoyed. — I say "empty astral," because it does not contain any cliché that I can use , since I know a magical method for evoking and densifying astral clichés. Why this surprise? What then is a hallucination, mirage, etc.? This is the unconscious invocation and materialization of an astral cliché, even if it is a partial and fortuitous invocation of an ignorant person; the essence of the phenomenon remains the same, even if it is generated by the magical and conscious force of a wise person. If we had been on our old Earth, I could have easily opted for the astral cliché of a palace, even that of Semiramis; I could evoke it, density it and make it a real building, for a certain time or forever. Then the building would already be ready, and I would only have to furnish it in the same way. In this cursed, newly-born world, there is not even an single piece of architecture ; I do not want the clichés of huts or hollow trees populated by " monkeys" . Nor is there any hidden treasure that could be used to make jewelry. As for the graceful wizards, we need to catch them first... This will be done, I promise! — He suddenly became animated shaking his clenched fist. — And since they are all artists, we will have decent closets and utensils.

Jan burst out laughing delighted.

— I hope that these happy times will come soon, and that fate will give me a wife, a beautiful blonde with a fair complexion and sapphire eyes. This is my ideal of feminine beauty.

Abrasack burst into a loud laugh of derision.

— I can only imagine the uproar that will ensue when I unite them with the knights of their ilk, amphibians from two worlds, who bear no resemblance to the sweet lords of the divine city, filled with virtues and ideals... But all that is for later, now we need to get on with the job of making sure our ladies are properly comfortable .

And indeed, the work continued. The palace built by Abrasack, even though it was made of precious stones, looked heavy, not very graceful, with its tetrahedral columns and flat, grotesque roof. Tableware made of gold and silver - essentials utensils - also lacked artistic finish.

CHAPTER VII

While Abrasack was preparing for his audacious incursion and embellishing the future home of the beloved woman as best as he could, Narayana's wedding to Urjane was being celebrated in the city of the magicians.

Urjane was wearing a simple, wide white tunic,with a sash of the same color; her head was covered by a long silver veil with a wreath of flowers, in whose chalices the blue lights flickered and from her neck descended the golden insignia that distinguished the daughter of a magician of higher rank. In the company of her parents, young friends and fellow initiates , the bride went to the underground temple, where Narayana, Udea, Nara, Olga, and some other close friends were already

The ceremony was celebrated by Ebramar, standing next to the mystical stone on which the name of the Ineffable shone. In front of a large cup filled with the primal matter of the new world, which was igniting and boil ing , was a chalice also filled with a substance that looked like liquid fire.

The bride and groom got down on one knee and Ebramar blessed them to the sound of an invisible choir singing a soft and harmonious hymn. Then, taking the liquid fire from the chalice with the help of a little crystal spoon, he poured it into the palm of his hand and, pronouncing formulas slowly, first made a sphere out of it and then, shaping two rings, he placed them on the fingers of the bride and groom. The dazzling rings seemed to be made of transparent gold, reverberating with multicolored hues.

He then molded two more spheres out of the same substance, and placed them on the bride and groom's heads; and they melted into them. Ebramar gave them to drink from the cup and placed his hand on their heads, he pronounced majestically:

— I unite you for a common life and work. Ascend together to the perfect light, to the Father of all that exists, and obey the sacred immutable laws instituted by Him. Be worthy of generating from your union, not only carnal and voluptuous , superior beings, brave and strong in their journey in the fight for good against the "beast" of man, which must be subdued in this new earth, where we have a great mission to fulfill.

Once the ceremony was over, Ebramar kissed the newlyweds, and they all went to Dakhir's house, which was completely decked out in flowers. There they were greeted by the Knights of the Grail, who joined them later at the banquet, which passed in a lively atmosphere.

When evening came, a flock of domesticated birds, similar to white swans, took the newlyweds by boat to Narayana's palace; at the entrance, they were greeted by the magician's disciples, who lavished them with greetings and flowers. As there were no servants in the house, the young people made their way through the silent rooms to their chambers. The entire bedroom was painted white; the walls, the curtains and all the furniture stood out for their refined simplicity. In a niche, adorned with plants, rested the chalice of the Knights of the Grail, topped by a crucifix.

From the moment Narayana entered the palace, there was a visible change in him. There seemed to be nothing left of the old jester and joker; his handsome countenance was serious and concentrated, and when he looked at his young wife we could see a great deal of disturbance.

Urjane! The happiness of calling you my wife is totally undeserved," he said, pressing her hand to his lips. — Despite the torch that adorns my brow, many human weakness still lurk in my soul , which I will try to master with your help, for you are the very embodiment of the harmony that emanates from your parents. May you be blessed to come to my house, my dear angel, and be patient with your imperfect consort.

— I love you as you are, and believe in you as as I believe in my love. And now come, let us raise a prayer! We will beg the Father of all existence , to bless our work on the path of ascension," said Urjane, pulling him towards the niche.

With all the festivities over, life in the city of magicians was going on as normal. The schools of enlightenment were already up and running, and in all fields of science, at all levels, the settlers brought from the extinct land were working very hard.

Narayana, the "most humane" of the magicians – as Ebramar defined him – opened a specialized school for the development of the artistic spirit. From among the Earthlings, he selected a small group of talented people, to whom he taught music, singing, declamation, sculpture, painting and architecture, all based on the esoteric laws of magical science. And for his fruitful and prodigal genius a wide field of work opened up.

— You will be a great administrator- Ebramar once remarked, smiling f approvingly , after having visited the school for the first artists of the temples and kingdoms of the new world.

Dakhir also had some disciples, but outside the school, because, as we mentioned before, he was doing important work.

Little by little, Kalitin became his favorite disciple; his humility, application, and willingness for scientific work made learning easy. Every evening, Dakhir used to give him two hours of a lively and fruitful talk.

Once, Dakhir noticed that his disciple was a bit anxious and distracted. After giving him a searching look, Dakhir smiled and said:

— I see you have a lot of questions. Why are you so embarrassed to ask? You know I will be happy to answer them.

Kalitin winced.

— Master, you read my mind, so… You already know that I have a disciple…

— Well, so what! There is no reason to be ashamed of it. On the contrary, I approve of you sharing the knowledge you acquire with a brother or sister in humanity. Now, what are your doubts?

— Well, yesterday I was talking with my friend about the origin of man, and Nikolai's opinion is that the entire human race, which populates this globe, was made up of spirits. that came from the dead Earth. I have a different opinion, based on some teachings received from you. I would like to give him a consistent and correct explanation of this very interesting question, and also to understand it better; maybe Nikolai is right, since we Earthlings, are here preceded by the pioneers sent from Earth, finally, I know that armies of disembodied spirits came here to be born.

So, master, if the information is not illicit, and if you are willing to free me from ignorance, tell me where the spirits who populate this planet come from.

You are on the right track. The aborigines who populate this world are children of that same Earth and reached spirituality by passing through the three kingdoms of nature. The cosmic spirits accompanied the ascent of these spiritual masses in the course of the lower incarnations, although the Earthly pioneers came later. Since our mission was to civilize this world, we had to make its inhabitants as much like us as possible.

— Thank you for the explanation. Could you give me an idea of how a spirit passes through the three realms?

— I will have to explain to you the evolution of the spirit itself on its way of ascension. Of course, you already know much of what I am going to say, but it will help to broaden your friend's horizons.

We will begin from the moment when the spirit is born ignorant, but endowed with all the instincts of good and evil. It is in a state of torpor; as if it had just woken up, just as when it is born in a body that the spirit does not recognize.

As soon as the indestructible spark forms its individuality, it sticks – if we may put in that way – to the atom of matter, which is his astral body, which, together with its individuality, is transformed and perfected. Subsequently, the spark and the astral body unite with the simpler and more ordinary matter, that is predestined for it on the planet.

This is what happened, by the way, with the psychic sparks that currently animate the aborigines of this globe. You know that a cellular system lies at the heart of every organism.

In the same way that a mineral is made up of groups of cells, although externally it appears dense, in essence it is porous and allows air to penetrate.

The center of the entire cell is an individuality that has not yet been revealed, whose sole purpose is to be a vital current, that is, to remove or attract various fluids, harmful or dispensable, for the maintenance or nourishment of this world. During its time in the inorganic environment, the astro spiritual essence reveals the existence of instinct, or that germ of instinctivity, which in this case your science calls the "chemical environment," which makes bodies attract each other, quickly or slowly, or separate in the absence of affinity.

Although this unconscious existence may seem incredibly long from a human point of view, it is nonetheless, quite tenuous, and it takes very little to break the connection between the individuality that has sprung from a its center, as long as it is not too tightly bound to matter by the spirits. Strong atmospheric tremors, earthquakes, etc., precipitate the transfer of these invisible inhabitants. Billions of intellects, ready to leave, break free and are swept away by whirlwinds that are formed, and their place is taken by others, who are on the first rung of existence.

Let us move on to the second realm. In the pilgrimage of life, passing through rocky minerasl forms, and so on, the indestructible spark gradually relieves itself of heavy fluids and acquires, among other things, the first sense - impressionability to external influences - touch. Mercury, for example, senses the slightest temperature fluctuations. Then the spark is ready to move on to the next level and test itself in the plant kingdom.

Based on of the immutable law, which applies to everything, all acquired habitability must be used in search of improvement, and each property meets a known need. Acquired impressionability is used by the plant to sense the environment around it and meet its needs, because every plant, down to the smallest, must grow and sustain itself through food. The being tests its first steps in order to meet these two needs, already showing its instinctive ability to know how to find the nutritious elements, choose the useful ones, discard the harmful ones, adapt to the environment, look for warmth, light, humidity, avoid obstacles ro development. In short, there are many evidences of its embryonic rational activity.

Even with all this, its individuality has not emerged, and the soul is in a kind of sleepy state, unaware of its personality, in other words, it acts on its instinctive emotions. However, the well-rooted, with developed stems and leaves, have greater clarity of the situation, and form a specific world, because their cellular life pulses with other invisible lives.

Hostile aspects also develop in the plant kingdom, i.e., a pair of plants can have antagonistic fluids; in this case they cannot support each other.

In this way, the model of the future human being is clearly outlined: the vegetable takes in water, feeds itself, digests food, sleeps, has a nervous system, is receptive to fluids, heat, cold and light; consequently it is ready to move on to the animal kingdom.

Animal life begins, of course, with the least evolved species, which gradually acquire the autonomy to move around. At this stage, instinct is a stepping stone to consciousness and discernment. In order to improve, work and develop their skills, animals awaken two great forces of nature : effort and self-preservation. He is forced to look for food and to defend himself against enemies, and thus to reflect and even use trickery . Later , the need to defend the female and her offspring beings, and another powerful driving force also emerges: love and the law of attraction.

During this period all the germs of good and evil begin to manifest themselves; the animal loves, hates, becomes predatory, jealous, grateful, vengeful, lustful and ambitious, but it still does not have free will. Its defects and virtues are curbed by nature, which preserves it from everything that may be harmful , but, as it prepares to pass into the human soul, and having acquired the powerful driving forces mentioned in rational life, the animal awakens the consciousness of responsibility. In the character of the animal its personality is already clearly denoted and, on the level of its understanding, it knows perfectly well whether it is doing right or wrong. Moreover, stubbornness, indolence, and insubordination are present in it, and it knows the fear of punishment. In the animal, conscience already presents itself as an incorruptible inner voice, which leads it to the necessity of doing its duty, and constitutes the instinctive basis of the human conscience, although on a different level of development.

— Forgive me, master, I have one more question: do animals have a spiritual language, in other words, can they, like human beings, exchange thoughts? — Kalitin asked.

— There is no doubt that, animals have their own spiritual language, though restricted, depending on the degree of development they are at. Understand this well: in every animal there lurks an identical divine psychic spark, the generator of the progress that a human being, or even a perfect spirit, is endowed with, into which it will have to transmute itself. This also means, that there is a common root of the language of thought, in which he must communicate on day; and being on the same level as his fellows, he understands them perfectly.

— Do animals have any notion of death?

— A normal animal, even if of a very small species, has the notion of bodily death, which it fears, as it tries to protect itself from it. In higher animals, there is even a awareness of Divinity, that is , of the force on which everything depends. This consciousness, , is undoubtedly undefined and obscure, but in any case, it is profound, so that in times of danger or misfortune it turns to it.

Speaking of the awareness of death in animals, I should mention that their perception at the moment of passing into the other world is identical to that of human beings at the same level of development. An animal experiences the same kind of dread, disturbance and strong shock, when its astral body is torn away; followed by oblivion. But, on the other hand, its awakening in the afterlife and the return of consciousness occur more quickly and more easily than when it comes to a bestified human being burdened by misdeeds. Now we come to the great moment, when the life of the human soul begins.

— And at the moment when the soul, by a strange coincidence, seems to recoil; for a great many human beings, especially the most savage ones, are more rude, hostile, furious, vengeful and cruel than the animals themselves- Katilin observed.

— It is true. The spirit of the animal, transmuting itself into a human being, becomes outwardly worse, because it is no longer contained by the wise laws of nature, which until then had created insurmountable obstacles for it.

But this does not mean he is going backwards, because the good qualities he has acquired lurk in the recess of his soul; he is dragged down to the point of dullness of reason, by unbridled sordid passions, which are allowed complete freedom. Only over time, in the trials of life, does he calm down, learn to control himself, begin to see everything correctly and master his instincts.

Imagine, for example, that all the mysteries of our science were suddenly revealed to the savage inhabitants of this world, and they see themselves as the possessors of the power we have. How would they use it? Appalled, not knowing what to do with them, and no longer restrained by obligatory obedience, they would become insolent, dissipative, evildoers, bringing danger both to themselves and to others, until they achieve equilibrium.

— I understand, master, but I still have a question you have never addressed. We humans have an enormous grace, that of having guardian spirits, invisible mentors, who inspire us, support us and protect us from enemies invisible to our rude eyes. And what about the animals? It seems to me thaat it has already been written that they become human, that they should also have a hidden protection.

— Absolutely right. All along the ascension path, the indestructible psychic spark has protectors, according to its level of evolution. The less developed the spirit, the less its individuality is delineated and, consequently, the assistance it receives; but as the consciousness of individuality sets it apart from the masses, it will be the object of attention. You will agree that to understand and guide the spirit of an amoeba, for example, is much easier than doing it with your own, my friend, and, that is why your advisor must have a different temperament.

In this, as in other matters of the world economy, there must be consistency. Thus, animal spirits are appointed to guide the first steps in the animal kingdom, , but they are much higher up the evolutionary ladder. This work not only develops their skills, but also serves as a useful occupation; at the same time, they are repaying what they have previously enjoyed .

Because of this immutable interaction, the great evolution takes place like a vicious circle, driven by a single principle, progressing slowly, but steadily; this is how it is, from souls that are not aware of themselves, still insensitive, but linked to the atom of matter, they help and support each other and slowly they become perfect spirits. The enormous upward spiral makes a detour, and those who have reached a certain height come back down to work, watch over and support those who are still climbing; the circle is closed , and this perpetuum mobile never ceases.

Dakhir fell thoughtfully silent, Kalitin also indulged in his ramblings; a minute later, he remarked:

— Thank you, master! The more you initiate me into the mysteries of creation, the smaller and more ignorant I feel. Blind, we overlook the mysterious ladder of perfection that unfolds within and around us. As we gaze into the past and look at what remains to be done, we begin to realize the infinite wisdom that created this movement governed by a very simple law, which keeps its effects, so varied and numerous, in perfect balance.

— Yes, my friend! The wisdom of the ineffable Being is inconceivable to us, who are mere atoms, even though His infinite goodness has provided us the strength to ascend and join Him through the rapture of the soul. Those who, in their ignorance, reject the existence of the superior Being, puffed up by their pretty human vanity and stucked in foolish ramblings, have always seemed ridiculous to me.

— You are absolutely right, master! Only ignorance can generate disbelief and non-existence; anyone who understands how wise and wonderful the laws that govern the development of the soul are, cannot be an atheist.

After a brief reflection, Kalitin added:

— Tell me, master, how could humanity, after so many centuries of progress and mental work, plunge into that social and religious chaos similar to what I experienced, unfortunately, on the extinct Earth?

I cannot imagine how your disciples could have reached this point of decadence, those chosen ones who were lucky enough to know you, to have you as their teacher and to understand the immutable laws that govern us. Even for the disciples here , inferior beings but enlightened by you, such terrible decadence causes indignation.

— We immortals are different beings, plucked by fate from the bosom of conventional humanity; I hope that none of you are among the remiss.

— Remiss? How do you understand it, and what did they do to earn this label? — Kalitin was alarmed.

Dakhir smiled dejectedly.

— To make this clear, I will explain the cyclical evolution of humanity in general terms. Furthermore, during the cycles, which alternate on this or another planet, the spiritual population changes and the same roles are played by a new cast of actors, climbing the social ladder of the Universe. So, the orgy you witnessed was just na extended repetition of a succession of similar events.

The picture I wanted to show you concerns the distant past of our ancient home, but it will be repeated in the distant future of the world in which we live. In the times to come, when the memory of us is buried beneath the ashes of bygone centuries, only folk traditions, tales and legends will be preserved associated with our knowledge, far away, obscure and incomprehensible.

Thus, at the end of a certain cycle of major catastrophes , the actors on the world stage are divided: some ascend to a higher planet, others descend to lower lands as promoters of progress, and the third, finally, although mentally evolved, but whose morality is still far from the desired level, stay on earth, constituting the so-called "fallen angels" – a mystery that is repeated in all worlds, both in our own and in the systems to which they correspond. Now imagine that the cycle is completed; the division is completed – some go up, others come down, and the armies of the third species are ordered by their superior judges and leaders, to remain on the same Earth in order to teach the people, who have just come from a lower planet, everything that the reason of the former has already researched, studied and assimilated in terms of faith, society, science, and morals. "Guide these weak minds and teach them what you have seen, known and learned" - that is the sentence. Now as for the "remisses", they do not seem very flattered by the mission entrusted to them, however great : they feel unhappy. They are far away from their friends, companions and even their enemies, in other words: from the entire spiritual family in which, for many centuries, they have concentrated their affection or their hostility. And you know that this last feelingt is the cause of many annoyances on the monotonous path of an eternal life.

They both laughed at the remark and Dakhir continued:

— Then our remnants, disgusted and full of disdain for the newly arrived spirits, are forced, for better or worse, to incarnate among these.

Spirits who are periodically swept away in rational migratory avalanches to a new world, are in every way inferior to their former inhabitants; they feel displaced, as if lost, without knowing how to take advantage of the benefits provided .

However, even though the fleshly mantle and forgetfulness do much to keep the " remisses" from being denounced , they have not lost the higher reason, the acquired knowledge, the intuition that animates their memories. As soon as the " remisses", are scattered among the masses, begin to recognize each other – not as individuals, but as their peers – they come together and join the fragments of the traditions that have been saved from destruction, forming a solid chain between them... They become masters of an ignorant multitude, to whom they have been summoned to guide and prodigalize the teachings.

Aware that the power over the human conscience is the most infallible, the "remisses", cunning and eager for authority, re-establish the priesthood and, from the back of the temples, shrouded in a veil of mystery, rule over the naive peoples, making them venerate and fear them, since they intercede for them with the Divinity, without which they would not survive. These legislators of the new cycle proclaim themselves – and with good reason, by the way – to be God's representatives on earth. Bad representatives, by the way! However, they were, in fact, appointed by the higher will to guide the lesser brothers and sisters, to stablish faith in God, the laws, to trace the path of ascent to Divinity and to promote the sciences and arts, of which they were the curators.

But instead of tolerance and love, which should be the hallmark of mentors worthy of the name , the "remisses" give wings to their vanity and selfishness, directing their wealth of knowledge and the forces of nature only to instill fear, seeking to solidify their power.

From the temples have come all those who are indispensable in guiding the destinies of peoples: kings, priests, scientists, doctors; but all of them jealously hide their knowledge; at best they begrudgingly share their fragments. and wherever their little brother's shrewd curiosity is directed , he always finds myself facing an impenetrable mystery.

— I do not think I understand you correctely," said Kalitin, taking advantage of a brief pause, "It seems to me that the servers you mention should be trained in centers of initiation… You seem to blame the " remisses" for hiding their knowledge under the veil of mystery, however...

He fell silent in confusion.

— Are you saying that we also act like this, and we should not judge the imitators? — said Dakhir , smiling mockingly, and making his disciple flush. — You don't need to justify yourself! From your point of view, you are right; but you know: in a song the important thing is the pitch. We measure truth by reason, and shroud only dangerous forces, because in the wrong hands they would be harmful and bring countless misfortunes. However, we are happy to spread the light, and we try to free everyone from ignorance . In short: we look for willing disciples; we do not reject anyone for fear of rivaling us. We prefer to elevate spirits rather than keep them in the dark, preventing them from satisfying their thirst for power and ambition. As for kings, priests or doctors, they must undoubtedly always be above the crowd in terms of knowledge, both spiritual and physical, and receive special training to fulfill their sacred commitments with dignity.

Returning to the question of the "remisses ", the positive side is that among them there are always highly evolved spirits who understand their destiny. It is precisely they who spread the teachings to their minors and accept disciples, being helped by missionaries. The latter, inspired by true love of their neighbor, come out of the darkness of the temples, proclaim the great truths and spread the immutable laws of concord and love. Among these missionaries are divine emissaries who open gaps of light in the darkness and drive progress for many centuries to come.

Time takes care of the rest. The degrees of knowledge that peoples attain and the social system, put in place by the rulers for their own welfare, promote habit, order and contribute to the development of intellects. Thus, the most energetic, persistent and sensible rise to the point where they become initiates.

Of course, these beginners are still overbearing and egoless in sharing their knowledge and enlightening the younger brothers and sister, and they shy away under the pretext of the oath of silence, exercising an even stricter domination than their predecessors. But the gap of light is open, and the army of masters is filling up with new adepts from the lower classes.

And even among the masters there are many transformations : a great number, after fulfilling their mission, leave the planet; others take on some special tasks and, under the aegis of a gigantic discovery, reveal a lost or forgotten scientific secret to their contemporaries.

This is how human development has been, enlightened and pushed forward by divine missionaries; and every time they rekindle the light of truth, the darkness thickens and faith begins to wane. I must make an observation here.

The first followers of any revelation, or, if you like, doctrine, once they have overcome the threshold of ignorance, become zealous and morally lofty, proclaiming the truth with their chests full, and promising to renew the world. With the disappearance of the great preacher and his first disciples, human being becomes accustomed to the light; subsequent followers end up forgetting the terrible cloak of darkness that enshrouded humanity, only seeking , without much enthusiasm, to enjoy the benefits obtained. In man, then, evil rises; the light, obtained with so much sacrifice, becomes a right of a few, which gradually fades away until it is completely extinguished, amid total indifference, disbelief, and rejection...

To understand this better, just remember what happened on our beloved dead Earth, in other words: how Osiris grew old, became stale and died, giving way to Jupiter, who in turn was replaced by the divine doctrine of Christ.

Note also that in every age of transition, men have furiously overthrown what they once revered; there is nothing sacred in the barbaric hands of the fanatics. But this crazy quickly volatilizes and, in the midst of new, transformed beliefs, the imitators of the past flourish.

Ingenious hands, highly intelligent heads usurp power, and the naive and ignorant masses are bound by shackles; then, those who shouted loudest against the atrocities and despotism of the temples, proclaim religious intolerance in all its aspects, and keep mankind, under the cruelest spiritual yoke for centuries.

Meanwhile, in this bloodthirsty school, skills develop; even those with a lesser gift for learning have caught up with their brothers and, breathing hatred and indignation, they climb the last steps that separate them from the "remiss".

Their beings suffered the most during the long journey of the arduous ascent; their intellect, heavier and less flexible, was imbued with vanity and narrowness. All they knew for ceratin was their knowledge, which they had acquired at the cost of many sacrifices; they only recognized the right to existence in what they could feel or prove with their imperfect instruments.

And since no scalpel is capable of discovering a soul in dissected matter, no microscope has ever provided them with the sight of an astral body, and they – much less – were not in a position to perceive the invisible, they concluded that only what can be seen exists, insolently discarding any spiritual principle of creation.

Presenting the laws of nature as na explanation - the ones they know, of course - they propagate materialism; non-existence takes the place of God; scientific intolerance, the predecessor of religious intolerance, reigns supreme and... And so we reach the end of a cycle.

The exact sciences – cruel, immutable and materialistic – grow and flourish; but in their ramifications, faith, shame and moral laws wither away.

A veritable orgy breaks out. Discoveries follow one and another and the terrible forces of nature are enslaved to dirty work; without knowing the laws that govern the giants of space, they are transformed into forced laborers; it does not cross their mind that the worst could happen, as with the sorcerer's apprentice who failed to tame the forces summoned.

Esoteric knowledge, which they used to use only in special cases and passed on only to trusted people, became the patrimony of the mob; by exorbitating it, becaus of undribled bas instincts, humanity was led to decadence, which you have already witnessed. In an instant, a new world catastrophe arises, putting an end to the criminal human species, its sciences, crimes, and abuses…

In this journey of humanity over the centuries, the moral and social history of the peoples, who replace each other on Earth, during the duration of a given cycle is included.

That, my son, is the thorny path of the lower nations that ascend to perfection by the invisible ladder. So it was, and so it will be; the interpreters change, but the roles and weaknesses remain the same.

And now it is time to part ways. Our conversation has gone on longer than usual, and if you want any further clarification, we can talk tomorrow.

CHAPTER VIII

Life in the divine city was peaceful, dedicated to work. The schools functioned well; in the great temple, work of great importance was being carried out. The hierophants felt that it was high time that tabernacles were set up in the forests and valleys, where the population could raise their prayers to the Divinity, begging them for help in pain, healing, curing diseases, establishing through faith and prayers an indissoluble contact between suffering humanity and the forces of good.

To this end, sacred statues were being made, which would later be installed near the miraculous springs, in regions prolific in medicinal herbs and other places of natural health treatment.

The production of statues was a very complex craft, involving a magical ritual, in which only chief hierophants and virgins of high initiation could take part.

In one of the caves, next to the temple, there was a workshop illuminated by a pale bluish light, where the raw material for the work was found: precious minerals.

On one occasion, Supramati was in the underground workshop with seven maidens, dressed, according to the ritual, in white robes, girded with silver belts and with bare arms . Supramati, also dressed in a white suit and with the sparkling insignia on his chest was working next to huge vats arranged along the wall.

To the substance in the vat - something like a light blue flour paste - he added a colorless liquid from a bottle with a gold stopper, cadentially pronouncing magical formulas.

The contents of the vat were transferred to a stone table and Supramati began to shape a human figure, at first very rudimentary, with only the head and torso outlined. The seven young women then, joined hands and formed a circle around the magician, singing a melodious song.

When this sketch of the sculpture was finished, Supramati took a piece of the dough, set it aside, poured a few drops of the primal essence, brought from the extinct planet onto it, and kneaded the dough. Then he made a sign calling one of the girls, and she divided it into two parts, one of which she shaped into a heart, and the other into a brain. Supramati placed the "organs" in their respective places in the body of the statue.

A few days later, the statue was ready. The statue represented a woman of heavenly beauty, wearing a long dress and a long veil on her head. The workmanship and the marvelous expression on her face mede it a true work of art. At midnight, Supramati soaked the eyes, the tips of the feet and the palms of the hands of the image with the primal matter, which had not yet lost its effects.

Once this was done, the girls took the statue into the adjoining cave, placed it on an altar that had been raised a few steps high, and around it they arranged tripods containing resinous twigs that were abundantly impregnated with a red substance, as ticky as tar, which also contained the primal essence.

When the tripods were lit, everyone left the cave and locked the door so that no one could enter for three days.

Once the deadline had passed, the cave was opened and a reasonable group of women gathered around the altar, mostly female magicians, but also made up disciples from the female school. In front of the altar, in front of everyone, stood the seven virgins who had taken part in the making of the statue; they were headed by Nara. From the crown that adorned her blonde head, golden beams sparkled. The women, holding crystal harps, were readying themselves with their hands on the strings, waiting for the moment to begin singing and lighting the tripods.

Nara got down on her knees and said a prayer, fixing her gaze on the statue, which then began to take on an extraordinary appearance. The body, behind the transparent veil, seemed to gasp, as if she were breathing, and her eyes seemed to be alive.

Nara stood up and turned to the women present.

She seemed transfigured. A phosphorescent mist emanated from her whole body, her breath seemed to be scorching and colored purple; streams of light poured from her slender fingers, and her head was girdled wit na igneous crown.

She prayed ardently and, in this powerful supplication, she cried out for the Divinity to send her its reflection, which would be engraved on the earth, to protect human creatures, the blind and the carnally and spiritually poor.

Then a violent roar was heard, the vault seemed to disappear; torrents of argent light poured down from above and over the beams, shimmering like snow under the sun, the golden image of a woman of heavenly beauty descended on the altar. Her translucent countenance breathed deep sadness; her large , incredibly deep eyes, radiated benevolence and mercy, compassionate for the afflictions and anguish of the human heart, which she would alleviate, already moved by the tears that would still flow at her feet.

As she got closer, the specter seemed to densify and incorporated itself into the statue; the forehead and chest – where the brain and heart were located – seemed to light up momentarily, enveloping the whole figure in an intense aurifulgent glow .

At the same moment, the arms of the statue rose and remained in an open position, as if to attract those who approached it, and in its eyes glowed sparks of life . After singing a hymn of thanks the women left the cave.

A few days later, a long procession of priestesses left the city of the gods and headed for the valleys. Some carried something wrapped in a linen cloth; others took turns carrying the float, where a long, bulky object covered in a silver cloak was . The morning promised to be a beautiful day; a cool breeze swayed the long transparent veils and white robes of the girls.

As they descended from the plateau where the city of the Magicians stood, the procession took a path and bravely entered the virgin forest. Apparently, the path was familiar to them and, after quite a long walk, they found themselves in front of a picturesque valley. Descending the verdant hill to the lake, the opposite side of which was surrounded by high rocks, the priestesses circled the lake until they came out at the entrance to a cave hidden by wild grapevines.

The grotto was spacious and apparently specially prepared; at the bottom, at the height of three steps, there was a marble altar, above which was a tall, narrow niche . The statue was placed in front of the altar and the mantle was removed, and it was immediately installed in the niche; above the depression, there was a fissure or crack, through which light escaped; suddenly, this was replaced by flashes of sunlight, which illuminated the statue and the whole grotto with a wonderful sapphire-blue light.

From the wall of the cave a spring gushed , whose crystalline waters flowed into a natural pool and, through it, into the lake.

Nara approached the fountain, sprinkled a few drops of primal matter into it, and then sprayed the cave walls and the earth copiously. The liquid was instantly absorbed by the rock and earth and, a few minutes later, the water in the pond seemed to boil, turning a light blue color. And – a curious fact – as it flowed into the pond, the water spring did not mix with it , tearing folds in a blue band to the opposite shore.

Nara continued her work, assisted by other priestesses, who brought her vials of the primal matter diluted in varying proportions, with which she watered the earth around the lake. These first sanctuaries, with their miraculous fountains, had yet another purpose: the people of early childhood, still crude by nature, with their obtuse and uncultured intellects, did not have the l slightest magnetic, mediumship or intuitive power; however, from that crowd, receptive beings -clairvoyant and salutators -, would be formed, in other words, the flexibilization of their spirits would be promoted, making them suitable to receive progress.

The powerful astral force contained in the primal substance, mixed with the spring water , would influence the astral body, protecting it from the most vulgar emanations, while the soil, impregnated with that incredible and tender substance, would produce herbs and plants - or even influence minerals - with vigorous therapeutic properties.

The use of these plants, as well as baths in miraculous waters, would have a surprising effect on the primitive population, making them more receptive to the fluidic irradiation, sharpening their good instincts, allowing the magicians to influence their astral organisms, so that they could then use them as a sensitive and flexible instrument.

In the tabernacles, similar to the one that had been set up, young girls and women would live alternately, disciples of a lower degree, with the mission of attracting the inhabitants of the valleys and forests to the place, getting them used to bathing and taking the therapeutic waters, collecting and using the herbs in medicine.

After blessing the young girl who would be staying in the cave, Nara returned to the city with her companions.

Ceremonies similar to this would be repeated frequently. All over the continent, in response to the magicians' orders, these natural sanatoriums were set up where suffering humanity could seek relief from their ailments. Many of those miraculous springs of complex chemical composition, which provide cures for thousands of sick people, are due to the benevolent actions of the ancient primeval masters…

Among the magicians working on the installation of the medicinal springs was Urjane, who had led this kind of expedition several times before. And so, once again, preparations were made for a new journey, which would take even longer, because the cave to be inaugurated was located in a very remote region. For such a trip, Urjane wanted to take advantage of Narayana's absence, who was leaving with the students from the art school on an expedition to get the materials he needed.

To Urjane's surprise, Dakhir provided her with a different list of personally selected girls who would accompany her. Soon after Narayana's departure, her father called her.

Dakhir was in his room, sitting by the open window, not working and looking worried about something.

After kissing her father, Urjane sat down in front of him and, since her thoughts were still on the determination she had received from her father in the morning, she immediately asked him:

— Tell me, why should I take the women I did not choose with me? Except for my friend Avani, all the others leave something to be desired, both in terms of knowledge and degree of initiation. Their will is less powerful, and so it will be more difficult for us to summon the divine recording. Besides, our group is smaller than usual.

— Your observations are fair, however, the order undoubtedly had very important motives, and you should have understood that," replied Dakhir sternly .

Urjane looked at her father in alarm.

— You are right. Forgive my intemperate question! From how serious you look, I should know that something is oppressing you. Are you not angry about some slip-up of mine, or disappointed in me for something? Perhaps, due to my ignorance, I have made a mistake. If not, what could you be worried about? Since we are immune to human weaknesses and worries... We do not fear illnessor death, at least not in the distant future; we are immune to human misfortunes, malevolence and hostility.

A smile flashed across Dakhir's handsome face when he heard those words. He stroked his daughter's silky head and said:

— Nodear, you have done nothing wrong, and I have no reason to be disappointed. True, none of the aforementioned misfortunes can befall us; but there are still trials, which can befall a magician as much as an ordinary mortal. The higher you climb, the more arduous the trials on the narrow path of ascent.

You forget that the reason we avoided a conventional death was to become legislators and enlighteners of the new world. The supreme will put us on this earth, not to live in palaces, enjoy the luxury and beauty that surrounds us, which is provided thanks to our knowledge and magical power. No, we are here to establish relations with rude and savage peoples, who are nevertheless capable of assimilating civilization. This humanity, which until now has led a practically vegetable existence, has matured, to be divide into nations, to form kingdoms and, when the proper level of its intellectual development has been reached, to begin the great spiritual enterprise of its ascension.

Dormant in its long vegetative period, the planet must awaken to intense intellectual activity; at the same time, the fierce conflicts of the passions - pride, vanity, hostility, and other low instincts – will erupt. Nevertheless, this clash will serve as an impetus for progress and will forge strong spirits that will lead peoples.

We are still on the bottom rung of the ladder; but, at the first tremor that will shake the masses of humanity, it is you whom fate has reserved for the sublime sacrifice of enduring an arduous but worthy ordeal. Will you submit to these designs without resentment or disgust?

Urjane raised her clear and gentle gaze.

— I am your daughter, and I readily submit to any sacrifice you impose ; I know that you would never provide anything beyond my strength.

— I thank you for your confidence, my dear child, and I am sure that you will be up to your mission, even if it is difficult . You will be deprived of the well-being you enjoy in this divine city; you will be away from us for some time and in a wild environment; you will have to be brave, support and lead, use your knowledge wisely and wait, humbly and patiently, for the hour of your liberation. And now, tell me, do you remember Abrasack?

— That disgusting disciple of Narayana, who kidnapped him and then ran away? Yes, I remember him. He always disgusted me, especially on the day of my engagement. Abrasack came with the other disciples to greet us, and I casually intercepted his scorching gaze, full of impure passion, which gave me goose bumps. But Narayana has always been blind to him, in awe of his intelligence," Urjane concluded bitterly.

Dakhir smiled.

— Narayana has his reasons. Abrasack is a man of unparalleled intelligence and gigantic willpower. Unfortunately, his morals are far inferior to his intellect; in spite of everything, his achievements will be enormous and his legendary name will cross the centuries, even if today he is nothing more than a criminal, blinded by pride and the insane passion you inspire in him. To have you, he is willing to take heaven by storm, but first he will kidnap you.

An intense blush covered Urjane's face, which alternated with an intense pallor.

And will you allow this ignoble act? I know I have no right to question the decision of the magicians, but in exchange for what do they want my shame? Will I, defenseless, have to be handed over, to satisfy the animal passion of that filthy man?

— Of course not! You will be protected against his violence, I will give you a gun, right now. Bring me the carved box on the desk.

Leaving the box on the windowsill, Dakhir opened it and took out a thin gold chain with a star-shaped medallion in the center of which a droplet of strange substance flickered and reverberated.

— Hang it on your lap! It is a very powerful talisman, activated every time Abrasack's aura collides with you, repelling him. If you want him to come closer, to talk to him or shake his hand, turn the star.

— And if he realizes that I am carrying the talisman. That animal will tear it off ; besides, he is smart enough to know the magical power of an object from the daughter of the three-fanged wizard .

— Fear not, he will never know. The star is invisible to his eyes. As for how to contact me, to talk to me or Narayana, or to see from a distance what is happening here, I do not need to tell you, because you have received sufficient initiation and you will know how to communicate with me to ease the anguish of separation.

— In any case, I will be away from you, mother and Narayana for some time, having to endure the presence and insolence of that disgusting man," Urjane muttered, and a few bitter tears glistened on her cheeks. — If I only knew how long my purge would last! — she complained.

— It will last as long as the struggle between Abrasack and Narayana lasts; the former will do anything to arrest her, and the latter to get her back. It will be the first conscious war on the planet, the first armed clash that will awaken courage, rivalry, competitiveness and pride, in other words, the impulses that rekindle the passions and potential of the human soul.

— But where will the armies come from? Abrasack is alone, Narayana too . Where will they find warriors ? The magicians, of course, will not fight, because their mental potential , thank God, is quite " awake".

Dakhir could not contain his laughter.

— Do not be so mean to us poor wizards, Urjane. As for the armies, do not worry: they will sort themselves out. Abrasack is not alone, you will be convinced of that in his palace; his armies will be made up of rougher and wilder beings, but who are already on the road to progress. Narayana, for his part, will lead the tribes educated by the missionaries.

— Poor Narayana, what a terrible blow my loss will be for him! And if I have to leave tomorrow as planned, I will not even say goodbye to him! Perhaps the intended kidnaping will still take time?

— Would you not believe that Narayana would have let you travel if he had suspected the plot? No, he is too "human" and would have done a lot of silly things. The work he will have to do to free you will serve as an atonement ; he is stubborn, obstinate and so sure of himself that he will not even accept advice or a warning from anyone. The hard lesson that Abrasack will have to learn will be a good one , and will make him more careful from now on.

Urjane sighed heavily.

— Thank you, Father, for the warning. At least now I know what awaits me and I will try to live up to the mission entrusted to me.

Dakhir gave her an affectionate look. The education and strict discipline at the school of magicians had borne fruit, sowing in the chosen soul submission to the higher will and the firm and serene decision to accept the trial, which, however hard , was already a step forward.

— We are apprentices of conscious effort in the laboratory of the Eternal and, that is why the knowledge we have acquired, my child, cannot degenerate into pride and serve only our own benefit; our duty is to bring light to the darkness and chaos where our inferior brothers and sisters are to be found. While we were weak, ignorant, and incapable of defending and guiding ourselves, we were victims of the elements, which decimated us; now we govern them in the same way that you will govern inferior beings. Courage! I am fully convinced that you will endure the ordeal required of you with dignity.

Bidding her parents a gentle farewell, Urjane withdrew. She felt the need to be alone and to pray; she accepted the test willingly, but her heart was squeezed at the thought of being separated from everything she loved.

Let us now return to Abrasack, who was feverishly continuing his preparations. The palace was now ready, except for some work on the inside, which was very difficult.

They also continued to build houses for their friends during the day, while at night they worked tirelessly in one of the city halls , illuminated by concentrated light, making furniture and crockery out of precious metals, whose rough workmanship left something to be desired.

One of the great difficulties was making cloth. They did not know how to make them, nor did they have any looms; meanwhile, the clothes of Abrasack and his companions were in tatters.

He then patiently set about researching a plant whose existence he knew, after having read its description in one of Narayana's manuscripts on the flora of the new world; and finally, he discovered it. It grew in a marshy place, in the shade of cliffs that protected it from the sun rays. Thick dark red stems crawled across the surface; huge white flowers variegated in colorful filigrees; the pumpkin-sized fruits were greygreen and had a sour, pleasant and refreshing t taste. The most curious thing were the roots. As thick as a human arm and rough as a turtle's scaly shell, they stuck out of the marshy soil, ending up in spheres even larger than the fruit. When they were carefully dug up, a strange material was found that wrapped the stem, resembling transparent threads, that could be unwound. In each bulb , there were six to ten meters of this crude, gauze-like material.

Once the material had been spread on the ground, the material dried quickly and increased in thickness, and on contact with it, you could easily take it for soft silk; if you layered it in layers, while it was still raw , the stratification disappeared and you obtained a satiny material that fused firmly together. It was an extraordinarily resistant fabric, of various colors, depending on the color of the chalices: pink, lilac, golden yellow and turquoise.

Once he had that wonderful fabric, Abrasack felt in control of the situation, and his joy knew no bounds. A large stock of plants was then made and fabrics of various densities and applications were produced.

Finally, everything was finished in Abrasack's house, and his supporters were finishing the decorations as capriciously as they could. Some of the aboriginal women had been taught how to make nails, which were made painstankingly in the workshops; they were used to join boards and other materials.

With satisfaction mixed with bitterness, Abrasack examined the poor, shabby dwellings where he intended to put Urjane and her companions. Despite the abundance of precious metals used in the decoration, the whole look was disordered and even laughable; in short: they were nothing more than the dwellings of savages.

And when Abrasack imagines the disdain and scorn with which Urjane would react to his humble "palace", he reddens with anger; however, nothing could make him hesitate in his decision to kidnap his beloved woman. For the time being, she would have to be content with his love, and as soon as the divine city was taken, he would compensate her for the hardships e she had experienced.

With the energy and determination inherent in him, he began to devise a plan to kidnap her. It would not be possible in the divine city; but he knew of the plans to set up shrines in the valleys and forests with the statues made in secret by the superior magicians.

Undoubtedly, so many years after his escape, many tabernacles should have been opened; perhaps, by good fortune, Urjane would attend them and visit the sick.

When he set off on his reconaissance expeditions, he always wore the fabric that made him invisible and approached the outskirts of the city of the Magicians, riding the Dark One, whose sight would not attract so much suspicion.

He became convinced that numerous tabernacles had been set up well away from the no-go zone. Later, he discovered that, in a valley between mountains, not far from where he had his headquarters, the earthlings were preparing a cave for a new sanctuary, under the direction of a magician and some initiates.

Hiding in a nearby crevice, he overheard the conversation of two young initiates, and found out that a ceremony would be held in a few days, with Urjane taking her turn. He also heard mention of some female adepts who would accompany her; Abrasack knew them all personally: they were as beautiful as celestial visions.

He returned home, overjoyed: apparently the occult forces were sponsoring his cause and that of his friends.

After talking to his friends and discussing the kidnapping plan, Abrasack thought it best not to get directly involved in the kidnapping of the young priestesses, as such violence could generate their anger and disgust. He would go outside and later present himself in the role of a liberator.

It was therefore decided that the aborigines would take charge of the imprisonment, whose repulsive appearance alone would panic the women, . The smartest savages were then selected; and it took a lolt of of work to make them understand what was expected of them; but, with the help of gifts, delicacies and promises, they ended up being seduced, and the fear of disobeying did the rest, for Abrasack provoked a mixture of dread and fascination in the savages, who habitually submitted to him as much as his companions.

With pain in her heart, Urjane prepared for the journey, whose unfortunate end she already knew. After praying ardently, she visited her magical palace, the place of her happiness and peace.

Since the destination was far away, the statue was loaded onto na airplane; it would be driven by Urjane and her friend Avani, who had also undergone the first initiation.

They woul not be accompanied by any of the men, since the journey would present no danger, as the savage tribes of the neighboring nations were considered peaceful and harmless; moreover, they had a feeling of respect, fear and adoration for the superior beings, regarding them as messengers of good health and many benefits. As for the wild animals, they did not inpire fear in them; the smell they emanated, as a result of the primal matter had taken, would send them fleeing.

Without a hitch, the priestesses arrived at their destination. The statue was installed according to the ritual described; in view of some issues to be resolved around the sanctuary, they would have to extend their stay for three or more days.

In the late afternoon, the priestesses retired to the cave to rest and sleep; by dawn, they were all up and preparing to go to a nearby stream.

Suddenly, they saw a terrified crowd of beings they had never seen before approaching. A group of hairy giants with the face of monkeys, armed with sticks and maces at their belts, came leaping towards the women.

Seized with terror, they had no time to flee; the savages threw themselves screaming at them, and raising each one in their colossal arms, their prey ran back. Leaping high, they reached the woods, and took refuge there with their spoils.

In vain did the young girls try to resist; in the strong arms of their captors, they looked like struggling babies; and and finally, mute with fear, they all fell into a kind of numbness.

The journey was long and terrible. The branches creaked under the giants' heavy feet ; the trees that blocked their way, were torn up by their roots, like bundles of straw. Finally, they descended into a valley, at the bottom of which was a lake . The descent was made over sharp rocks, but the giants, with the agility of the monkeys, leapt over them, letting out guttural grunts from time to time.

When they found themselves in the valley, the forest dwellers stopped indecisively; in the meantime, Abrasack and his companions emerged from the bush Pretending to be surprised, they threw themselves at the giants, swinging their axes.

Immediately, dropping their precious cargo, the kidnappers fled in a stampede, shouting loudly.

Abrasack and his friends then began to lift the priestesses off the ground. They were all dressed in their best clothes; Abrasack was even wearing a silver Grail knight's tunic , stolen before the escape. Their appearance was decent enough, if it had not been scorched by the looks with which they devoured the beautiful maidens shivering next to Urjane and Avani.

Trembling and barely able to contain his happiness at finally having gotting the woman he wanted, Abrasack bowed to Urjane.

— Allow me, noble Urjane, to express my esteem and joy for having freed you from the hands of these savages.

— Ah, is that you Abrasack? I thank you very much, and I must admit that those disgusting creatures that attacked us have scared me to death. But who are these people accompanying you? Do they belong to any race from the extinct planet? They are not the ones we brought back from there!

— No, they are my friends and companions. I will tell you their story later; you and your friends must be exhausted with nerves, so I suggest that you rest. Allow me to accompany you to the humble house of the banished fugitive, where you will find shelter.

— I thank you and gladly accept the invitation," replied Urjane in a cold but mesured tone.

Abrasack's devouring gaze and the effluvia of his tempestuous passion, when they reached the pure and sensitive organism of the initiate, were the cause of an inexpressible exhaustion.

— The way here is difficult, so let me to offer you the services of our winged horses," added Abrasack, lifting Urjane, who, however, did not put up any resistance.

Each of his companions approached a priestess; and only then did they realize that one of them, Avani, was missing a partner. Abrasack hesitated for a moment, but soon proposed decisively:

— I will take both of them. Let us call for a ride.

He whistled loudly, joined by his companions; minutes later, the winged dragons pointed into the sky and landed obediently on the earth.

Abrasack mounted the Dark One, palced Urjane in front and told Avani to settle in the back, holding on tightly to him. The detachment took off .

Urjane was calm and impassive. She had expected the events, and the awareness of her strength, and the certainty of her father and Narayana's protection gave her back her emotional balance. The ordeal had begun and all she had to so was endure it with dignity.

Curious, she began to observe the unknown plains overflown by the winged dragon. Soon they reached the endless virgin forests; Urjane was surprised that in some places there were clearings marked by rudimentary huts with flat roofs, inhabited by the same species of hairy giants that had carried out that kidnapping.

After landing, Urjane found herself in front of the entrance to a large flat-roofed house; a few white stone steps led up to a gallery, supported by tetrahedral columns; a number of plants, in tubs, gave the room a certain life .

Abrasack led the visitors directly into the hall of the house; in the center was a table, set in advance, probably for a banquet. The crudely finished dishes contained fruit, bread and boiled vegetables; in odd jugs, eager to look exquisite, adorned with colored gems, there was milk and a strong drink, produced by the host himself.

Urjane's countenance frowned in annoyance as she gazed at those elaborate delicacies, ; , she let herself to be led to the chair, which was a little higher than the others, resembling a kind of throne. Abrasack sat between her and Avani; all the others sat down, so that a lady was interspersed with a knight.

Pale, the poor young ladies cast worried glances at the strangers next to them and sometimes at Urjane. Mastering her restlessness, she accepted the glass of milk and the fruit.

Half-heartedly, Abrasack seemed to be impatiently examining the meeting impatiently, thinking about the best way to begin a definitive explanation; in his nervousness, he had forgotten that the wizard could read his thoughts.

Suddenly, Urjane interrupted his thoughts:

— Everything here leads me to believe that you premeditated the banquet. I have heard that you are quite good at fortune-telling; could you not have foreseen our misfortune and our arrival at your home?

Abrasack's tanned face flushed, and a disturbed spark flashed in his black eyes.

— You were not wrong, noble Urjane. I really did see you coming; so, I salute you all as good geniuses, who have come to put an end to our solitude, and who, with skill and beauty, will adorn our monotonous life as hermits.

Driven by the will of destiny to enlighten the inferior peoples, still in their animal state, we were unable to find consorts in their midst that suited us. You have solved our problem. Your companions, elevated, beautiful creatures, made into divine vision, will become faithful wives of my friends; young, handsome and energetic, they will not be undeserving of them. From their union will come new divine generations, who will reign over these savages, civilizing them.

You, Urjane, will be my queen; and if what I can offer you at this moment seems too little and too meager, in the future I will lay the world at your feet; for now," he raised his cup, "I drink to the health of the divine wives and to this day of our marriage.

Urjane listened to him without interrupting; among her young friends, there were shouts and cries of indignation.

— Traitor! Ungrateful! You kidnapped us with the help of those disgusting servants, and now you and your cowardly accomplices want to abuse us? Or have you forgotten that I am the wife of Narayana, your benefactor, who armed you with the strength you exorbitantly use? — Urjane was indignant, measuring Abrasack with a look full of contempt. — Give us back our freedom, otherwise your ignominious act may cost you dearly.

Abrasack crossed his arms and, insolent and defiant, looked at Urjane.

— If I had been afraid of the consequences of my act, I would not have fled the city of wizards and... to this day, I see no reason to regret it. I hope it will be like that forever. Do not be angry, Urjane! You and your companions belong to us irrevocably; thousands of my servants, fearsome and terrible, will be watching the palace and the houses of my friends, with orders to finish off anyone who dares to approach one of you.

You and your friends will be our wives; give up resisting uselessly now. Friends! Take your chosen ones home, as beautiful and comfortable as circumstances allow. Very soon, the hands of the sorceresses will adorn everything with their marvelous works of art.

Abrasack's accomplices, who had been waiting feverishly for that moment, each snatched their priestess and took them away, disregarding the tears and the desperate resistance of the virgins struggling in their arms. Only Urjane, Abrasack and Avani stayed in the room.

There was a heavy silence . Urjane got up, pushed back the chair and, leaning back in it, waited serenely for the outcome; only her rapid breathing and the expression of anger in her eyes betrayed her disturbance.

— Well, Urjane, will you submit voluntarily or will I have to use violence? You will be mine, that is for suret! — asseverated Abrasack in a deaf voice.

— I cannot be your wife, because I am united to Narayana; and to be your mistress of my own free will would be too much to expect from an honest woman who had just been initiated ," Urjane maintained calmly.

Abrasack's face lit up and, visibly furious, he took a step towards her; but at that moment Avani stepped between them and forced him back.

— Stop, you insane creature, and do not aggravate your guilt with the irremediable crime of attacking your benefactor's wife! I sense that you need a life partner; take me, then, in your place, and release her to her husband and family. Despite the violence you have resorted to in order to take possession of us, I will be your wife and try to soften your cruel heart and moderate your daring acts. Give up, Abrasack, the unequal struggle against beings before whom you are nothing but a pygmy. Establish your power over these primitive peoples, enlighten them, suggest the Divinity to them and, perhaps, you will be forgiven this great sin, that of your disobedience. Do not begin your reign with such a clumsy and ungrateful act!

Abrasack stepped back and, surprised, looked at the enchantingly beautiful young priestess in her burst of generosity.

Her bleached lilac face flushed a soft pink , and in her large eyes, dark as a moonless night, he could see the greatness of her pure soul. Yes, she was as beautiful as Urjane, but she did not inspire him with love, while the one who hated him had enslaved his soul forever.

He sighed and replied after a minute's hesitation:

— I thank you, Avani, for your sensible words and for the generous offer, but I cannot accept it. I have loved Urjane ever since I saw her, and this love has become fatal in my life. She has been the inspiration for all my actions; I have risked everything to win her, and I am prepared to defend my possession tooth and nail. Fate has been my ally until now, and I am sure it will be in the future, to make what I have planned come true.

Since fortune exempts you from being the wife of a mortal, I designate you, Avani, as the goddess of the temple I have erected, which lacked a priestess . You, predestined to be always beautiful and young, you will reign in the temple, and the people will deify you; the people will bring you offerings and venerate, in your person, the unprecedented divine beauty.

Well, that is enough for today! I am generous, and I understand that you, Urjane, must get used to your new living conditions and rest from the many emotions you have experienced today. I will accompany you to your quarters.

He took a small horn from behind his belt and blew it. Almost immediately, two furry giants opened up a kind of curtain, where the repulsive giants armed with gnarled sticks stood in full view. Abrasack motioned the wizards to follow him, and they did, submissively. Grim-faced, they crossed the gallery and entered a spacious room with a door and a large window.

— Both by the door and under the window, my faithful servants will be watching, so do not even think of running away," he warned in a threatening tone.

Bowing, he left. Avani dropped onto the wooden bench and covered her face with her hands; Urjane began an inspection of the room.

Apparently, the decoration of the room had been a lot of work for the host. Chiseled wooden trim adorned the walls, along which there were a few chairs, a bookshelf, and a chest in gold and silver; but they were all rather bland artifacts. At the back, there was a large low bed with a baldachin and curtains made from the amazing fabric made by Abrasack; the blankets and sheets were also maded from it. In the center of the room, a table with baskets contained fruit, a jug of milk, honey and a vase of wonderful flowers.

After the inspection , Urjane sat down next to her friend and said in a gentle tone

— Do not cry Avani! In order to endure the ordeal worthily, we must have courageand coldblood; crying will do no good. Let me thank you with a kiss for your great selflessness.

— What good has my good intention done? The stubborn rascal will not let you go, and for the height of insolence, he wants to force me to perpetuate a profane comedy; to play the Divinity. I will never let that happen. I cannot hold back the tears just thinking about you.

Urjane thought for a moment and pondered :

— Do not worry about me! I will be able to defend myself against this paranoid and his violence. As for the strange idea that haunts this despot. Of making you a goddess, I think I had better consult my father, which I will do as soon as it is dark.

Talking and consoling each other, they waited for complete darkness to arrive; to their disappointment, an electric sphere suddenly flashed in one of the rooms. It illuminated the room with silver light.

Urjane, however, began the invocation. As soon as she had finished pronouncing the formulas and drawing the appropriate Kabbalistic signs with the small magic stick she kept behind her belt, there was a deafening roll of thunder and a crackling sound; the room was swept by a fierce gust of wind. Then, a kind of sphere erupted, flaming and incandescent; it swirled for a moment, wrapped itself in a whitish mist, densified, took on a human shape and... A few steps away from the friends, the slender figure of Dakhir appeared.

Urjane wanted to throw herself into his arms, but he quickly raised his hand and said:

— Do not touch me, I am impregnated with electricity. Although you have not invoked me directly, I have come to support you, dear children, and to show you that you are not alone or abandoned.

— I know Dad, that I am here to fulfill the plans you spoke to me; Avani, however, feels very depressed about the role the insolent man wants her to play.

Heartbroken, Avani relayed the conversation with Abrasack about his plans with her; Dakhir listened attentively and said in a serious tone:

— Your role would be unworthy and unholy, if your soul overflowed with pride and dared to think of yourself as a divinity, before whom the poor innocent savages would prostrate themselves. As long as you, with faith and humility in your heart, pray for them, heal , comfort , and enlighten them, using your charm for good, you will have fulfilled your task. Another purpose, no less important, will be achieved naturally, beyond your control. For the primitive and brutish people, you will be the personification of a superior, unseen and pure beauty, . As they raise their prayers and contemplate you in adoration, they will engrave your image, thus creating the first astral images of beauty, which in turn will be reflected in their descendants. Their appearance is fearsome, because it is the result of the brute forces of nature. Therefore, I think you should play the role that was devised by this criminal but brilliant genius man, whose lack of wisdom is compensated by spiritual intuition.

You, Urjane, will also have a lot of work to do here. By now, you must have understood the criteria that guided the choice of your companions, compelled to be the wives of Abrasack's friends. Console and guide them, suggest that they commit themselves to bringing these men to their senses, cultivating their spirit for the good. That they never hate or think of taking revenge for the violence perpetrated.

The primitive peoples that surround them present themselves as a wide field of work. By taking advantage of your influence over Abrasack, or in other words, the passion that inspires him, you will be able to direct this man's enourmous qualities towards the good, achieving a great feat. You have plenty of time , because you will not soon be fighting the great battles that will mark a new era . For us immortals, time is the least important thing. Here is a small gift for you both , which will help you consolidate your supremacy," Dakhir continued, placing two crystal vials capped with gold stoppers on the table. — A drop of this liquid, diluted in a bucket of water, is enough to obtain a remedy for diseases, wounds and so on. And now, so long and be strong!

He blessed his daughter and her friend and then disappeared.

Urjane and Avani, accustomed to the orders of superior magicians, thanks to their strict discipline and unrestricted obedience, did not even think of protesting. Still distressed, but resigned, they talked for a while, lay down and fell asleep.

CHAPTER IX

For a few days, the two prisoners were completely alone. Neither Abrasack nor any of his friends, showed up. Every morning, one of the host's friends mutely brought them the daily meals; in the gallery and under the window. Their master's disgusting servants continued to watch them.

Finally, one morning, Abrasack appeared, overjoyed, announcing that the temple was finished and that he had gone to fetch Avani to take her to her new workplace.

Without exchanging a single word, Avani kissed her friend and left with Abrasack.

When they left the city, not far from the protective walls, they took a desert path criss-crossed with rocks and came to a narrow crevice, through which a slender person of medium height passed. The crevice stretched across the entire rock massif, ending in an open space, in the center of which there was a open space, where grotesque steps of a ladder could be seen. After a fairly long descent through a winding passage, they reached an opening the width of a door, enclosed by a curtain. As soon as Abrasack opened it, Avani was stunned.

She found herself in front of a huge grotto, lost in the distance, supported by natural columns and forming a vault, as if in a cathedral. By some strange quirk of nature, the light penetrating through an invisible crack was a light blue that gave the entire interior a heavenly color ; the transparent, sapphire blue water, gushing from an abundant fountain, bubbled into a natural tank in the center of the grotto. It was impossible to know where the excess water would end up.

Hidden by a curtain, the entrance was one a level above the floor; next to it, inside a high, deep niche, was a baldachin in the shape of a throne.

In front of the niche, at the height of two stone steps from the floor, there was an elongated, tetrahedral altar made of solid gold, interspersed with two bizarre triptychs. On the altar, there were also various objects for the worship of offerings.

I discovered this cave by chance and ordered it turned into a temple," declared Abrasack, overflowing with satisfaction. — My intention was to make it into a statue; but first, fate sent me a deity in the flesh . We did our utmost to give order to the temple. Enthroned in it, your mission will be to bestow spiritual wisdom on the people, who will take you as their goddess. All that is left now is to show your living facilities .

He took her to an adjoining cave, also illuminated in blue, provided with as much comfort as could be offered in those circumstances.

— In that box you will find all kinds of powders, herbs, and everything else you need that I can offer you," added Abrasack, pointing to a large box next to the wall. — Your worship begins at sunrise and lasts until three o'clock in the afternoon; after that, the entrance to the temple will be forbidden, so you can rest and do whatever you want. Urjane will be able to visit you. In the evening, if you wish, you can visit us. Escorted by guards, of course. Your worship service begins tomorrow.

After waving goodbye, he left.

Some time later, the savages began to gather in crowds on the wide plain that stretched out in front of the cave entrance, which was obstructed just as much as the mountain peaks by huge blocks of rock.

The inhabitants of the small town and many other neighboring villages were there; those who lived further away sent their representatives to the meeting organized by Abrasack.

The crowd of feathered giants was churning like a raging sea; everyone was eager to know why the king had summoned them.

Suddenly, Abrasack came down from the heights, riding on the dragon. Landing in the middle of the wilderness, he announced loudly to the people that the great God – of whom he had already told them that he rules the universe, and who with his hands had created everything that was visible, including them – had spoken to him, Abrasack.

God, who dwelt behind the clouds, in a palace of indescribable beauty, said that the Gaia people (that is what the simian giants were called) would be worthy, from that day on, of a glimpse of the visible divinity – the only daughter of the great God; she would descend from her father's palace, to inhabit the underground palace, a path that he, Abrasack, would show them. They could go to this personified and living deity with their requests. The next day, at sunrise, he would take them to the feet of the deity, but until then they had to remain there, in the valley.

Just as Abrasack was speaking , dark clouds covered the sky and a terrible storm broke out; flashes of lightning tore through the sky in all directions and the rumbling thunder shook the earth.

The mob would have dispersed in terror, if it had not been for an imperial order that had nailed them in place.

Finally, at dawn, the storm subsided and Abrasack reappeared. Before he had terrified the people, he now set about calming them down, explaining that the storm had been caused by the descent from heaven of the daughter of God; that he would lead the subjects to her, that he would answer their pleas and help them in all their needs.

At the end of his speech, he led the crowd into the grotto, which, in spite of its dimensions, had no room for so many people. Some of the natives remained outside waiting for their turn. Abrasack lit the tripods, laid flowers on the altar and, climbing the steps, opened the curtain, woven with golden threads, concealing the niche where Avani was.

Serene and concentrated, the young priestess gazed thoughtfully at the mob of hideous giants swarming at her feet; at Abrasack's command, they prostrated themselves and lavished glory on her in disconnected exclamations. Alva, translucent in her white robes, Avani, in fact, seemed like a celestial being to the poor ignorant savages.

After everyone had been able to visit the grotto and gathered in the valley, Abrasack, without any embarassment, taking on the role of interpreter of the divine will, told them that every morning, from the rising of the sun – the dwelling place of the great God and Lord of the Universe – until sunset, the divine daughter would be visible, and that everyone should bring her daily offerings, daily of flowers or fruit, explaining their needs to the deity, while the sick would have to bathe in the natural reservoir.

On his return home, Abrasack decided to visit Urjane. With Avani away, he had a clear path to happiness.

Urjane, sitting by the window, seemed immersed in sad reflections. When Abrasack appeared, she stood up and measured him up with a stern, cold gaze; he came closer and stared at her, full of passion. Some unknown force seemed to keep him at a distance; but, absorbed in his impetuous feelings, he did not even notice .

— What do you want from me? — the young woman asked coldly, making him shudder and blush.

— I have come to demand my inalienable rights of possession. My friends have their wives, so you will be mine.

However, I am magnanimous and will let you get used to me little by little. Right now, I just want to kiss those pink lips, those sapphireblue eyes, those black locks and prove you that my caresses are second to none. What I feel for you is very different from that lukewarm, insensate feeling of your demigods, semi-species.

As he said this, he was about to throw himself on Urjane and wrap her in his arms; but the young woman's gaze, stern and piercing as a dagger, stopped him in his tracks.

— Never dare touch what is your master's domain! Have you forgotten that I am the wife of Narayana and the daughter of Dakhir, the magician of the three flames? They will know how to defend and free me. Your passion is nothing more than an obsession of vile instincts, but inspires nothing but disgust in me.

Urjane's voice and her burning eyes showed such contempt and disgust that Abrasack recoiled, as if struck in the face; his throat tightened, he seemed to suffocate. Standing up in a flash, he measured her in turn with an angry, arrogant look.

— Excessive pride prevents you from being reasonable, my beautiful Urjane. Do not forget that no one has freed you so far, and you are in my power. So, you reject a peaceful solution? Well, I do not need it. You will be mine, for better or for worse. I will not submit to your whims, much less to the authority of the sorcerers.

He turned and left angrily . Urjane breathed a sigh of relief; but she felt dissatisfied with herself. Why had she not hold back in her threats, openly expressing her contempt and dislike for that dangerous man? It was very likely that his disordered emanations had na efect on her.

Urjane got down on her knees and prayed ardently. Calmed and invigorated by the prayer, she r stood up and resolved to be kinder and more restrained in the future.

In Abrasack's room, he was waiting for Jan, sitting at the table and absorbed in apparently dark thoughts. When the leader arrived, he raised his head and, whe he saw his friend's dejected countenance and the anger that falred up in him, an enigmatic smile slipped across his face. However, without making any comment, he went straight to the subject that had brought him here.

Abrasack gave a few brief instructions, slumped down in his chair, wiped his hand across his forehead, as if chasing away a fixed thought, and said:

— You look worried, brother. What happened? Or has your honeymoon been covered in clouds? I have noticed that you all say nothing about your marital happiness; for some time now, I have only seen grumpy faces.

— You are right, the bad weather covers your friends' marital firmament and Jan sighed heavily. — Only in one respect have you kept your promise; our wives are wonderfully beautiful, but their temper leaves a lot to be desired. Instead of taking care of the house and beginning to decorate our homes, as they were suppose to, most of them sit around disconsolately, bemoaning their lot. This hurts even the most unassuming pride, not to mention the fact that they practically do not hide their intentions to flee, which forcies us to lock them up and make sure our " monkeys" do not let them out of our sight.

Oh! Your Urjane, at least, has the justification of being married; my Sita is unattached, though ... Hell, I am no worse than anyone else! She is a charmer, I am crazy about her... And she cries rivers of tears, blaming me for the crime of her dishonor. It is enough for me to snuggle up to her to start uttering, I do not know how, the scornful words that force me to retreat from her. I will go mad! And Randolfo, irritable and irascible as he is, seeing his beauty turn into a vale of tears, became furious and gave her a good beating. From then on, she hardly opens her mouth; as soon as she sees him, she hides wherever she can.

Abrasack let out a loud laugh.

— Well, that is too much! They are not used to this kind of treatment. As I have already told you, I will be with you tomorrow and then I will teach you a formula that will break the enchantment Sita uses to protect herself.

When night fell, Abrasack took some talismans and quietly crept into Urjane's room. Carefully examining the interior, he saw that she was sleeping. Like a shadow, he crept over to the bed, stopping a few steps away from her, as if spellbound, unable to take his eyes off her. He had never seen her as beautiful and seductive as she was at that moment.

A small electric glowing sphere on the ceiling illuminated her with silver light; Urjane was the marvelous statue of sleeping Psyche herself. The light robes outlined her divine forms; her graceful countenance breathed in deep repose, her long, downy eyelashes casting a shadow on her tender, rosy cheeks.

A burst of passion overwhelmed his heart and mind. Nimbly, raising his hand, he traced a cabalistic sign in the air, pronounced incantations that would keep Urjane in a deep sleep, and threw himself upon her. At last, he could embrace his beloved and cover her seductive little face with kisses.

However, something totally unexpected happened. No more than two meters separated him from his prey; suddenly, a pale blue light flashed from Urjane's chest, hitting Abrasack in the chest so hard that he staggered and, as if swept by a gust of wind, fell into the far corner of the room. Trembling with fury, Abrasack stood up, stunned, and resumed his attack. Urjane seemed not to hear his fall and continued to sleep calmly.

Now Abrasack tried to act more carefully. There was no longer that clear light, but there seemed to be an obstacle between him and Urjane. She was so close that it would have been enough to stretch out his arm to reach her; but he struggled uselessly with the invisible wall that protected Urjane's bed.

However, Abrasack was not a man who gave up easily. This time, with strength of will, he suppressed his rage and called on his knowledge and magical strength for help. In vain, however, were his terrible conjurations and summons by the elemental spirits and demonic forces: all his efforts were useless. From the enormous effort of his will, the veins in his forehead and neck swelled like ropes; sweat rolled down his body, sprinkling his livid face, like that of a corpse, while his chest weezed and heaved, . Forgetting all caution, he shouted in a hoarse, broken voice the formulas that, in his opinion, would have a fearsome power.

But… Nothing helped. The invisible wall withstood the most furious attacks and seemed to protect the sleeping woman so well that she did not even wake up from her slumber.

Finally, Abrasack was convinced of his defeat; he was on the verge of completely exhausting his strength. Staggering like a drunkard, he dragged himself to his room and fell over the first chair. It would be impossible to describe what he felt at that moment and, if Abrasack had been an ordinary mortal, he would have died of a heart attack.

For the first time since his escape, he was clashing with a power greater than his own; he realized then that the knowledge of which he was so proud was of little value; and that, in the face of the giants he was defying, he was nothing more than a powerless pygmy. The pain of his own insignificance overwhelmed him; his skull felt like it was being crushed. Groaning hoarsely, he clutched his head and, like an inert mass, collapsed to the ground.

Urjane, however, had not even looked up . Sensing that Abrasack would make a nocturnal incursion, trying to take advantage of her sleep, even though she had gone to bed, she decided not to sleep and to stay alert. His protective talisman was hidden under her tunic, as instructed by her father

Her keen ear picked up Abrasack's almost silent footsteps; she saw him enter and, through half-closed eyelids, with her heart pounding and pretending to be asleep, she followed the fierce struggle taking place two steps from her bed. Only she could see an incandescent film protecting her, where, like a stone wall, the demonic forces summoned by Abrasack were bumping into each other.

Finally, her kidnapper staggered out of the room. Urjane got up, knelt down and prayed feverishly. Not only did she thank God for her salvation, she also prayed for the man, blinded by impure love, whose defeat and suffering she had just witnessed.

Back on his feet, Abrasack felt shattered and weak, as if after a serious illness; the blow of the reaction had been so strong that even his immortal organism had been shaken. He settled into bed and began to reflect; sleep was not coming , but his mind was working as well as ever. And these bitter, angry thoughts, which stormed like waves in a storm, caused him almost physical pain.

Jan, who had just arrived, understood immediately, at the first glance at his friend's pale, transfigured face, that his love affair was going badly. Without revealing anything , after discussing totally unrelated matters, Jan asked him to teach him the magic that would prevent Sita from interposing the fluid obstacles. Upon hearing the request, Abrasack burst out laughing.

— I cannot help you, dear friend. As a friend and cousin, I confess that as of tonight I no longer believe in my knowledge... At least in certain fields. I will dedicate my life only to revenge. I will use all my science and energy, solely and exclusively, to accelerate our attack on the "divine" ... Ha, ha, ha... City, and I will reduce this nest of tyranny and damned science to ashes.

His friend shook his head disapprovingly.

— 'Do not get carried away , Abrasack! Do not waste your gifts. From what I can gather from your words and your state, you must have suffered a huge setback, facing powers greater than your own; but let this serve as a warning to you. Think carefully before waging war against those who, according to your own words, are powerful and immortal.

— We will see! Only the future and the decisive fight will tell us who will win. Even if they are immortal, and I cannot kill them, I will make them suffer until they reveal all their mysteries to me.

And he clenched his fists.

— I will be traveling today to look for allies. I discovered some time ago that, not far from here, in the coastal region of the volcanic islands, there are certain giants, who are nothing more than dwarf kings to our "monkeys". They are more difficult to tame, such is their ignorance; but I know their primitive language, and I have found a way, it seems, to tame them and subject them to our will. Their incredible physical strength will be of great help to us when we go on the attack.

I am leaving tonight, taking Randolfo and Clodomiro with me; you will be in charge in my absence. Your duty of look after Urjane needs no comment. Be careful not to interrupt the military training of our " monkeys", or the manufacture of weapons.

In fact, in the evening, Abrasack left with his two companions, without saying when he would return. Jan zealously carried out the task delegated to him.

He was an intelligent and energetic person. He was endowed with many virtues, not fully developed, and although he was not as brilliant as Abrasack, he was more conciliatory, calmer and not so presumptuous. In an flash, he realized that the woman who had been able to stand up to his fiery cousin must possess wealth of knowledge and, perhaps, could help him soften Sita's heart and also restored peace to his friends' homes .

— Where will all this lead," he lamented, "since the damage has already been done? Sita, my wife, whom I love madly, accuses me of having dishonored her. Yes, but I wanted nothing more than to legalize our union and perform all the rituals laid down by the magicians, if I knew them. My friends are in the same situation. Not all of them, however, are as patient as I am; one of them, with a very explosive temper, even beat his wife.

— Shh! It is going to be hard for him to win my friend's heart like that! — Urjane thought. — But you're right: you cannot repair what has already been done. I will do my best to convince my friends to submit to their God-given destiny and do their duties with dignity.

I will talk to Sita today, or you bring her here. I would also like to visit the others, if I could walk freely around the city, without fear of the giants. do not be afraid, I will not run away, even if the opportunity arises. I give you my word of honor," she assured him, smiling.

Jan assured her that she had nothing to fear and offered to accompany her to show her the city, the houses of her friends and to show them the best way to the temple, where Avani was .

He also told her that the temple was full of people at worship times . And that the " monkeys" never tired of marveling at the goddess and inhaling the aromas coming out from the grotto.

Urjane expressed her desire to visit Avani first, and Jan took her to the grotto, which was empty of people at that time .

According to Avani, the aborigines were very respectful. Due to the large influx of sick people, she needed someone to help her with the cures, since, since her status as a deity condemned her to apparent idleness.

— I will come to help you, because I am not doing anything either, and my admirer is away. I will also try to get more help," Urjane said: after a brief reflection.

Urjane began to visit her friends, who had become victims of Abrasack's marital projects.

First, she went to Sita's house and, with her characteristic vehemence, gave her a long reprimand, reminding her of the principles of the esoteric school where she had received her education.

— What was the point of studying so much, learning all those laws that guide us on the path of ascension, if, in the first test, all that bliss comes crashing down, and, from the depths of her soul, the low and abject instincts, that I thought she had mastered come pouring in, unbalancing her harmony, blocking the only gifted path of a woman who has reached the threshold of higher initiation.

Urjane knew how hard Sita's misfortune was – a trial imposed by a higher will – but it was up to her to take the initiative to turn it into a mission .

To educate and enlighten the man to whom you were united, to bring him up to your level – and not down to his deficiencies – this was a worthy and fruitful task for a woman. The great Magi would undoubtedly approve and bless this assignement, which was carried out scrupulously , and in due time they would consecrate that union contracted that union contracted under exceptional conditions, but enlightened and purified in the joint work of improvement.

Similar speeches, varying according to the case, did not fail to have their due effect on the souls of her friends, oppressed by despair, shame and resentment, who were gradually being driven away; Urjane watched with growing joy, as suffering and well-meaning hearts submitted to fate. the girls also agreed to take turns helping Avani in the temple.

The next day, overflowing with happiness, Jan came to thank Urjane. He had an enlightening conversation with Sita; she was calm, conciliatory, and he hoped that soon there would be full harmony between them.

From then on, Urjane began an intense activity and, as well as sowing peace in her friends' homes, she helped Avani. After making friends with the natives at the temple, she learned their language and began to visit their homes in the city and nearby villages. The savages treated her with respect; even though they feared her, they obeyed her in everything, thinking of her as the sister of the "goddess."

She taught them to weave baskets, loincloths, ropes and similar artifacts; she also made them learn some non-complex trades. Her most successful activity was making head, neck, and hand ornaments from the feathers of dead birds and colored gems. In spite of the repulsive appearance of the natives, a desire to please others emerged in their brutish souls; the men never missed na opportunity to dress up, as much as the women.

Urjane and Avani spent their afternoons together, trying in long conversations to kill the agonizing time of banishment and stifle their longing for the divine city. Eventually, some events testified that they had not been forgotten . For example, they once found in their rooms a supply of robes, some magical devices and brief instructions on how to carry out the works.

Abrasack was still absent, but he was much remembered in the conversations between Urjane and Avani; both regretted that that man's colossal energy and powerful mind were directed towards evil, and that his torpid inclinations were nourished by such impure and useless passion.

Finally, he returned with his two companions, apparently pleased with the results of the journey.

He told Jan about the giants he had encountered, many of whom were more repulsive and terrible than his " monkeys," real monsters, in the literal sense of the word. With long tails, thick and short limbs, like clawed paws, their male representatives had horns. They got around on all fours and, when they stood up, they were frightening because of their size. They walked by leaning on tree trunks, that had been uprooted . They fed on the raw meat of animals killed by stones or suffocation.

— I have never seen such underdeveloped creatures; our " monkeys", are erudite compared to them. What is more, they are practically devoid of the gift of speech, if we can call a few guttural grunts a language," added Abrasack.

— My God! And you have been among of this scumbag so long ? What do we need them for? I'm surprised they have not killed you! — Jan exclaimed.

Abrasack laughed.

— They tried; I had to give them a few electric shocks to make them understand who they were messing with. You will see how useful they are in practice; be sure! No wall in the divine city can resist their force.

Jan shook his head.

— And how are you going to get them to take part in the attack, since they are so obtuse?

— There is a force – the magical force of music – that pacifies and attracts them all, like insects to the light. With my harp, they will follow me to the end of the world. They will do whatever I command ; like snakes, obeying their charmer, they will never harm you.

Jan's report on the latest changes in the city left Abrasack possessed. His heart contracted with fury and resentment when he learned that Urjane had established peace and concord between her friends and their kidnappers, even though she had not shown the slightest pity or justification for her feelings.

His later meeting with Urjane was tense. He reproached her for the coldness towards him and described her actions, which culminated in his friends' happiness, as a way of showing her humiliating contempt for him.

— Happiness! What happiness," said Urjane, "when my friends are the unfortunate victims of a cruel and infamous betrayal? Ther is simply nothing that unites them indissolubly to the divine city, and I have only tried to help them to submit to their inglorious fate; in this way, they will willingly influence and regenerate those beings whom fate has placed as intimates. As commendable as this very difficult task is, to say that there is any happiness at all is strange, to say the least, strange, if not absurd.

— Would it cost you to take on a no less praiseworthy mission, no less praiseworthy, that of trying to regenerate myself? I assure you that your existence would be much smoother than if you were married to Randolfo, for example.

— I am married to Narayana and I love him; your insolence, in wanting to possess the wife of your benefactor, makes you doubly repugnant. Not to mention the gulf that separates us, of purification and initiation," Urjane concluded.

Abrasack gave her a dark look .

— Then there is only one thing left for me to do: force the wizards to reveal to me the arcane science that would allow me to become your equal.

It is my desire to rule this world, where I have been brought. I want to be god and lord of these infernal peoples, whom I will enlighten; and, as the only reward for my struggles and sacrifices, I want your love. And what I want, I get.

Urjane said nothing, and Abrasack withdrew gloomily, like a heavy cloud.

He did not consider himself totally defeated, even though his subsequent attempts to possess the young woman, using cunning or force, were unsuccessful. Urjane seemed protected by an invisible wall, and he was forced, incubated with rage, to give up the fruitless attacks.

Filled with hatred, he actively resumed his preparations for war; in his moments of greatest distress, he began to visit Avani; her serene gaze, her invariably friendly welcome, and her deep and harmonious voice had a calm effect on him .

He once proposed to take his harp and play for her, while she, sitting on the throne, would listen to him like a benevolent deity.

— It would do us both good, and I would be grateful. But will you play and sing the melodies I ask for, which have a special healing power?

— as long as I am offering, I will certainly grant your request," Abrasack assured her good-naturedly . — I must say that I am not so ignorant in the art of harmonic vibrations and their effects," he added.

— Excellent, your participation will be valuable!

And so, little by little a friendly relationship was established between Abrasack and his lovely prisoner. One day, when he was too gloomy, nervous, and irritable, corroed by contained anger, Avani, who was watching him, suddenly asked .

— What is wrong with you? Has anything extraordinary happened?

— Nothing extraordinary. I have just spoken with Urjane. Her heavenly beauty has enslaved me; but her hatred and contempt for me leave me possessed, all the more so because of the insurmountable wall that the tyrannical magicians have imposed between us, the cause of almost physical pain.

Avani shook her head.

— You are wrong! Urjane neither hates nor despises you; she has compassion, but can do nothing about it. Judge for yourself how unworthy it was of you, after receiving knowledge and being initiated - the first condition for taming the inner beast - to nurture an animal feeling for someone else' s wife .

Nevertheless, you may have a wide field of work ahead of you; to contribute to the progress of this humanity, to promote enlightenment and wise laws in this virgin land. Would such a mission not fulfill the greatest of ambitions?

Even the magicians would be willing to help you in this endeavor, yet you want to turn the savages against them. Do you not understand your folly in declaring war on the inhabitants of the divine city, on those giants of knowledge whose power is equivalent to the forces of nature? Make sure the magicians do not turn on you, otherwise they will break you like a stick and turn you into nothing. He who strikes with iron will die with iron! Submit to them, give Urjane back her freedom, and perhaps they will forgive you!

Abrasack was thoughtful; a minute later, he shook his head, defiantly.

— Thank you for your words of friendship. Perhaps you are right; sometimes, I also wonder if it would not be crazy to undertake this adventure. But I cannot back down, I have burned the last cartridge! The magicians' humiliating disdain has wounded my pride and rekindled my thirst to measure my strength.

I will take revenge for their arrogance and I will raise millions of giants against them, I will take the city and I will wrest from them the mysteries that they hide so much from me. Oh, they will pay dearly for erecting the wall that separates me from the woman I adore!

He raised and shook his fist, and wild hatred shone in his eyes .

— I will never free Urjane, I cannot have her, but, nevertheless, I am happy to glimpse her radiant beauty and hear her voice, sweeter than the song of the spheres. Knowing that she is here, even if it is under a poor roof, the only one I can offer her, at least I do not suffer from jealousy, when she is with Narayana. And he quickly stood up and left the cave.

CHAPTER X

The kidnapping of Urjane and the young priestesses who accompanied her caused a great stir in the city of the wizards. The news was brought by the young woman who stayed on the spaceship and witnessed the attack; she quickly returned to sound the alarm.

The greatest disturbance, however, was expressed by the earthlings, who could not understand the apparent indifference with which the magicians treated such an unspeakable crime. As for Narayana, the disappearance of his wife shook him so much that there was a moment when the wisdom and discernment attached to the magician's will seemed to collapse, giving way to the mad fury of a mere mortal. Soon, however, this furious impulse subsided under Ebramar's deep and stern gaze, warning him.

— Are you not ashamed of giving in to feelings that you should already have mastered?

— You are right, master! My recklessness and foolish stubbornness got a deserved punishment. I failed to realize that I was protecting a scoundrel, and now you have given me the proof of my blindness. But is my fault so great that I must pay for it with Urjane's dishonor? Can Dakhir allow his daughter to fall victim to the animalistic passion of this ungrateful evildoer?

— No, Dakhir will be able to defend his daughter's honor; all the other events, however, will take their own course written by fate, whose blind instrument is Abrasack himself.

— Perhaps it is the will of fate, set by our higher mentors, that I stay here planting bananas, waiting for " fate" or "its instruments" to return Urjane to me," Narayana observed, and a convulsive twitch of his lips betrayed his disturbance.

Ebramar put his hand on Narayana's shoulder and said in an affable tone:

— My prodigal son, when will you realize that haste is the enemy of perfection? No one is asking you to remain impassive in the face of these disturbing events; you must strive to free Urjane, but do not do it so hastily; use the powers at our disposal. Can I read the "why is that" in your eyes?

Because, my son, our task on this planet has a special character. We are legislators, called to lay the foundations of a civilization. This means watching over and guiding the movements that will accelerate the development of mental activity. Unfortunately, this acceleration requires a war . All spiritual or political crises in worlds as yet unevolved, as the one we are in, or the one we come from, they are accompanied by fatal clashes of the human masses. For peoples already well developed, war is a reaction, a bloodthirsty awakening of inert and dull tranquility and insignificant interests. War shakes and regenerates peoples called to play a historic role in humanity; it mows down and leads to annihilation obsolete, morally and physically decadent peoples.

The giants, a primitive generation of the chaotic forces of nature, are a world of inferior beings. By their nature and constitution, these beings are obtuse and incapable of developing an expanded intellect, while their great numbers and phenomenal physical strength represent a great danger to their weaker neighbors, reserved for later development.

These pioneers of mankind lived in an atmosphere saturated with emanations of crude forces, deadly to weaker beings. They have already fulfilled their role, as colossal organisms condemned to digest what has bee discarded by the chaotic forces of nature, and they must disappear. Such a cleaning of the planet, from harmful and costly animal races is necessary, and Abrasack will contribute to this work. We will not have to look for the monsters in their lairs, they will bring them here, and we will liquidate them.

— How can the scoundrel establish a relationship with those horrible creatures, when each one alone can crush him like a worm? How can he subdue them? — Narayana asked furiously.

— It is clear that it is not physical strength; which proves that he has enormous willpower and remarkable intelligence. He will be an enemy to match," smiled Ebramar, smiling. — Now, calm down! I am sure you understand the importance of future events, and you agree with me that personal interests must take second place to our mission as legislators.

Narayana was crestfallen; a minute later, he stood up and an ecstatic energy shone in his dark eyes , typical of his character.

— Yes, master, I understand. Starting tomorrow, I will begin recruiting an army against the ingrate. May my long separation from dear Urjane serve me as a deserved punishment for my stubborn blindness, and the hour of her rescue will be all the sweeter.

— That is how I like you! — added Ebramar. — Now go to Dakhir! We have already made a list of your likely helpers. Dakhir will give you useful instructions and reassure you about Urjane.

Two days later, Narayana, in the company of his friends and brave helpers, went to the place where the first conscious army of the new planet would be assembled.

After a few weeks, Udea, having taken Narayana to the tribes he had colonized, returned to the divine city. The next day, we found Dakhir, Supramati and Udea on the terrace of Ebramar's palace, as well as his master, the latter reporting on the expedition.

He was pleased with the progress of the colonies, that were prospering under the wise rule of the kings, his descendants. It was precisely from this nucleus that Narayana had decided to form his future army.

The kidnapping of Urjane and the young disciples from the initiation school continued to unsettle de earthlings.

The young priestess' testimony about the hairy simian colossi made the earthlings' hair stand on end; their suspicions that the insolent figure of the rebel Abrasack was behind the whole story were not unfounded. On the other hand, it was an unsolvable enigma that the hierophants let him go completely unpunished.

The topic was the subject of endless conversations and aroused an alarming interest in Kalitin. At one of our daily meetings, he wanted to talk to Dakhir about it.

Despite this decision, he was embarrassed before the magician, because both his own curiosity and his concern seemed absurd to him. If his powerful protector and Urjane's father remained calm, carrying on with his routine duties, then it could be inferred that the superior magicians felt they were in control of the situation.

Dakhir, watching Kalitin and leafing through a manuscript, then said to him:

-Your conclusion is correct, my dear Andrei! We are calm, because we have enough power to defend ourselves against the attack of the inferior creatures.

We are aware that Abrasack is preparing for war, certain of taking the city with the help of the numerous horde of giants and monsters he has trained . However, as these masses are of no use in this incipient age, and their numbers are too great, they are doomed to annihilation, or at least to be reduced to a minority doomed to definite extinction. The cosmic forces we are subjected to, will do their job, and you will witness, I hope, the destruction of this avalanche of monsters.

— Thank you for the explanation, master! What a grand and terrifying spectacle the annihilation of these legions of giants by the elemental forces will be; they will be slaughtered like a bunch of ants! — Kalitin commented, shuddering slightly.

Only the dangerous and harmful beings will be exterminated. I should add that the same basic procedure applies to all the lower worlds; but the cosmic forces are not always appealed to, because in other cases, wars are used . We are now dealing with primitive races, colossal offspring of the crude forces of rich nature. It can also happen that, over the course of centuries, some cultured nations fall into atavisms, threatening other peoples around them; then the same law that I have just described applies.

The peoples condemned to extinction begin by losing their religious sentiment, which leads to moral decadence, because the soul is no longer guided by divine laws. Little by little, their brains degenerate. Their faculties are concentrated on only one thing : material interests. Their brain only function in industrial production; they reveal an incredible aptitude for mechanics, chemistry, commerce, the generation of comfort goods; at the same time, the intuition of the divine is waning, the radiations emanating from exalted faith are exhausted and all the arts take on a pseudo-real and decadent orientation. Under the mask of pseudo "artistic truth", music becomes noisy, disconnected and irritating; painting and sculpture serve as a cult of indecency; literature becomes deformed, idealizing vices and moral degradation. And for a long time, no one realizes that, underneath the prosperous and highly "cultured" appearance, physical and moral degeneration is being perpetuated.

Society gives itself on to animalistic passions; an unheardof arrogance takes over human minds and cruelty becomes as necessary as satisfying hunger or thirst, ready to reveal its dangerous madness.

A nation made up of these barbarian hordes is always a threat to the people around it, all the more dangerous if it is rich, disciplined, possesses technical advantages and psychic drive.

At such times, immutable fate sheds light on the spirit of extermination. Circumstances invariably lead to the outbreak of a great war, which is far too bloody, and its victims are countless, especially the dangerous disruptors of the general peace. They number in the thousands and are always defeated.

Kalitin took a keen interest in the subject and the conversation went on for a long time. Since coming to the new world, the young astronomer had made enormous progress and Dakhir was happy with his application and observant spirit, which was always evolving.

There was silence. Dakhir was examining the contents of the desk and took out an instrument he wanted to explain to his disciple.

Kalitin, who was attentively watching all the magician's movements, abruptely bent over the master's hand resting on the table, and asked a little hesitantly:

— Master, let me look at your hand. I have been wanting to do so for some time, because it looks very interesting.

— Please look as much as you like. What did you find so curious about it? 'It has five fingers, like yours, although it differs a little in shape,' said Dakhir good-humoredly, holding out a hand that was smooth, thin and well cared for, just like like a woman's.

— Oh, no! There is a big difference, and not only in the hand, but between our bodies in general. Your skin looks different, less dense, and I have even noticed a few times that it phosphorizes; also your hand... Look how much lighter it is than mine, which resembles the paw of a rough peasant next to the hand of an aristocrat.

Dakhir burst out laughing and slapped his disciple's robust hand.

— In fact, you are right! An inattentive observer would not have noticed such a subtle difference. Yes, my body has a different composition. Over the centuries of my existence, it has changed a lot; not because of the death of an ordinary mortal, but because to its astral activity, like a gelatine melting in hot water, my rough flesh has gradually melted. In a way that was imperceptible even to myself, the dense and heavy particles of the fleshly were blown away, like flakes swept away by the wind, and in their place a tenuous ethereal envelope appeared , replaced in turn by a more delicate and pure body.

This transfiguration of matter, as I have already told you, is a consequence of astral work, which calcines the crude particles of flesh. On our old Earth, this happened to those uninitiated in our mysteries, through reincarnations or ascetic life and tireless, fervent prayers.

As proof of what I am saying, it is enough to remember the beasts in the circus, which, instead of tearing apart the saints and the martyrs, would l lie down meekly at their feet. The pagans attributed this to the "sorcery" of the Christians; but the cause was quite simple: purified by prayer, the martyrs no longer emanated the smell of human flesh that excites the voracity of the wild animals.

Here, I would like to make a digression on the subject, which will be useful to you when indoctrinating your own disciples. I want to talk about the influence of food and hygiene.

— Thank you, master, the question comes in handy! Not long ago, I almost got into an argument with my two pupils. They were furious with me just because I forbade them to eat meat and because I told them to bathe three times a day, according to your instructions.

Make them see that bloody flesh not only impregnates the physical body with its disgusting smell, but also the astral body. When man dies, he leaves on Earth only the physical remains, his psychic part; however, his spiritual body, saturated and burdened with that stench, drags the foul-smelling emanations into the afterlife, binding it to the lower parts of the astral plane. it is precisely for this reason that we demand an exclusively vegetable diet from our disciples, which provides hygiene for the astral body and the necessary lightness for its rapid evolution.

Only absolute hygiene, maintained by frequent ablutions or baths, facilitates metabolism and purifies the aura with healing effluvia. As long as people lived outdoors and abided by the law of ablution, even if driven by religious canons, mankind was less subject to various diseases. Sweat should also always be removed, as it closes the pores, causes fermentation and generates toxic substances and harmful bacilli.

Like it or not, we draw life lessons from our old earth, because in the new world everything has yet to sprout. So you may remember that in ancient times people ate a bit of everything, drank strong wines and, in spite of everything, enjoyed perfect health; there were rarely any diseases that claimed humanity.

The reason for this is that life was in the fresh air, with frequent ablutions. You may be aware that, in recent centuries, weak and degenerating mankind has been cooped up indoors in warm clothes. In this triple crust of walls and garments, people lived without even suspecting what cloaca they were in, actively generating all that miasma, the consequence of impure instincts, unbridled passions, hatred, envy, and profanity – as seen in people's favorite expression: " to hell with you". Instead of crying out to God in a moment of misfortune, man cried out to the devil.

Oh, man would have been horrified if he had been able to see the thousands of spirits attracted by the insults, curses, and impurities of their evil emanations. But people see nothing and quietly breathe the air contaminated and then complain of sudden pains, dizziness, or lack of sleep.

Only prayer, holy water and pure air can cleanse such a " repository", where everything overflows with astral slag, nourished by the emanations of the inhabitants and the contaminated air; in these conditions, the fluidic population can become vampire beings, harmful and dangerous , to the point where they have to be expelled by fire.

Thus, the belief in holy water or sacred water is not a superstition. Water is a substance that provides the greatest assimilation of astral light, pouring out in radiant streams of prayer – a kind of accumulating and distributing force for the lucilating currents of gifts.

Dakhir was silent for a while, apparently deep in thought; he wiped his hand across his forehead and turned to Kalitin, who was waiting for his words, mute and respectful.

— We have totally deviated from the subject of the progressive regeneration of the astral body through work, prayers and the ascetic life.

— Yes, master, you have told me that your body has gone through several incarnations.

— Three, my friend. And as the very being of my immortal body changed, so did its organs . Thus, the heart no longer played the leading role. It no longer had anything to fear for itself or for others whom it loved; the rigid discipline, imposed on the soul, tamed the "beast" in man and subdued the passions; now the heart only feels pure and lofty love, and its calm and quiet beating only regulates the phosphoric substances into which the blood in our veins has become, irrigating the brain, now our most important organ. And the more perfect it is, the more strength it gives us to concentrate and release the colossal power that governs the elements.

The stomach has also been practically suppressed, as food serves us only to nourish the tissues; the spine is our electrical network; the muscles are the distributor of phosphoric material.

Even carnal relations, in the unions of higher-level magicians, are different. Like the fakir of old, who with the radiant force emanating from him made a plant grow, blossom and bear fruit, in the same way, the radiant force that unites consorts fertilizes and brings birth specially chosen beings, missionaries predestined to perfect humanity.

Undoubtedly, what I have just said applies today to superior magicians; but among humanities that have reached a high degree of perfection, as on Jupiter and other similar planets, human multiplication only takes place in this way.

Progress is the law of the universe. The more man works on the astral plane, the more he shakes off his animal passions to work in the spiritual field, the more he draws phosphoric substances into his aura and organism, the more his body is transformed, his blood is changed and his power is increases.

The faces of the saints is always enveloped in a radiant glow, and the contact of their hands heals. These superior beings, endowed with divine breath, have the power to rehabilitate the functioning of organs tainted by disease; the deaf begins to hear, the paraplegic to walk, the internal ailments subside.

Prayer, as you can see, is the first magical formula humans have found to fight against the flesh that suffocates and sucks them in. You know that sounds contain a fluidic substance of varying combinations, produced by vibration, just as a dynamo generates electricity. Prayer, by the essence of its chemical composition, generates vibratory, phosphoric and radiative currents, assimilated from the four elements. These four currents take the form of the Cross, rotating rapidly. The purer the prayer and the greater the impetus, the more vertiginous its rotation; crackling and sending out luminous beams, the fluidic mass rotates, introducing heat and useful particles it contains into the body. The pure radiation of the speaker spirals up in the form of light blue waves and joins the divine breath. This serves as a connecting wire or, if you like, a telephone, through which the creature gets in touch with its Creator and the Holy Protectors.

As a result, after fervent prayer, man feels tranquilized and invigorated; sometimes they feel exuded, and this tepidity enlivens them and helps them to get rid of fluids and other impurities that cause illness.

The sign of the cross is a magical sign that surpasses all others, a center of convergence of the cosmic currents of the four elements that make up the formula of prayer. Through intuition, man has always surrounded this mysterious symbol with a crown of rays and the cross corresponds to knowledge, the strength and faith of the one who uses it. Whether it is a simple wooden cross or a jeweler's gold one, the meaning of both is identical and they have the same power. The sign of the cross serves both an ignorant person, who does not know the mystical power, and a magician; it unites him to the Divinity, protects him against satanic beings, or impure and chaotic forces; it summons the spirits of the four elements to gather around the symbol drawn by man for his own help. Only through the hands of those who understand the importance of the sign, represented with reason and faith, does the cross become an unbeatable weapon.

This symbol, I think, may be called the signet of the Eternal. It is the foundation of every creature, a symbol of eternity, which expresses and encloses the four elements, in which all the modifications of matter take place , the source of spiritual and physical life.

— So, is the study of the cross a specific science?

— And huge! In the past, certain parts of this science were passed on to the higher initiates in the shelters of the temples; in all the doctrines of antiquity, this mysterious symbol, a powerful talisman against the attacks of all that is impure, played an important role.

— Yes, Andrei, it takes a lot of work to reach the pinnacles of this science ; starting as a neophyte, right up to the level of magician; even though I have worked hard, I am far from understanding this marvelous science in all its magnitude.

CHAPTER XI

Life in the city of the Wizards was quiet. There were classes in the schools; the hierophants were imperceptibly finalizing the defense of the city against the hordes of Abrasack, who were engaged in preparations for the attack.

Dakhir and Kalitin did not interrupt their usual daily lectures on the most varied subjects.

— You told me, Master, of the disbelief that has plagued the Earth, contributing significantly to breaking the link with the Godhead. It is true; in my time, to believe in the Creator, in the holy protectors and in prayers was seen as archaic reminiscences of ridiculous superstitions.

Thank God, I have completely rejected these misconceptions and today I venerate what I used to demean... But I do not understand one thing; you, our masters, have faith and devotion, yet you do not call yourselves saints.

— Simply because we are not," laughed Dakhir.

— Why not? You are so charitable and even wiser than most of the saints whose lives I have read about, insisted Kalitin.

— I like to see, my son, that you always want to get to the point. In that case, I would ask you to answer me, what is the difference in the paths of ascent between a life dedicated to holiness and one dedicated to scientific work? Please.

Katilin remained mute.

— Look. There are two paths leading to the same goal: perfection.

Holiness leads to an ideal morality through the education of feelings and instincts; it enlightens the heart, sharpens concentration on prayer, builds self-denial and self-sacrifice for the benefit of others. It also provides an insight into the intricacies of the soul, that is physically and morally martyred in self-denial. In short: it is an education of the soul and, at the same time, the knowledge of the Divine greatness, of the Creator' s supreme creation – His indestructible spark.

The journey of an adept, a scientific journey, seeks above all to develop reason, to learn the principles and laws of nature that govern cosmic forces. In other words: it is a quast to learn about the evolution of the Universe and of man, to learn about the greatness of the Creator in His laboratory.

To sum up, science speaks to man's reason, while religion, that is, the precept of holiness, speaks to the heart. We are all endowed with reason and heart, although the former is usually dulled and there is a greater predominance of people with charitable heart than with lucid reason. Most people only understand with their heart; few are capable of theoretical concepts. It follows that religion is necessary both for intellectuals incapable of isolating themselves from the body - and for the masses - for whom the pinnacles of abstract ramblings are not accessible. Thus, magic, being a dangerous science, that breaks weak minds, cannot be accessible to the masses, being restricted only to persons of strong mind and spirit. But, for perfection to be achieved, the human spirit must possess the two branches of knowledge in equal proportion; thus, the righteous devote themselves, later to science, while the wise embark on the pursuit of knowledge, self-denial and love of God and neighbor.

I should also add that the one who becomes an adept, not being an righteous person, has a much greater risk of stumbling on his way and exorbitating his knowledge, because in the recesses of his soul his earthly passions still lurk. On the other hand, a saint is quicker to divest himself of his human weaknesses and self-abnegation lifts him higher into the clear spheres of the adept's science – at least in the first steps of knowledge – because he will have to sacrifice himself if he wishes to ascend the steep path of perfection. Are you satisfied with my explanation?

— Perfectly master, thank you very much!

— But tell me what exactly is troubling you, and I will try to dispel your doubts.

— You read my heart, dear master. Once, Nivara referred to a printed passage from the astral clichés that link us to our Mother Earth. He said that this image, with which the Earth has now been graced, comes from another similar world, totally destroyed and dissolved of its primordial substances.

— What is so amazing about that? In the great economy of the Universe, each particle occupies its proper place and works to preserve the general balance. The igneous image with the astral cliché cannot be destroyed, because it contains the primal substance, that is, the elemental forces. The film spirals around the orbiting planet and the astral clichés imprinted on it materialize as they appear. It is like an extensive school program for creatures of various abilities.

— Yes, that is clear! However, how can this be reconciled not only with the concept of justice – as I understand it – but also with the principle of free will, or responsibility for our actions? In this second case, spirits are forced – if such a comparison is possible – to play the role of actors, obliged to live and behave on the basis of the cliché drawn up by someone else; they also have to bear, fatidically, the effects of the acts carried out by "others," tyrannically becoming evildoers or saints, according to the engraved cliché in spite of their own will?

— My, where have you been! If everything was tyrannical , as you say, if someone had to play a role according to a script printed on a cliché, that would be really unfair. However, fate is only mapped out in general terms; then you have to understand that such sensitive matter, capable of recording even the oscillations of a thought, must at the same time be delicate enough to yield to a fresh impression, without damaging the first. The two do not mix, because the chemical composition of each individuality is different.

Only a few clichés, imprinted by the higher will, remain in somewhat unchanged; sooner or later they are revealed depending on the performance of the new cast of actors in the drama.

For this reason, since time immemorial, there have been incredibly correct predictions of certain events in the distant future; any errors only concerned the date of their occurrence.

Both prophets and clairvoyants had and still have the ability to glimpse astral clichés, but often without understanding . Some details of the picture, because what they saw had not yet been discovered at that time, or rather had been rediscovered, and they described it using metaphors.

As always, I have to bring up an example from our old Earth. Thus, the great clairvoyant - author of the Apocalypse - referred to a copper horse, sparking fire, which was actually a steam locomotive –a discovery in future centuries. Another humble clairvoyant called Suffrano, trying to decipher the time of the event from existing evidence, said: "When men fly like birds with the swiftness of swallows, and chariots move without horses, such a thing will happen...". This means that he could not name – and there was no way – cars and airplanes, which he could, however, see in operation.

Let us now look at the issue from a differenht perspective and decide whether it is in fact violence and injustice for living spirits to become interpreters of a script printed on the astral cliché; or whether they are not formed according to the principles of the law of magnetism or attraction, through incarnations – a form of general evaluation of the forces and in the particularities of previous existences, as microorganisms in higher and lower beings.

Every soul is drawn into the fluidic sphere, full of lived impulses, where the preponderant attractive influence of one of the elements reigns. Fire and air are higher elements; water and earth are lower. No spirit with lofty tendencies and goals will be attracted to the lower plane, and will never submit to an influence that does not dominate it.

According to the perfect harmony of fluidic and karmic attractions etc., based on the unity of peoples, groupings of people and the constitution of families, each spirit is attracted precisely to the environment to which its abilities and moral forces are most suited; at the same time, this corresponds to the existences of atonement or trial.

In the first periods of existence, the lives of the spirits are always less complex; but in the great laboratory, the enormous workshop of planetary life, there will be vacancies for everyonel, according to their abilities, level of development and need for work on the path of ascension.

It is a mistake for you to think that the spirits are thrust against their will into the current of a certain cliché. No, the spirit is drawn to the battlefield itself, where it must measure its forces, according to its tastes and tendencies. As a tenor, who cannot sing like a bass, a tragedian cannot play the role of a comedian; a porter cannot be a prince; a evildoer cannot lead the life of a saint – so, too, everyone takes on a role that they can, or think they can play.

The play is the same, the role is set, but the actor can enhance it or even, to a certain extent, change it, giving it his own individuality . If he plays it well, so much the better; if he plays it badly and still thinks he is the best, he must begin again… And that is it .

Peoples, like some individuals, are subject to the same laws; they have their own cliché, their own karmic conditions and their rational temperament, the nature of which I have already outlined to you when discussing the transmigrations of a spirit through the three kingdoms.

The predominance of this or another element in the composition of their astral body is of great importance in the tendencies and distinctive traits of a people.

The best endowed peoples are those in which the influence of the fire element predominates: we call them solar peoples. They are religious, believing, full of benevolent impulses, gifted with abilities in all fields of science, born artists and endowed with unparalleled courage; at the same time, they are calm and obstinate like a flame, they do not let go of their prey. Being mystics, dreamers and deep thinkers by nature, the solar peoples provide the greatest number of saints, outstanding men, phlegmatic, even if sometimes in poor health.

The peoples who have left the aerial corporations long for regions of light. They are also gifted, with a lively and jovial intelligence, albeit licentious, because they are fickle and sometimes passionate. From them come innovators, fanatical adherents of religious sects or impassive freethinkers.

Those in whom the water element predominates are outwardly as calm as an ocean on a calm day; but at their core they are treacherous, ambitious and t deceitful. Since water is their native element they are above all intrepid navigators, merchants and scientists who excel in practical sciences.

The element of "earth" attracts vulgar natures; the people, in whose astral zone this element predominates are usually heavy-bodied, voracious, covetous, bloodthirsty, selfish and cruel ; their minds are heavy, hard, arrogant, and malevolent, their attitudes towards others are disdainful. These peoples are not very religious, they are the ones who provide the most atheists and apostates, and they favor the forces of evil, among whom sorcerers and servants of Lucifer abound.

Future nations are formed on the basis of the deeds of their previous existences, in accordance with the karmic law.

The astral cliché of one nation or another is not the result of their slavish obedience to the impressions of their cliché; it is the impressions themselves that correspond to the tendencies, character, and temperament of that nation; on the other hand, the impressions experienced by that nation are so closely aligned with the events recorded that they are practically identical to them. As far as isolated individualities are concerned, it is clear that each one tries to fit in with their own tastes and ideas, looking – like choosing the right outfit in a store – for an existential cliché in which they hope to do well or to atone for their burdersome past.

Among the billions of spirits hovering in the orbit of our old Earth, and among the elemental spirits working for its transformation, the rulers will elect the coming planetary peoples, according to their past deeds. This will be the subsequent population to prepare for a new evolution; made up precisely of the cast of actors from that same cliché that is linked with the resurrected world.

— You told me earlier that the cliché, linked to Earth, comes from another destroyed world. How many times can it be used, and does it always pass directly from one world to another?

— It is used as many times as necessary and, once it has been used, it returns to its place in the archives of the Universe, from where it can be removed if necessary. I should add that the film of the astral cliché is indestructible and, after the annihilation of the planetary system, it returns definitively to the archives, where it remains as a document of the past. With the new creations, the conditions are different, or the previous impressions no longer meet the needs of the humanities in formation, which, even though they go through a course of learning, have different subjects.

— My God, how interesting and complex this is, yet how simple and grand! Happy is he who can understand at least a particle of the mysteries of creation.

— Anyone with good can come to know the truth through hard work," said Dakhir .

— Is that so? Some people are incapable of understanding the meaning of the simplest and most ordinary routine," exclaimed Kalitin. I remember a colleague on Earth. He was a very good person, but deaf and blind to any question of an abstract or esoteric nature; I always liked to delve into old books, because the past excited me, which at that time was totally inexplicable.

I happened to come across a very old book on the occult; it talked about many incomprehensible things and, among other subjects, about reincarnation. The transmigration of the soul through three realms, the cycles and so on. These three questions fascinated me; so I later talked about it with the colleague who worked with me at the astronomical institute. My God, he was furious! The thought that he could have been a pebble, an onion, or an owl – the relationship, by the way, is his own – made him indignant; in the same way he would not admit the cycles. And if I had not been a peaceful person, the scientific controversy would have ended in a fight; even so, he created certain embarrassments for me with my colleagues. But then came the catastrophe , and he probably perished, without changing his point of view, since I do not know if he took the primal substance.

Andrei fell silent and sank into sad thoughts.

— Yes, how stubborn the blindness of some is; but that is a consequence of karma: it is useless to convince them, because their previous existence clouds their reason. No free-thinking mind can reject the phenomena shown by nature itself so clearly. Let us take, for example, the enigmatic process of man's formation as proof of his passage through the three kingdoms. The infinitesimal tiny nucleus of the future human being is made up of three elements, the same elements that make up the Earth, on which he is predestined to live. The spermatozoon resembles a plant; one end is the spheroid head, the other, the tail. Dissecting it, we see that the remaining part looks like a bulb, consisting of a series of thin integuments, enclosing a liquid substance.

Next, the embryo begins to project its limbs outwards and becomes defined . Then the embryo develops into a fruit, acquires the shape of a tadpole, living as an amphibian and develops in the so-called "waters". From time to time, the embryo acquires the properties of a human being, it is seized by the first shudder of the eternal breath, it moves... And the divine essence is incorporated into the fetus, where it remains until the moment of man's physical death, when it becomes spirit again.

Just as a fruit develops in the liquid medium of its mother's womb, so the earth matures in the ether of the world, or astral fluid from the bowels of the Universe.

These cosmic unborn babies, like their pygmy inhabitants, are initially nuclei and only later embryos. Little by little, they mature and develop mineral species, plants, animals, and humans; they are born, grow, age and die at the end of their existence. In this way, the cycles follow cycles, encompassed to infinity.

The embryo develops in its pre- maternal sphere; the individual in its family; the family in the nation, the nation in humanity; the Earth in our solar system; the system in its Universe;

the Universe in the cosmos, and the cosmos – in the first and only impenetrable and infinite cause.

Oh, how great is this knowledge of the life of worlds and beings; how simple the basic laws and how diverse the consequences! And this diversity is already bewildering, scrutinized within our tiny and restricted horizons, who will say of the unknown and unsuspected wonders of other worlds and systems sailing through infinite space, like translucent archipelagos! Oh, how I would love to go somewhere like that one day!

Dakhir smiled wistfully.

— When you are ready to be a space tourist, you will no doubt go to the accessible systems, where you will be able to see many wonders.

And the more you ascend, the better you will understand the mechanisms of the laws that make faith, prayer, and the practice of good necessary, in other words: everything that precipitates pure and ardent outpouring, a counterbalance to evil and a balancing factor on which the existence of the world is based.

These effluents serve to contain the currents of chaotic and pernicious forces and beings that operate within the unsubmissive atmospheric masses.

There matter roars and rumbles in its ordinary state, populated by spiritual monsters whose horrifying aspect it would be difficult to describe; there, in their state of primitive power, the elements rage, unable to break out of their planetary limits. But wherever the attraction exerted by the divine current – an obedient, harmonious and powerful force – is delayed or interrupted, a breach is formed through which the disconnected forces of chaos erupt with their unbridled elements, which, like a hurricane, annihilate everything in their path.

— Is this what explains the so-called "miracles", the miraculous healing...? If I understand correctly, physical and moral illnesses signal chaos, the disintegration of the main elements of our tiny human cosmos, while the pure ecstasy of prayer attracts the current of divine grace, providing a cure for illnesses, or, in other words, restoring harmony and balance.

— Your observation is correct. Not only the powerful prayer of higher beings – the so-called saints – but also t those of ordinary mortals, who was overcome with pain; the rapture of the believing soul causes the astral body to separate from the ordinary flesh; at such moments, the spirit of man plunges into the affluent divine current, or into the aura of the saint, for whom it cries out, finding there all the chemical substances necessary for him, or for the one for whom he prays.

Based on what has been said, you will understand the great responsibility of being the legislators, and how essential it is to firmly entrench divine laws to ensure the prosperity of the planet. The correct action of the pure astral currents must be consolidated with the faith of the peoples, with the joint prayers of the multitudes, with the persuasion that all support must be sought from the forces of good and that, to receive it from above, it must be deserved.

Where faith is weakened, low passions run wild, orgies and profanity are promoted, and lustful animal instincts flourish; there, under the influence of the disintegrating breath of evil and disharmony, an environment is established for chaotic spirits, incapable of surviving outside the disordered currents. Then storms, floods, droughts break out; the temperature gets out of control; epidemics strike. It is then said: " such a country has been struck by the wrath of God".

A messenger sent by Ebramar to invite Dakhir to a meeting of magicians interrupted the conversation. Narayana, who had just arrived in the city, wanted to ask his friends and superiors for some advice and report on the latest events.

In the city founded by Abrasack, life was painfully monotonous, especially for the female prisoners, who took little interest in the war arrangements being finalized at full speed.

For the young priestesses, treacherously kidnapped by Abrasack and begrundginly made the wives of the insolent rebel' s companions, daily life was too hard, especially during the first year of their abduction. They were hit by a hurricane of heavy and material feelings and currents, filled with vulgar passions, which changed everything externally and internally.

For Urjane, the ordeal was very painful. She was oppressed by the long separation from Narayana and her parents; but without weakening, she patiently found peace in intense activity. If, in a moment of weakness, the separation from her beloved seemed too torturous, she repeated her father's motto, when he alluded to the anguish of their secular lives:

— Let's go to work, friends! People who work eat up time!

— Abrasack's relationship with the young woman was somewhat curious. Convinced that his attempts to possess her would not succeed, he would not agree to let her go ; always suspicious, he watched her gloomily, even though she did not even think of running away. In their rare encounters, Urjane received him in a friendly way; she would talk to him with the best of goodwill and tried to lift him up. It was precisely this conciliatory gentleness that irritated the proud and explosive Abrasack: in the face of his intemperate fury that impassive docility.

— I would give anything for your love; I do not need your magnanimity tempered with contempt," he said angrily one day, as he left.

Usually, after such scenes, he would take refuge in Avani's house; the pristess' deep and clear gaze had the property of calming him down.

— How good and patient you are, Avani, and I did not even deserve this! — He once said.

— Since you have turned me into a diva, I will fulfill this role, and the first virtue of divinity is patience," returned Avani seriously and thoughtfully.

And so time passed. Abrasack now had a well-trained army; although armed with rudimentary weapons, the monstrous strength of the giants represented a threatening power.

An unexpected incident brought Abrasack out of his state of relative tranquility. A detachment of his army, led by one of his friends, fell victim to an attack by an unknown troop, whose warriors proved to be more skillful and better armed, although the enemy lost out in stature to Abrasack's giants, inflicting a heavy defeat on them with heavy casualties.

According to his friend, the commander of the enemy troop was a tall person, wit a bronze-red complexion , a pointed helmet and a necklace of precious stones around his neck; his commanders, also of a reddish complexion, turned out to be very shrewd. Armed with bows and arrows, they fought with incredible skill and mobility.

Abrasack was baffled. So the wizards had deceived him by denying the existence of relatively cultured peoples on the new planet and unleashing those fierce hordes against him?

That had to be ascertained as soon as possible. But his magic mirror only allowed him to see the huge groupings of red-skinned men described by Clodomiro; as for their origin – whether or not it was a fluke, or the will of the magicians – he could discover nothing. As the clashes recurred over the weeks, usually in favor of the Reds, and one of the giants' villages on the border with the forest was even seized and burned, Abrasack became alarmed.

He then decided bring forward his incursion into the city of the wizards and, without wasting any time, began the final preparations. His entire army would be sent to the place where he would await the arrival of the monsters, commanded by Abrasack. To defend the city with his prisoners, there would be a reserve detachment , well supplied with ammunition and commanded by one of his friends.

Finally, one morning, the astonishing army left the city. Abrasack and Clodomiro headed for the rocky islands in pursuit of the horned monsters, whose task was to destroy the city of the wizards.

While Abrasack's preparations were underway, Narayana wasted no time either. He set up his headquarters with the civilized peoples of Udea who, divided into tribes, were essentially dedicated to livestock and wheat cultivation.

With his characteristic talent for organization, Narayana was able to quickly train the masses, developing their warrior spirit and courage. He soon selected the most gifted and made them commanders: precisely those who led the successful attacks against the savage hordes of Abrasack.

His army was ready to go on campaign against the " monkeys", when Narayana suddenly received an order from the superior magicians to take the armed forces to the outskirts of the divine city, camping there.

Sudden news spreadt through the city, announcing an imminent threat to the reigning peace. On their way home from work, the workerstold of seeing armies of hairy giants in the woods, similar to those that had kidnapped Urjane and her companions, accompanied by unusual monsters of immeasurable stature, horned and horrifying. From the looks of things, those disgusting hordes were heading towards the divine city.

Two days later, we could clearly hear the deafening rumble of the moving masses and the distant, disconnected voices; black clouds as if they were looming on the horizon, spreading in waves across the plain, framing the plateau on which the divine city is located.

As far as the eye could see, only the enemy masses emerged . Like an unbridled avalanche, the hordes advanced, tearing up trees in their path; the earth shook under their thundering footsteps, and the disconnected cries, as they merged, resembled the roar of waves crashing on rocky shores; a nauseating smell poisoned the air for long distances.

In front of the black masses of simian giants came the legendary monstrous beings, crude and disgusting creatures of a primitive nature.

The huge colossi were covered in long hair; some had the bare skin that was spotted like reptiles; most had curved horns and all had tails that dragged along the ground.

With their hands, which used to be clawed paws or curved claws, they lifted and threw huge blocks of stone and tree trunks uprooted like toys. This sea of creatures gradually surrounded the city.

Above , mounted on winged dragons, swooped Abrasack's companions, commanding the masses, and above them all loomed the audacious rebel himself.

Dressed in white and visible to all, Abrasack rode the Dark One; well-trained, he obeyed any signal from his legs. The commander-in-chief wielded a crystal lyre sparkling with hundreds of brilliants; from his neck hung, linked by a gold chain, a kind of magical bugle, the sounds of which sent the warrior spirit of his fighters into a rage.

Dakhir, who was monitoring the advance of the attackers, ordered his assistants to open a hatch in the parapet of the tower platform. Outside, a medium-sized airship was swinging, equipped with devices at the ends, from which bundles of thin metal rods hung.

Four people boarded, and the ship gained altitude. Dakhir and an adept settled down to the devices; Kalitin and another disciple were ordered to pilot the ship according to the magician's instructions.

Almost at the same time, other aircraft of identical construction took off from the other towers, scattering in different directions.

As soon as the horned monsters began to climb the steep rocks on the slopes of the plateau where the city was located, Dakhir's ship appeared above the first ranks of the enemy; a strange and awesome spectacle began. The metal rods spat out beams of sparks, hitting the enemy's closed ranks with unusual hisses.

Almost simultaneously, gaps formed in the middle of the attacking masses; the monsters seemed to have evaporated, leaving no trace.

As the boar glided along and the guns fired their deadly sparks, the enemy monsters vanished or melted into thin air. Everywhere the projectiles ended up falling, the roaring masses simply disappeared with the blocks of stone or tree trunks they carried. The ground, on the other hand, was covered in a thin layer of white ash.

Terror gripped the survivors. Screaming and howling, they fell back against the masses of simian giants, bringing disorganization to their ranks.

The scene was terrifying. In the general confusion, the crazed creatures began to push and trample each other, disappearing in clouds of sparks.

Abrasack's friends were perplexed and mute with terror as they saw the annihilation of his army. Their winged horses began to show a dangerous attitude, throwing themselves in different directions and refusing to obey; finally, half-cowering, they took off in flight towards the forests.

In the meantime, Narayana's army began to descend from the mountains, animated by the warlike impetus. As soon as the new combatants appeared, the spaceships stopped their work of devastation, which had already been completed. A bloody battle began. The army of the " monkeys", totally depleted, thought more about fleeing; however, the instinct of preservation made them repel the attack, and the confrontation would have cost a lot of blood, if an unexpected circumstance had not put an end to the fight. Dark clouds quickly covered the sky and a storm was unleashed; the darkness was such that nothing could be seen, and in this hurricane of the raging elements the fighting ceased of its own accord.

Finally, the thunder and roar of the storm quietened down; a pale glow illuminated the battlefield and the survivors of Abrasack's pitiful army stampeded, roaring with fear, towards their forests. On thier own, moving across the land caused them enourmous discomfort and fear, and as soon as they found themselves under the canopies of the leafy, gigantic secular trees, they climbed them and, leaping from branch to branch, headed for their villages.

Abrasack resisted as long as he could. He soon became aware of the terrible force at the service of the wizards to defeat him; he had heard the others talk about it, but how could he master it? — It was a mystery.

A mad despair came over him. He execrated the hour in which he had taken the primal substance; the immortality for which he had so longed now seemed like a curse, it made him surrender, bound hand and foot, to the authority of the implacable judges who mocked his insurrection. Suddenly, in a exterminating ship , he spotted Dakhir. A furious hatred shook his whole being, and a thought flashed through his excited brain. Who knows, since he was immune to ordinary death, that unknown force, which pulverized even primitive giants and massive rocks, could also give him the death he wanted, freeing him from imminent punishment. Dominated by this will, he wanted to maneuver the Dark One to descend into that whirlwind of beams; but, for the first time, it refused ro complay with his order, so a confrontation began between the two, and the animal came out on top.

Snorting and tearing the air with its mighty tail, the dragon soared into the air and rushed into the woods, threatening to strip its rider bare.

Not even Abrasack could explain how he had reached the city; his head was spinning, and only a blind instinct for self-preservation made him cling tightly to the mad animal.

Having recovered, he found himself lying on the ground near the entrance to the temple. Night had descended. Screams and howls of pain could be heard throughout the city; hairy figures were running around aimlessly.

In a superhuman effort, Abrasack got up and dragged himself to the temple. His tattered clothes were dirty with mud, his whole body ached, his breathing was intermittent, but he did not seem to notice anything.

A single thought hammered at his throbbing head.

"I have been defeated; I am powerless. I have been forced to go on living and to submit to the diabolical punishment that was planned."

The temple was empty. Herbs, flowers, and a bundle of resinous branches were burning on the altar; a few lamps fixed to the rocky wall spread a weak bluish light.

Avani finished arranging the fire on the altar, said her prayers and retired to her niche.

Urjane, who had just been with her , told her that it seemed that Abrasack and his companions had suffered a setback, judging by the fact that they had returned in a daze, locking themselves in their homes. Among the " monkeys", in her words, there was a desperate panic; none of them could say what had happened to Abrasack.

— We already knew about the defeat of the unfortunates. Did he have to wage a just war against those whose power he knew? I am so sorry! — Urjane concluded.

— Like Icarus, I imagined that he would reach the sky on wings of wax... However, he has a strong and courageous spirit, and it would be a pity to let that strength be extinguished in vain," Avani observed.

— You are right. Narayana would not have insisted on protecting him, if he had not perceived in him a chosen spirit, eclipsed by unfortunate circumstances. Well, I'm going home now, something tells me that we will soon be freed.

He said a gentle goodbye to her friend and left the cave. Just as Avani was going up to the niche with the intention of returning to her room to pray, Abrasack entered the temple.

Pale and staggering like a drunk, he approached the altar, but collapsed on the first step.

Avani rushed downstairs and, when she was convinced that Abrasack had lost consciousness, she moistened a towel in the reservoir and rubbed Abrasack's dusty face with it. Then she took a flask from behind her belt , poured a few drops on the flames flickering on the altar, and a life-giving aroma invaded the cave. Taking a goblet, half-filled with red liquid, she turned to Abrasack, who, his eyes already open, rose with great effort.

— I'm thirsty. — he stammered.

Avani brought the splint to his lips and he drank greedily. Suddenly he grabbed his head in his hands and, choking, he cried out in a broken voice.

— They have won, I am just a fugitive without my power.

— It is part of human life to stumble along the way. Your pride and impure feelings have caused you to use your knowledge for evil; repent, then, and reconize your impotence, so that you will have the indulgence of your judges.

— Indulgence? — he laughed dryly. — It will undoubtedly be expressed in diabolical punishment.

— Be ashamed, and do not forget that your victors are superior beings, incapable of petty and cruel feelings. The punishment meted out will only serve your ascension; the more sincere your repentance, the more lenient the sentence will be. Only rebellion and stubbornness deserve severe punishment. I know that you fear Narayana's just wrath , but no vile revenge will guide an adversary as worthy as he is, and if you show sincere repentance , he will forgive, as a father forgives his prodigal son.

— You have no idea how hard it is to humiliate me and recognize me as a powerless plaything, subject to destruction by the hand of his owner," Abrasack whispered darkly.

Avani shuddered and turned away from him.

— So do you not realize, Abrasack, that it is the spirits of darkness that guide you? They are the ones whispering to you pride and rebellion. Expel the lugubrious advisors, spawned by passions, impure instincts, exaggerated arrogance and ambition for power. Drive away these ignominious servants. May they die of inediacy, deprived of the nourishment of the exhalation of their passions.

Mater your pride, purify yourself and pray! You have built a temple for lower begins to learn to worship the Divinity, but you have forgotten yourself.

Or have you forgotten the importance of praying, drawing light, warmth, and strength from the Almighty's focus? Why not make use of that sublime grace, which benefits every soul? Why not make use of that talisman granted to all the weak and disinherited, but which has been snatched away from you by immeasurable pride and fatuity? The magicians themselves and higher hierophants submit in silence before the Divinity to draw strength and wisdom from the source of sublime light. And the higher they are on the ladder of perfection, the more humble they become, for true greatness consists in the awareness of immeasurability of the path to perfection. Believe me, I only wish you well; resign yourself and pray, and the forces of good will protect you, inspiring you and raising your light.

Abrasack remained silent, his terrible excitement giving way to great discouragement. Avani knelt before the altar and began to pray fervently.

In the divine city, the unbridled elements soon calmed down and the rising sun covered the battlefield in rays, where thousands of living creatures perished without a trace, apart from a thin layer of ash.

The magicians gathered to discuss the future, Narayana, who was present, did not seem to be in the best of moods.

— Did you have to unleash the storm and the darkness, preventing my army from playing a decisive role in the fight? Why did I make the effort to recruit the army, if everything could be done with the help of the ethereal force?

— When will you stop being frivolous? — Ebramar retorted. — You know very well that no one stood in the way of your warriors to measuring their strength against the enemy and testing their courage. Besides, everything that was useless and dangerous has been annihilated. Further carnage will be unnecessary, as the population of " monkeys", as Abrasack calls his subjects, has been reduced. As for his soldiers, who already have a high level of intellectual and physical development, they will be used to form future kingdoms.

The wounded will be picked up and given medication; the corpses must be disposed of to avoid the risk of contamination. Calm down, then, and send your commanders back to their homes; then take two aircraft and go to rescue Urjane. Also bring our female disciples with their families. And do not forget your former disciple. We will have to re-educate him, since you have given him immortality.

A few hours later, two aircraft landed in a small clearing in front of Abrasack's palace. The joy of Urjane's reunion and Narayana, after such a long separation, was immense. Once the initial excitement had subsided, they talked freely. Narayana i found out about her companions and announced that, if they wished, the magicians would give them back their freedom, taking them away from their imposed husbands. Urjane smiled.

— I doubt they want that. They have made great sacrifices to improve and develop their men; they also have children with them and have already adapted to this life. However, I do know of one wish they want the union to be made sacred by the wizards through a appropriate ritual, and for their children to attend school.

— Well, the magicians will decide their fate; my order is to take them and their families to the divine city, so I will send people to fetch them.

Grim, mute and sullen, Abrasack's companions came with their wives, pale and alarmed. Narayana, who had known the women since childhood, embraced them and their children, and then announced that, following the magicians' orders, they should return to the divine city, where the masters would decide their future.

— Well, now I need to look for my worthy leader - said Narayana, and his face became cloud.

it was hard to look at his disciple, whose perfidy had robbed him of the happiness of being fascinated by success, revealing that he was unworthy of his protection. Urjane read his thoughts and gently squeezed his hand.

— True, Abrasack's decline was great, overshadowed by the arrogance and lustful feelings that enslave imperfect men. However, it was not all useless that he had been your disciple; he is a strong and powerful soul, with an active intelligence; so, he will eventually shake off his blind impetuosity, repent and emerge victorious, regaining your trust ; and, if he is given a mission, he will undoubtedly fulfill it worthily.

— Let us hope that you are right. I will intercede for him with the masters; they will decide.

When Narayana, Urjane and other adepts entered the underground temple, they found Avani kneeling before the altar, over which hung a radiant cross.

She was immersed in an ecstatic prayer; the silver rays radiating from the cross enveloped her in a bluish mist. Abrasack lay motionless by the steps; the terrible agitation and inner struggle he had gone through the day before had left him cataplegic.

Narayana ordered him to be taken to the airship and, after talking to Avani for a while, they all headed back to the city of the magicians.

CHAPTER XII

When Abrasack woke up from his long fainting spell, his body had regained its former strength, his soul, however, seemed tired and his head heavy; the anguish and discouragement he felt were the result of an enormous moral and physical upheaval. He was in bed, in a totally unknown place, wearing the "garment of the repentant ."

He got up quickly to familiarize himself with the place. It was a large cave, carved out of a rocky massif and illuminated by a lamp on a ledge. It was a installation devoid of comfort, even if it was not totally austere. In addition to the bed, there was a large table surrounded by chairs, some books, manuscripts, ancient papyri and other office materials. Adjacent to that cave was another, smaller one; there, there, a crystal-clear stream of water gushed from the wall into a large tank used for bathing ; next to another wall, there was a bookcase and a huge chest made of aromatic wood, filled with black and white linen garments.

At the back of the first cave, a step up from the ground, was an altar with two golden candlesticks between its edge. With red wax candles, and right there was a finely crafted gold chalice adorned with gems. Above the altar, next to the wall, was an artistically crafted engraving, whose white surface, tinged with a substance reminiscent of mother-of-pearl, stirred as if under the action of the wind and reverberated all the colors of the rainbow.

The only way out was an archway leading to a large balcony with a wooden parapet.

As he stepped out onto the balcony, Abrasack saw that this dwelling was perched on top of a pointy cliff that bordered a chasm; on the other side, all along its lenght, rose curious cliffs. A river was crashing down into the depths of the unfathomable abyss.

He leaned on the ledge and gazed at the gloomy panorama; only the roar of the waterfall or the occasional cry of a nocturnal bird, probably nesting on the rock, broke the deadly silence.

— First prison and then the gallows! — Abrasack burst out laughing.

He returned to the cave, dropped into a chair and clutched his head with his hands; a minute later, he remembered the table full of books. They probably gave me a task. What is this literature about?

Moving his chair closer, he began to leaf through the manuscripts and then realized that he needed to do some mental work before appearing before his judges.

Suddenly, out of a lifted roll of manuscripts a sheet of paper fell, the title of which read in large letters : "The purification of a delinquent adept".

" The most serious crime related to initiation is the abuse of power, favored by sacred science, in order to satisfy abject and immoral passions, . The adept who has committed this culpable act, endowed with knowledge, but who has tainted his soul and plundered his virtues, will undergo the work of purification in oeder to restore his lost clear strenght.

"He should give himself to meditation and develop the greatest possible sensitivity in order to grasp the radiant force and mentally reproduce the prayers described below.

" When he acquires sufficient power to raise a cross with his mind on an altar and contact the elemental spirits, protectors of the sacred symbol, he must, with his help and obstinate work, open the way to the Divine Spirit of Christ."

"If, through a threefold aspiration of deep repentance, ardent faith and the ecstasy of prayer, he manages to invoke the image of The Savior in his soul, and then imprint it on the substance of the engraving, the chalice will be filled with the divine essence, the adept will drink from it, and the evil excrescences accumulated by his actions, will be burned away by the celestial flames. Then he will regain the purity of flesh and spirit, with its former virtues, and will recover the supreme powers."

Abrasack, motionless, breathing heavily, he kept his eyes on the message that presented the program of the tests imposed by the judges.

A few moments later, he stood up feverishly. His head burned; his soul boiled with bitter despair. What was required of him was beyond his strength, he would never be able to do it... With that impossible program, they were mocking his impotence... It was just a hypocritical way of sentencing him to eternal seclusion.

His breathing became difficult he imagined he was suffocating. Almost instintively, he ran to the balcony and leaned on the ledge.

The cool night air invigorated his soul, the storm was still raging; he cast a pitiful glance over the desolate landscape, lit now by two moons. The sharp rocks cast strange odd shadows here and there; only the vague lapping of the water broke the silence.

He really felt defeated. The veil of pride, presumption and rebellion, which had hidden his mistakes, broke into pieces; tears of shame and repentance shone down his cheeks.

— Forgive, O All- Merciful Judge, my sinful faults against Your holy laws," he stammered, gazing hopefully at the cross.

This impulse of repentance completely exhausted Abrasack's strength; he fell on the altar step, and his exhaustion gave way to a deep, restful sleep…

It was very late when he woke up. As he got up, he stretched and wanted to go to the adjoining cave, when his attention was drawn to a stony table, that he had not noticed the day before. As he approached , he saw a sheet of paper on which was written:

"Eat as much as your body needs, which is used to heavy, filling food, because you will need much strength in the future."

There were two baskets on the table: one with bread and the other with eggs, fruit, butter and honey; there were also two jugs: with wine and milk.

Looking at the bountiful delicacies with a half- melancholy, halfironic look, he went to the adjoining cave and took a bath. Changing into a linen robe, Abrasack knelt before the altar and began to pray.

After the prayer, he ate a piece of bread and drank a glass of milk, returned to the table with the books and reread the program of purification of the delinquent adept. Rereading it once more, he propped his face on his elbows and covered it with his hands.

It was no longer fury or indignation that overflowed from his soul, but a deep discouragement, the consciousness of weakness and impotence.

To unite with the divine spirit of Christ, to evoke his image, and yet with such force that it is imprinted on the substance of the engraving? What purity and strength it would take to do that! No, no, I could never do that...

— Try it! Everything is difficult at first, but willpower and patience will overcome any difficulty," whispered a vibrant voice, as if from afar.

Abrasack stood up and his eyes lit up. So, he was not alone in his ordeal; someone shared his fate...Supporting him in that moment of misfortune. Who was this friendly soul? He seemed to recognize Avani's voice ... Whoever it was, they came to him, encouraged him, wished him success.

From then on, Abrasack began his work. He read and he studied the books and manuscripts that provided him with valuable information; and if he ever felt weak or tired, a friendly voice encouraged him.

Finally, the night that became memorable for the repentant adept arrived. Filled with the ecstasy of prayer, in a sincere impulse of humility and repentance, he rejected all petty ambitions forever, begging only for the grace to be able to continue steadily on the path of ascent to divine light and sublime knowledge. Suddenly, an incredible phenomenon occurred.

Ethereal waves swirled around him with dizzying speed, shimmering lightning streaking through the air towards the engraving. A roll of thunder shook the walls, the interior of the painting was filled with splendid light, and, against that radiant background, the figure of the Redeemer was seen in all His supernatural splendor.

With divine docility and infinite love, the great eyes, immeasurably deep, gazed the prostrate adept; one translucent hand rose to bless the repentant sinner; the other held the chalice...

Suddenly, the vision faded and went out completely. The light inside the engraving was extinguished. But in the oscillating background of the pearly substance, the image of the Son of God was alive.

With his soul throbbing, Abrasack contemplated that divine image, smiling mercifully at him. Then he deserved the grace to assimilate the translucent image with all his fibers and print it. He had fully endured the prescribed ordeal, for the golden chalice on the altar was filled with purple liquid. Abrasack took in that mysterious substance, which spread in a vivid stream throughout his body, giving him a sensation of strenght, that he had never before experienced , lightness and well-being, despite feeling dizzy. Involuntarily, he leaned over the nearest chair. The earth seemed to slip away from his feet, the walls of the cave swayed and seemed to move away; suddenly, an arched door opened in one of them, revealing the staircase up which a group of boys from the school of adepts had been climbing . They were carrying certain objects that Abrasack could not make out because of the commotion; they were bright costumes, similar to those worn by wizards. The young men took Abrasack out of his robes and dressed him with the new ones.

Stunned, Abrasack mutely offered his services. As soon as he was fitted with a fine silver belt, Narayana appeared smiling at the doorway. On seen him, Abrasack fell to his knees and laid his head at his feet. Gasping with shame and repentance, he muttered at great cost:

— Master, will you ever forgive my vile ingratitude?

Narayana hurried to lift him up and kissed him.

— I have nothing to forgive you for. This hour has redeemed everything , justifying before my masters my protection and trust in you. Now stand before your judges.

Abrasack had no idea that he was being held in a secluded wing of the magician's palace .

They went down the stairs, through a long corridor and into a large vaulted gallery. There wa melodious music and joyful, triumphant singing ; girls from the magicians' school were throwing flowers at their feet.

The legislators' court was a spacious arched hall. The ceiling, columns, and walls looked like a lace of wood; the inscriptions on the carvings, excetuded in precious stones, spoke thoughts of supreme wisdom.

The hall ended in a semicircle, where in the form of an amphitheater, there were cairs. There, the judges presided; in the top row set the hierophants, whose countenances were shrouded in a bluish mist; a little lower down were the other magicians, and on the bottom tier was Ebramar, who was to pronounce sentence.

Pale and fretful, Abrasack stood before the court, waiting, his hands folded across his chest. Ebramar seemed to be surrounded by a light, transparent mist; six sparks formed a fiery crown on his forehead. His deep gaze stared searchingly into Abrasack's anxious eyes; and finally, he spoke in an affable tone:

— Welcome, prodigal son. You have thrown off the shackles of darkness, returning to the light and the dignified work of God's dwelling . Getting rid of the excrescences of so many impure passions was an arduous task, but a magnificent spiritual work. I congratulate you on fulfilling it as expected; with your soul purified and ennobled, you were able to assimilate the image of the Redeemer; your faith and love were strong enough to indelibly imprint the divine image on the radiant matter of the engraving. So accept the invisible symbol that will place you in the same ranks as the servants of truth.

Abrasack knelt down and Ebramar touched his forehead with the magic sword with a fiery edge. Immediately, on Abrasack's forehead flashed a bright star wrapped in a Kabbalistic symbol, as if drawn by fire.

— Entangled in the darkness of pride and ambition, you wanted to become king; now that you have rejected this, this reign is given to you as proof of your powers. There are many mature peoples on the planet who will have to be governed with justice, receive the laws, assimilate the idea of God and other fundamentals of initiation. One of them is entrusted to you, and I expect you to govern it with the wise exemption of priest, king and legislator; there, the first divine dynasty will be founded by you - one of those that existed in the awakening of mankind, as the popular legends of all nations testify. You will receive detailed instructions as you begin to prepare for your new mission.

Come now to receive our kisses, and then we will celebrate the return of the brother who has regained our trust.

After blessing Abrasack, the high hierophants and most of the wizards who had presided over the Areopagus left; a large group of Ebramar's disciples and friends, and Abrasack's former schoolmates , made their way to the wizard's palace.

Along with Nara, Edith, Olga and others, there was also Urjane .

Narayana took his former pupil's hand, led him to his wife and, smiling mischievously, teased:

— Have you quickly forgotten your deranged expassion, so much so that you only greet her with an indifferent bow?

— I want nothing more from Abrasack than a good and lasting friendship, even if I protest that he treats me with indifference," Urjane replied good-naturedly, holding out her hand to her "kidnapper".

A dark blush covered Abrasack's pale, emsaciated face.

— The ordeal imposed on me cured me of all my foolishness. If the worthy Urjane presents me with her invaluable friendship and accepts the pledge of my loyalty, this day will be the happiest of my life, and proof that her noble heart has forgiven my ignoble act," he said in a low voice, kissing Urjane's hand respectfully.

The lunch passed in an atmosphere of great animation; at the end, Ebramar, in the company of Narayana and Supramati, took Abrasack to his office and announced that from the following day preparations would begin for his new position, under the direction of Supramati and Narayana.

— But first, we must take certain precautions regarding your companions, summoned from space and materialized with the help of the primal substance, as well as the fate of the Simian people that you have managed to subordinate to yourself.

The way in which you led the army to dominate the savage tribes, sowing the first seeds of civilization, is a testament to your skills as a governor, and it would be a pity not to take advantage of them.

— Have any tribes survived? — Abrasack asked restlessly.

— Yes, we have only thinned them out; an explosion in their numbers would be dangerous and unnecessary. The survivors will be divided into two parts and later transferred to the other region of the continent. As climate change has greatly influenced the growth of the race, a region with a cold temperate climate will accelerate their extinction. With intensive miscegenation, we will later significantly improve the species .

For the time being, these simian people are in the care of Jan D Igomer; we think, however, that it is you would like to take them with you, a fair and natural thing to do. Since your companions have always worked under your guidance and know your system, they will be able to carry on the task you have started. Select six of them for the role of responsibility, so that one pair directs the destinies of the native populations , and the remaining two help you in the government of the city and village to be founded.

The other companions you can take along with the respective consorts that you have taken care of providing for them; they will contribute to the development of the aborigines.

I must say that the unions perpetrated under constraint were legalized and made sacred by divine rituals, with the consent of the spouses. By the way, it is time for you too to find a partner too, a queen for the future kingdom and mother of the divine dynasty. I offer you the opportunity to choose one of our young women and receive the consent of your chosen one.

I already have my chosen one, as long as you approve of her, and I can deserve her as my wife. I would like to marry Avani. She was the kind genius who helped me with her advice; moreover, it was her prayers that helped me purify my soul, enlighten my reason and tame my "beast". I am what I am thanks to her. I have a great love for her, and I am infinitely grateful ; if there is no obstacle, I will seek her approval. I do not know if I can, but at least I will try.

— You have my permission and I hope you will unite. Love and recognition are the best accomplices on the road of life - Ebramar concluded - and I hope you will unite.

After discussing a few more details related to the decisions taken, they parted; Narayana took Supramati to his house.

— I think Avani is with Urjane; I am going to arrange for you to meet her and sort things out. Do not be nervous, I know everything will work out. When a woman takes such an interested in a man's fate and worries about his recovery, it is because she likes him. Her gratitude is a great opportunity to consolidate her authority over her husband.

Never forget Abrasack; despite the magician's spiritual eminence, she will never cease to be a "daughter of Eve", so do not try to betray her; one day, you will come around to my words .

Abrasack could not contain his laughter.

— Well, the lesson I have had has probably cured me of all levity. Avani is so far above me that it will be difficult not to submit to her authority. God willing she will agree! — Abrasack sighed.

Leaving him in one of the rooms on the fgirst floor, Narayana went to his wife's room, fifteen minutes later he returned cheerfully.

— Go to the balcony, there you will find Avani, ready to talk!

Visibly upset, Avani was sitting in the chair by the parapet; next to her it lay a gift, carelessly dropped. It was a cloth embroidered with silky, metallic threads, an ornament of flowers and butterflies from the extinct planet.

Abrasack approached quickly, pulled up a chair and took her hand.

I have asked permission to talk to you about a subject on which our future will depend. I love you and would be infinitely happy to have you as my life partner. I hope I will not be condemned for my words after you have witnessed the mad passion I had for Urjane. I swear to you that that impure and criminal feeling has been mastered and forgotten; you, whom I dared to make into a deity, have enslaved my heart. I learned to value your patience, kindness, nobility and remarkable intelligence, while your docile authority treated my spiritual wounds in the most difficult moments.

He fell silent and looked at her anxiously. Avani blushed.

— Do not blame me for taking Urjane's pain, whom I adore. If I had thought better, as any sensible woman would, I would not have offered myself to the inconsequential and passionate man instead of her. And, by the way, the exchange did not seduce him.

By the way, I must admit that you ahve done surprisingly well out of the whole situation: you gave up a normal wife, making her a " deity". It was a brilliant idea.

Avani let out a little laugh; Abrasack did not hold back either.

— Since my pride has been spared," she continued seriously, "I feel no anger towards you.

Relieved and happy, Abrasack drew her into his arms and gave her a kiss, sealing the consent.

The next day, as agreed, he went to Supramati's house to receive the proper instructions about his future activity. This work excited him; the mission entrusted to him would open a vast horizon of dignified works.

The magician welcomed him jovially and made him sit down at a table cluttered with manuscripts and devices whose use he did not know.

After making some preliminary observations, Supramati opened a map before Abrasack and said:

— Study this map of your future field of action! The country, as you can see, is cut out by a great river; the land is fertile, rich, and good to be populated. it is home to a primitive people, but one that is ready to receive the principles of civilization. In addition to your old companions, you will be taking some Earthlings to help you. Assign them the tasks you deem necessary and show them the way . All orders will come from you and they must obey you unconditionally.

We will leave you a code of general laws that will serve as the basis for future legislation; it is up to you to apply it according to the characteristics of the unborn people, inherited from their previous existences in the three kingdoms, and the result of planetary, cosmic, karmic astral cliché, etc influences. Being a priest, a a king and legislator, you must study all these details in order to use them in the field of religion, sciences and the arts, so that they serve as a subsidy for the betterment of the people. Needless to say, all this will require a lot of energy and obstinate patience. I should add that the support of legislation must be underpinned by veneration of divinity, awareness of life beyond death and responsibility for one's actions. What is good and what is evil must be clearly defined, so that people are aware that they will provoke the divine wrath if they disobey the laws. They are issued to repress the animal passions, which are responsible for cosmic disorders –

like the dirt thrown down the well and which leaves the water fetid and saturated with harmful miasmas — these laws must be seem as divine or as commandments from the Divinity.

Religious services, based on a specially developed ritual, must include acts of purification. It is well known how important chants, aromas and recitations are in these cases. Their composition is aimed at creating a combination of sounds that will attract beneficial effluvia from space to humans, animals and plants.

— I believe, master, that certain moments in human life should be marked with ceremonious rituals, especially the passing, as a stop to earthly impunity, Abrasack observed.

— You are really right, my son! Allimportant human moments must be duly marked with a ritual; this is not human mumbo-jumbo, but has a profound arcane meaning.

So, firstly, it is birth, the joining of the spirit with its new body, which needs blessing, like a new dwelling that you want to be accessible to receive the effluvia of the forces of good; the second phase is death, a separation of the earthly body with the astral one, which detaches and begins to live in new conditions, resulting from man's earthly actions.

As for the arts, necessary to refine people, Narayana will give you instructions, as well as the architectural manual .

From that day on, Abrasack set to work with enthusiasm. His desire was to faithfully carry out the entire program , as a way of meeting the expectations of his masters.

One afternoon, going over the map of his future kingdom, Abrasack said to Narayana:

— Did you notice that this region is very similar to one in our ancient world - Egypt, to be more specific - which was flooded in the catastrophe just after you rescued me.

Narayana smiled.

— There is certainly some resemblance. In fact, this Syrian deserves to have a civilization that is just as great , a monumental science and, above all, that lasts a long time, because no religion, no system of government of our old Earth has ever reached such heights as Egypt. According to certain incomplete calculations– and many confused ones at that – by some Egyptian and Greek historians, Egypt had its national monarchs – the Pharaohs – for twenty-three thousand years; and what is more curious; in the secret archives of the temples, there is still data on the divine dynasties, whose origin dates back to the secular reigns of the first sovereigns…

CHAPTER XIII

The day of Abrasack's departure finally arrived, also marked by two consecrations: that of king and that of his marriage.

Inside the gigantic temple of the City of the Magicians, all the inhabitants flocked; two hierophants introduced Abrasack.

After the sung mass and the prayers of those present, the hierophants took Abrasack to the Sancta -Sanctorum, where Abrasack received the mysterious magical consecration that qualified him to carry the heavy burden of king.

Abrasack came out concentrated and visibly nervous. He was now wearing a white garment edged in purple; on his head was a large crown set with precious gems , from his neck hung a necklace with several turns and on his chest was a gold insignia . In the meantime, two young adepts had placed a portable altar on a platform in the center of the temple, over which a flame was flickering in a crystal bowl.

While the new monarch was in the tabernacle, Nara and Urjane brought Avani. Wearing a wide, simple tunic, girded by a golden sash and covered by a veil as silvery as mist, the young woman was charming, yet serious, thoughtful, without stopping to pray.

Abrasack took her hand and they both climbed the steps leading to the altar. There they were waited by one of the great hierophants; who placed the bride and groom's hands together over the flame and recited the formulas that fused them by indissoluble fluidic bonds.

The flame suddenly extinguished and the cup was filled with a purple liquid emitting steam. Having tasted its contents, the hierophant placed the rings on them.

Again, joining their hands, he walked around the altar three times, pronouncing solemnly:

— As the Universe that revolves around the arcane center, dwelling place of the Ineffable, so you, particles of the Ineffable, so you, particles of the Divine, orbit around your destiny. May the road of life, to be walked together, be eternally flooded with the clarifying light of goodness, and may it guide you to the next rung of the ladder of perfection.

At the end of the ritual, Avani descended from the platform; one of the adepts replaced the cup with the Code of Laws — a heavy, bulky book of solid gold.

With his hand resting on the book, Abrasack pronounced an oath in a loud voice, heard in the back rows, to scrupulously fulfill the divine commandments, both in private and social life, severely punishing their violators, or those who used their knowledge and power for evil.

The ceremony was followed by a banquet and those present joined in a fraternal feast behind long tables set up in the palace courtyard.

Abrasack and his friends, along with their wives, sat next to the magicians. At the end of the meal, Abrasack prostrated himself before each master and thanked them exaltedly for the graces he had received.

when they said goodbye, the newlyweds received a brotherly kiss from everyone; Urjane's kiss on Abrasack made the new monarch happy and grateful.

The travelers settled into various aircraft and the air fleet soared towards the new field of work.

One afternoon, in Ebramar's office, some of his friends and disciples were gathered, waiting for Narayana and Udea to return from an important expedition.

The two arrived soon; Narayana as always, cheerful and animated; Udea, serious and thoughtful.

— We have fulfilled our task, master – Narayana announced, with an air of satisfaction. We have just divided that territory into two great kingdoms, with the help of the surveyors: one for Udea, the other for me.

As they were examined Narayana's kingdom plans, he pointed to a place marked with red pencil and said:

— Look, Ebramar, the capital's foundation stone will be laid here. The site is incredible and the location is wonderful. From the shores of the sea rises an altiplano with forests at a height of five hundred meters ; further on, a mountain range extends and there is a huge lake that can supply the entire city; the mountains can house temples and caves for the storage of archives. From above, the panorama is grandiose, and high up I will build myself a palace . Oh, I hope you like the capital "Urjane", when you come to visit my kingdom.

— I think you will do well. — Ebramar assured him with a cunning smile.

— Do not laugh, dear master. You know my love of the arts and you have always supported me in this passion. And now, I would like to make a great request of you.

We have your promise to visit our kingdoms to evaluate the work done. I would like you to take the opportunity to bless the laying of the foundation stone of my capital and of the temple to be consecrated to the cosmic forces, a visible manifestation of the work of the Ineffable. What is your answer, Ebramar?

I will take your request to the hierophants and give you an answer later. And you, Udea, do you have any special request?

— No. I am entirely in the hands of my mentors and would be honored by your visit — replied Udea.

Leaning on his elbows, Udea seemed to be deep in thought. Ebramar, observing his pale and worried face, asked:

— Are you thinking of leaving? In fact, I think you should quickly assume your role as king and legislator — remarked Ebramar .

— I am practically ready. By the way, I would like your advice on the Earthlings I plan to take.

He read some names.

— Your choice is the right one; I would not have made it any better. But you forgot the main assistant: your queen and mother of the divine kings, who will be in charge of women's choice and all women's issues. Have you elected her yet? How can you rule without a life partner and a helper in your work? — Ebramar observed, sternly.

Udea sighed.

— I do not have anyone in mind; and it is a very difficult choice, even if it is necessary . I beg you, Ebramar, help me with this delicate matter! I fear that my long and hard atonement has coarsened my soul… I am unsociable… of little conversation... and boring, in other words: I will be an unbearable king. What woman will want me, especially for centuries on end, when tolerance and much affection are needed?

— The existence of defects only means that the magician must correct them, replied Ebramar. — But let's get back to the main subject! It seems to me that you have a special interest in Ariana, Sunacefa's daughter, judging by the amount of time you spend talking to her, compared to the other girls.

— It's true! Ariana is charming and knows how to be cheerful or serious when the circumstances require it; however, I thought that she was meant for Sandira, Supramati's son.

— I do not deny that it was considered, but the plans were changed. I have reason to believe that the young woman is interested in someone else.

— Ah, so this also applies to me too? — Udea blurted out, with a somewhat undefined expression on his face.

— No doubt about it! But imagine Ariana's strange inclinations! The man she likes is unsociable, taciturn, even boring, and he will definitely be an unbearable husband; in spite of everything, I know she will be happy to accept the proposal of her small-talking admirer, and the future does not suggest the slightest fear for her, said Ebramar, staring at Udea's flushed face with a mischievous look.

— Thank you, Ebramar! Since Ariana is intimate, it does not hurt to ask for her hand. If she accepts an owl husband, the problem is solved, and after the wedding I can leave… — Udea concluded, visibly annoyed.

Two days later, Udea's engagement to Ariana was celebrated in Sunacefa's palace and, a month later, the wedding ceremony took place; a few days after that, the aircraft took the third colony of legislators to their field of activity.

CHAPTER XIV

It was a wonderful evening, warm and calm. The rays of the setting sun were playing brightly over the colorful palaces of the city of the Magi; the air was scent with soft fragrances from its vast flower gardens.

A fairly large group was gathered on Ebramar's large terrace. Besides the host, there were Supramati and Dakhir, some of the great magician's disciples and friends , members of the Egyptian hierophant's collegium and female representatives of the higher school of initiation, including Nara, Edith and Olga.

After the frugal dinner, they discussed the details of the planned excursion .

— We will start the excursion from the kingdom of Udea, said Ebramar. — This morning I received word that he is waiting for us in the mountains, near the headwaters of the river that irrigates most of his domain. Then we will go to Narayana, who informed me in his letter that he is finalizing the preparations for our reception.

The sun was rising and flooding the green valley with light, cut by a wide river that was already navigable, judging by the numerous boats moored on the shore. Painted white, with a high curved prow, they were equipped with cloth balcachins to protect the travelers from the scorching sun.

A group of men in simple, dark clothing, girded by leather belts with finely worked buckles, had gathered on the shore.

Udea was standing on a mound, wearing a white tunic, edged in gold, girded by a golden belt. His beautiful countenance had changed a lot. As before, he exuded strength and youth, but his former expression of tiredness and dejection gave way to an energetic serenity; his gaze was still stern, but in the depths of his large, clear eyes there shone that tranquility which only a happy life could provide.

— They are coming! Udea rejoiced, pointing to the fast-approaching aircraft ; which soon landed near the group of men.

On the balcony at the bow was Ebramar, in the company of several wizards and hierophants.

Udea hurried towards them and helped them disembark.

— Welcome, my friend and all of you esteemed masters! I am very glad that you have honored me with your visit to see my work, he said, kneeling down to receive the mentors' blessing.

Ebramar lifted him up and kissed him; all the others also placed their kisses on him. Udea introduced his companions, who prostrated themselves before the hierophants. Splendid lights emanated from all of them, especially from Ebramar; his clothes seemed covered in diamond dust.

At the end of the ceremonial reception, Ebramar asked:

— Well, my friend Udea, how do you intend to transport us? Is that what the the boats are for , or would you rather go by plane?

— If you do not object , I would like to take you to the capital by river. It is the best way to get to know a part of the country with its cities; later we can visit other provinces to get a better idea of the current system of government and its results.

— That is fine with me, and I think the brothers also agree, said Ebramar.

So, once everyone was into the boat, strong rowers propelled them swiftly along the gentle surface of the river, which gradually widened.

Along one bank was a low mountain range; on the opposite side, as far as the eye could see, stretched an endless plain. A wide network of irrigation canals cut through well-cultivated land. From time to time, uniform villages and flat-roofed houses could be seen, isolated by lush gardens. The villages were surrounded by huge belts of fruit trees, bending under the weight of the most diverse fruits. In the center of each village there was a masonry building with an obelisk bearing an inscription plaque; next to it there was always a much larger building.

On the mountainside, quarries alternated with extensive vineyards; on the lawns, cattle grazed.

It was the wheat and grape harvest time; work was going on everywhere; some were harvesting and gathering large bales, others were picking grapes. Only sporadically, a group of villagers looked curiously at the fleet, saluted the king and prostrated themselves before those unknown "gods" who accompanied him.

— I am pleased to see that your subjects are not basbaques who are too upset for any reason, Ebramar observed.

— I gave orders for the work not to be interrupted, so that you can see the people going about their daily business. The most curious are the women, old people and children, he said, pointing to a larger group.

Standing on the shore, the representatives of that race were not particularly beautiful . The men in linen shirts were tall, strong and stocky, with broad, beardless faces, small, intelligent eyes and dark, slightly reddish complexions. the women, wearing colorful skirts, were also hideous.

— At least you know how to be obeyed, which is a sign of hard work, Supramati considered.

— Yes, I have done my best, and I am not short of work, thank God! I'm glad I have my staff to help me with my tasks. Even so, I am afraid I have forgotten something. Perhaps I did not understand all the teachers' instructions; I would, however, be infinitely happy if my work was approved.

— From what we have just seen, you knew how to establish order, instill obedience and foster progress, leading the country to abundance, indispensable conditions to solidify the nation's future prosperity , said one of the hierophants.

In the meantime, the boats were moving downstream, widening to take in numerous tributaries. Now the flowing current, pushed by a cool morning breeze, was already rolling with an audible rumble.

The edge of the mountain snuggled up to the bedrock and the hills gave way to granite cliffs with unusual contours.

— We are close to the country's main sanctuary , where the four elements of the Omnipresent's visible thought are venerated, Udea announced. — Every year, large pilgrimages go there, seeking healing and other graces from the gods and cosmic spirits. The people love it. Would you like to visit the place, or would you prefer to do so on another occasion if you honor me?

— Certainly now! — almost in unison the magicians returned.

The boats docked on the shore, the wizards descended, and were received with deep reverence by the people present; a group of women i sang a melodious solemn hymn.

Udea led the way, followed by the priests and priestesses of the temple. The magicians entered the interior of the rock, through a narrow entrance that was locked from the outside with a heavy metal beam. A natural winding corridor led to a strange-looking cave. A vault of colossal proportions was lost in the darkness; through four slits, arranged in the shape of a crucifix and corresponding to the four cardinal points, beams of light of different shades filtered through: red, blue, white and yellow-orange, passing through green. All these lights were concentrated around a white marble column that supported an enormous sphere that flickered like mercury, whose surface oscillated and reverberated multicolored.

At the back of the cave, a few steps above the floor, stood a kind of altar with statues adorned with flowers and wrapped in curtains. The priests and priestesses, standing on the steps and around the altar, sang a hymn to the gods, lords of the cosmic forces and servants of the Great Invisible God, executors of His will and embodiments of His divine breath.

When the hymn ended, Udea lit resinous branches on the altar, poured incense on the flames and offered fruit, honey and milk.

It was with great reverence that the magicians attended that first liturgy. Udea gave way to Ebramar and a hierophant.

After a silent prayer, Ebramar raised his hand pronouncing mystical words and, in the niche above the altar, a gleaming white cross appeared into the air. Then it was the hierophant's turn, who raised his hands upwards and, singing a sacred prayer in a slow tone, suddenly made a wide band of seven colors appear around the cross.

Udea emotionally thanked the masters for the grace he had received; , after blessing the public present, thye magicians returned to their boats.

Finally, they reached the capital, spread out on both banks of the river. towering over the metropolis were the royal palace and the huge buildings of the initiation schools, of simple but solid construction. The houses, made of brick, were also humble, but quite large, with backyards surrounded by gardens which, it seems, were obligatory even for the poorest inhabitants. In fact, the whole city looked like a lush garden, such was the profusion of plants and flowers.

The entire population was on their feet, squeezing in the path of the procession that was heading for the royal palace. There, Ariana was waiting for them in the company of two sons and a daughter; the latter and her older brother were already married and had children.

After a meal offered by the hostess, most of the visitors retired to their specially reserved quarters to rest. Ebramar, Supramati, Dakhir, Sunascph and other close friends to the king gathered in Udea's office, where a friendly conversation ended.

— His whole face is an expression of contentment at having defeated the shadows of the past, Ebramar observed, smiling.

— You are right, my master and friend, I am as happy as a mortal or an immortal can be, he added, laughing. — In Ariana, I have not only found an excellent wife and the kind genius of my home, but also a collaborator and advisor in my work. Afterwards, I love this intense life; the country provides riches that I want to see enjoyed by the working people .

I am delighted with how this infant nation has progressed. It is a paradise here now, compared to when I came here! And that terrible isolation in the middle of the foggy swamps, the inhuman struggle against the forces of nature! Now I am in a privileged position; thanks to the help of friends and companions, a lot has already been done, but there is so much more to do that I am ashamed to rest, Udea confessed.

What we have seen today already tells you how much you have worked and advanced in recent times, said Supramati. — Apparently your work is magnificent; but we know nothing of the internal structure and the laws that sustain order in the construction itself, he added.

— I see. You are curious about the ethical aspects of my work. Tomorrow I will show the mentors the legislative statutes and, on the journey across the country, you will have the opportunity to see the machine at work. With your permission, I would like to give you a brief account of my achievements and ask for some advice.

— Of course, do it! Your testimony will help us understand some details, Ebramar said promptly.

— Thank you . This is how I will begin my story. When I arrived here with my helpers, we found a barren and virgin land, populated by savages, beings at the lowest level of civilization. They walked around naked, killed on any pretext and were cannibals. The situation was worse than I had imagined.

Among my savage subjects, there were remnants of the populations of the sunken continents, even more primitive creatures whose hideous appearance and ferocity frightened everyone. My first concern was to clean up the mess; so, I decided to annihilate those people who were useless and incapable, due to their physical nature, of assimilating a high culture. This was the most difficult part of my projects, so I decided to start a war.

Even though I was aware of the basic axiom that forbade the practice of killing, there was no way I could avoid it in such remote worlds, where war was an attribute. The taste for fighting, the cruel desire to take the lives of others, goes back to ancient times and its origins are lost in the infinite past. If, already in a drop of blood, battalions of white and red blood cells clash ferociously, devouring each other, war between humans is inevitable.

My attempt achieved the expected result; the primitive monsters were decimated and my benign subjects feasted on the bodies of the wounded and even the dead. I decided to take advantage of that cannibalistic " feast" to take the first step in the difficult and grandiose transformation. The expedient was cruel, but I could not delay if I wanted to achieve my goals.

I caused a disgusting contagious disease to spread, which covered the whole body with ulcers, causing terrible suffering. I found the right moment to consolidate power. The whole country was temporarily divided into provinces governed by my assistants, who, after bewitching the imagination of the savages with paranormal phenomena, began to send me help. The methodology was as follows: those who used human flesh died, those who did not use it in their diet ended up surviving , albeit weak and sickly.

It was suggested that the cause of the deaths was the use of human flesh, and that the corpses were particularly toxic. Obtuse minds could finally get the message: there is nothing like physical suffering to change attitudes. So, for the next generation, human flesh became aversive.

By subdividing the populations into tribes, we concentrated our efforts on developing agriculture, as it was my goal to educate the subjects on a diet based on plant foods, making them peaceful, active and hard-working people, in a healthy and clean environment, preserved from the demonic influences of the astral world.

Food of animal origin is extremely harmful to the health of the body and is also harmful from an occult point of view, because the blood of sacrificed animals allows umbral spirits to condense their fluidic bodies and, in humans, it excites cruelty towards the lower brothers and sisters. This condition is particularly dangerous in relation to more evolved animal species, since human ferocity turns them into satanic beings, boiling with hatred and eager for revenge.

My people are vegetarians. Well-developed agriculture provides an abundance of products; we have made great progress in fruit growing, wine growing, flowers growing and of dairy farming; you may have noticed the number of grazing cattle that provide us with milk and wool for fabrics. We make shoes, belts and other artifacts from the skins of lost animals.

Thanks to all this, crime is a rare phenomenon; the legislative system in place, which prevents the progression of crimes, also contributes to this. The laws are severe, even crude, in cases of abuse and disobedience; but, in my opinion, a benevolent sentimentality would be harmful to a people at this level of progress, still susceptible to animalistic bloodthirsty instincts. Thus, the first measure applied to those who commit crime is their expulsion from the tribe, because every crime contaminates, the criminal's breath exudes putrid miasmas of impure desires, anger, rebellion against the laws in force and hostility towards their neighbor. Such individuals spread the contagion of crimes; by violating the cosmic laws, hereditary diseases are spread; it is therefore necessary to isolate the agents of this spread. Thus, in every province there are institutions where criminals are confined and forced to repent ; only those who manages to master their passions and correct their faults return home.

Special attention was paid to religion, devotion and faith in divine forces. Remember how I said that in every village there is a small temple painted white? Well, there is always an official next to it, whose job is to be a priest, doctor and mentor; two or three officials, depending on the need, manage agriculture and livestock, take care of mining matters, trades and so on.

Every day, at dawn, before work begins, the inhabitants gather in the temple and, together with the priest, say their prayers; then the superior or priest – as the priest is called – reads out to those present the 21 divine commandments, engraved on the obelisk, which recount all the man's obligations towards his neighbor and towards Divinity, so that the precepts are always fresh in the memory of the people. In his role as physician, the priest looks after the parishioners' health; as a mentor he provides them with notions about medicinal plants; for those who show an aptitude for learning, he teaches them the first rules of writing.

The most intellectually advanced are sent to higher education institutes, where career officials are trained.

The whole country is subdivided into 21 provinces, each administered by a governor and his assistants; every month he makes a round of his domains to inspect the work carried out, resolve disputes and, if necessary, apply punishments in accordance with the law.

You will have the opportunity to see the public tranquility and how everyone carries out an activity according to their aptitude; loitering is not tolerated.

— You have not told us anything about the importance given in your kingdom to the arts, to the healing power of colors, aromas... Dakhir asked, seeing Udea very thoughtful.

— I must admit that, due to the little culture of the people, the arts have not developed as they should. Painting is in its infancy, but sculpture and architecture have already evolved significantly, as I have worked hard to achieve .

I have made sure that music, that double-edged sword, is restricted to certain occasions. The harp is sung and played at liturgies, festivals, dances and after work, but the musicality leaves something to be desired. Any new rhythm is subject to regulation, to avoid prematurely exciting so many different senses.

To extract the aromas, we use flowers. They grow everywhere, and their cultivation - which is obligatory - is restricted to permitted species, based on the criterion of the healthiness of the fragrances. Both in the main temple and here, in the palace, we grow the plants that are used in higher magic. So, recently I managed to produce a curious shrub whose iridescent flowers sing, or rather generate melodic vibratory ; their scent seems to exude breath, condensing into droplets of dew. However,

I need to improve its tone; I also need to improve the transparency of the scent droplets. I must have overlooked something and I ask you to help me solve the problem.

— We will certainly do our best to help you in this very useful and interesting work, which I approve of, Ebramar assured.

— Thank you very much. All activities give me great pleasure; I pity the ignorant, for whom nature is deaf and dumb.

What a wonderful vision he who attains knowledge and develops his five senses, becoming capable of learning and seeing everything around him! For him, all of nature overflows with life; every little plant breathes, exudes its color, aroma and light; and the more you learn, the more discoveries you make and the more fascinated you become with the inexhaustible wisdom of the Almighty.

The next day began with a visit to the main temple, an imposing and majestic building, supported by tetrahedral columns. Its interior was decorated with sacred objects; in the tabernacle was the image of the people's hidden Divinity .

Dense crowds of inhabitants lined the streets and the temple, falling to their knees as the hierophants, who were considered divine, passed by.

In the center of the temple, the waters of the reservoir were considered consecrated by the gods. Newborn babies were baptized there, and given names; the same water was used to cure the sick and bless houses. In short, all the spiritual needs of the people were met at that time.

Pleasant and soft aromas permeated the sacred place. As the procession entered, Ebramar raised his hand; radiant flames immediately burst forth from all the tripods.

They then proceeded to offer flowers, milk, wine, butter and other products of the earth, singing hymns to the glory of the gods. The chants of the priests and priestesses stood out for its imposing, serious melody and acted as a calming effect on the crowd.

At the end of the ceremony, while Udea took the magicians to the male initiation schools, the queen went to show the magicians the female schools, where she was the superior mentor and where singing and harp lessons were given, along with the first trades and the basics of occultism.

— And so, my illustrious masters, have I fulfilled your prescriptions without omitting anything important in my task?

— On behalf of everyone, my son, I must say that you have solved the problem of the young nation's education with great wisdom, began Ebramar. — And on many issues, you have done more than we expected. Thus, with small resources and great simplicity, your subjects have made incredible progress in the art of weaving, producing resistant and beautiful fabric. In the same way, we can praise the arts applied to ceramics, the dyeing techniques. As for their orchards, the results are even more remarkable. The fruit tree without seeds, that you have developed is the proof of your persevering work. I have the impression that you were inspired by the banana trees of our extinct planet, judging by the rhizomatic form of multiplication, absence of seeds and bulb, and with an arboriform root .

In short: we can only praise your work. Your people are religious, humble and extremely clean. It will outlive many others, even if they surpass it in terms of material well-being and wealth.

So, receive the reward for your secular work! With the permission of the chief hierophants, I shine the second magician's torch on your forehead.

Moved, Udea got down on his knees and, when the second golden torch flamed across his face, Ebramar kissed the disciple and said:

— May the first divine monarch of this golden century receive my praise; these memories will live on in the memory of popular legends for time immemorial, telling that there was a time when peoples prospered and were happy, when the gods acme down from the heavens to talk to humans, ruling them and teaching them.

CHAPTER XV

On the pinnacle of the mountain gleaming in the sun like a colossal gold sapphire, the royal palace shone next to the temple with red columns, like ruby carvings, glimmering among the lush green of the gardens.

Three fortified walls surrounded the city, dividing it into three concentric parts; at the foot of each wall, wide canals fed the waters, whose course, starting at the top of the royal residence, cascaded down .

Beyond the limits of the lower wall, the richly colored villas of the public men spread out from every corner, variegated like inflorescence on the heights of the tress on the horizon.

It was a celebration in Urjane. All the houses – even the humblest, riverside ones – were decked out in green; the richest houses were decorated with multicolored pennants and wreaths , covering doors, walls and roofs.

The entire population was on its feet and the crowds lined the shores of the seaport, now criss-crossed by numerous boats.

Another part of the residents crowded along the wide road and staircases that went up from the valley to the magically decorated royal residence. At the top of the palace's astronomical tower fluttered the blue flag, embroidered in gold with a chalice topped by a cross, which was shining under the rays of the rising sun.

Soon, a sailing boat appeared on the horizon, rapidly approaching the harbor.

It was a boat of peculiar beauty; all carved in wood, with gold designs, it looked like a jewel with red sails.

In front of the command bridge, the wizards, Udea with his wife and other travelers were standing, looking curiously at the shore.

— What a wonderful view! How beautiful is this city that rises in terraces among gardens and waterfalls, topped by a magical palace. It does not compare to ours, where everything is so simple and shabby, remarked Ariana.

Udea smiled.

— You are right. But what can we do, since you have chosen such a prosaic husband who prefers practicality to beauty; now you will have to make do with what we have. Narayana, as I already told you, is a gift from fate; he is an artist attracted to beauty, like bees to nectar. He is a true legendary hero of the future, whose memory will hover in the imagination of the peoples, wrapped in the enigmatic veil of fairy tales.

— And there is the hero himself, coming to meet us, added Ebramar, and turning to Ariana, he added: I do not share your opinion about your kingdom. There are many picturesque places of wild beauty there.

He fell silent; Narayana's boat had just approached them at that moment.

In two leaps Narayana found himself on the bridge and respectfully greeted the magicians; he kissed Ebramar, Dakhir, Udea and Supramati. He was radiant. His happiness was reflected in his large black eyes; the Grail knight robes, which suited him so well, accentuated his classic beauty even more. In fact, he had made a few changes to the brotherhood's trivial attire. On the chest of his silver tunic was embroidered a kind of eagle or falcon with spread wings, and on the top of his helmet was a pointed crown.

— If your kingdom or capital, that we can see from here, is as graceful, rich and comfortable as the boat that came to fetch us, it is a sign that your civilization is a success – observed Ebramar, in a breezy tone.

But, in his agitation, Narayana did not notice his breeziness.

— Yes, master, I have done everything possible and impossible to develop the people quickly. What a wonderful race! It reminds me of my ancient countrymen, the Greeks, a richly endowed, passionate, warlike and impulsive people who will have a bright future. As for wealth and comfort, that is the least of it.

The soil provides us with an abundance of products; metals and stones, in most cases, are already in a malleable state, making them easy to use. Well, here we are! — he said, approaching the edge of the boat and raising his arm.

Immediately, a choir of countless voices rang out a hymn of welcome; the complex melody was performed with rare perfection. In the harbor, warriors stood magnificently decked out in light armor, reverberating in scales, in their golden helmets and armed with spears, broad-bladed short swords, bows and quivers of arrows.

The children covered the path of the illustrious visitors with flower petals; they soon took their seats on litters carried by eight porters, and the procession set off, protected by an escort and followed by an huge crowd.

In every part of the city, fortified by the walls, the procession of priests, priestesses, and magicians was greeted with chants under the chords of harps; the inhabitants fell to their knees at this passage .

They reached the top and headed first for the temple, a monumental building, made of transparent material resembling ruby.

At the entrance, Urjane and her two sons were waiting for them. Richly dressed and beaming with happiness at meeting her parents and friends again, she was more charming than ever.

At the end of the Mass, everyone headed out to see the city. Many things seemed to have been inspired by memories of the extinct planet, still alive in Narayana's soul. Thus, on the edge of the upper wall, just below the royal palace, he built a riding field, a series of public gardens and another building: an old idea, to which he had given a different solution.

It was a hotel, a shelter for foreign travelers, or for those passing through from provinces far from the kingdom, where they stayed as government visitors. The building was colossal, with every possible comfort and adapted to receive around a thousand travelers, who could stay there on a business trip from a week to a month.

The upper town was home to most of the civil servants and the arts and sciences schools..

Behind the next wall, the industrial life of the city was concentrated, already well-developed. There were schools for trades and factories for clothing, fabrics, household utensils, etc.; there were also barracks, as Narayana had a large army. In fact, only the well-equipped and armed royal guard was quartered inside the city; part of this guard had its garrisons near the palace and its detachments took turns guarding it. The rest of the army was distributed across the provinces and frontiers.

Finally, inside the lower wall , as well as in the valley and the seaside regions , lived the poorest part of the population, who made their living from fishing and sailing. Their houses were built closer together than the fortifications above, were more humble and not so luxurious; but they were very clean and had their own well-kept gardens.

Narayana's engineers used a very ingenious system to supply water to the huge city, which had around 100,000 inhabitants.

A pippeline was pulled from the volcanic lake to the special reservoir at the base of the plateau where the city was located.

From this main reservoir, suspended in the excavated rock, there was another five hundred foot high pipe, which carried the water with extremely high pressure to the place where the royal palace was located, and from there it was distributed to various parts of the city, supplying the houses of the inhabitants and the public fountains.

The temples, all equally majestic, were served by a special caste of priests; the people worshiped the solar disk as a symbol of the superior and invisible god. This disk, made of solid gold, was installed so that the first ray of the sun of the spring equinox would fall on it.

In the evening, a lively conversation took place on the terrace about the Magi's impressions of the city; they asked Narayana about the details of the system of government, aspects related to the liturgy and the faith professed .

— For the priestly caste, that is, the lower-level initiates, I introduced the cult of fire and the sun, since light and heat are more suitable symbols for the intelligence of the infant people to intuit the cause of the creation of the Universe. Despite the incipient level of the priestly caste, a more significant and profound and precise symbolism was suggested to them. Thus, without revealing the very essence of the mystery of the trinity of the One, these symbols represent the Higher Being in his cosmic power as Creator, Protector and Destroyer. I believe that I have not overstepped the boundaries of my mandate by revealing this to you...

— Absolutely! We would even like to learn more about this pre-initiation system.

— I have designed it so that those who are more developed than the rest of the crowd, those who are more active and more eager to rise, have the opportunity to enrich themselves with greater knowledge. I also put an end to bloody sacrifices. Offerings to the deity are limited to flowers, fruit, milk and aromatic essences; I have not managed, like Udea did, to ban the use of meat in food. The abundance of fish in the sea and rivers is a lure for my fishermen; likewise, the forests, full of birds, attract hunters and provide the people with cheap and healthy poultry .

I do not share Udea's opinion that meat is so harmful, and I believe that in the not-too-distant future, his people will also use it.

— It is possible, but for the time being, they can do without this food that excites animal instincts and perversity; I hope that in the course of centuries of vegetarianism a respected and peaceful generation will bear fruit . In time, all our work will be forgotten and human life will take a new direction, said Udea .

— In any case, I managed to weaken the meat habit by instituting periods of fasting; not to mention that the meals themselves are strictly regulated. There was no point in prescribing abstinence from meat, as was the case on our poor Earth; gluttony led to creation of the most exquisite delicacies , and people filled their bellies imagining that they were keeping the fast . In addition, during the initiation period, vegetarian food is compulsory.

Everything in the country belongs to me, i.e., crops, the pastures, the cattle, etc., are the king's property . The nation is subdivided into thirty-two provinces, each of which has its own governor, appointed by me, who is responsible for the well-being of his subjects.

The governor is advised by a council of peasants, local worker's representatives and a collegium of initiates, made up of an astronomer and some scientists in the occult art of invoking rain and preventing cataclysms, in other words, the controllers of the agents that influence plant and animal life.

Most of the product of the land are consumed in the province that generates them, but there is also barter.

A portion of what is produced is made available to the king and central government; then the province's harvest is distributed among the peasants, including the governor, who receives his share according to position, which ensures their well-being. Any increase in the volume of agricultural production or natural resources is distributed proportionally among everyone, so that the people are interested in the work.

To this day, this system has proven to be efficient and, as a result, poverty does not exist in my kingdom, much less the misery, or a proletarian class, that exists on our extinct Earth.

— May God grant that the system of government in place will continue to flourish for a long time to come! We also hope that the ruling class will continue, for many centuries to come, to be imbued with its sacred duty to serve the people, not sloppily leaving the great mission on the shoulders of the mediocre, indulging in rapaciousmess and the exclusive pursuit of their well-being and pleasures.

The following day, the Magicians visited various provinces of Narayana, just as they had done in the kingdom of Udea, and were convinced of the order and wealth that prevailed; they were also struck by the fact that the population was more evolved and agitated than the peaceful peasants and shepherds of Udea.

In this case, music played a very influential role . Every neighborhood had at least one school where singing and different instruments were taught. The working day usually ended with songs and dances; festivals were marked by sung religious processions; the dances surprised the Magicians by their refined rhythm and their plastic beauty.

On the eve of the last journey, at night, Ebramar and Narayana found themselves alone in one of the magi's chambers. Narayana watched his friend and protector leaning against the windowsill and immersed in deep thought.

— Dear master, he said after an anguished silence, "why is this shadow of sadness clouding your eyes, the stars that have guided my life? Are you upset with me? I have put all my strength into making my people progress, I have concentrated all my efforts and knowledge to stand before you dignified by the duty I have done.

Ebramar turned around looking with infinite love at his "prodigal son", who had been arduously led through the waters of human temptations weaknesses; how happy he had been to see the magician's torch appear on the his spiritual son's forehead!

— No, my dear son, I have nothing to reproach you for, but to praise you for your enormous work. I would just like to make a small remark about a certain oversight.

— What master? Forgive me for this unintentional fault! — Narayana exclaimed in alarm.

Ebramar put his hand on Narayana's shoulder and said in a friendly tone:

— You fool! I have already told you that I have nothing to reproach you for, because how can I blame you the fiery soul, enraptured by the fine arts, hovering over the mob you have been forced to govern. I enjoy painting myself, and I understand the power of beauty and the fascination it exerts on the soul; I will not be the one to judge you for not being able to resist the approach of the works of art, whose marks you still bear. Only this understandable and... forgivable infatuation made you forget safety regulations. Think of how many new feelings you have prematurely awakened in the souls of your people.

— I see. Are you talking about music, aromas and the effect of colors? Do you think I have exorbitated these three powerful forces, given the unpreparedness of my people? But I repeat, master, this race is extremely gifted and only needed a little push. I thought I was doing the right thing by awakening their reason, shaking up their senses, creating new desires in order to achieve the desired effects. An example of this are the women; beautiful and shapely, they looked like living statues; they did not give a damn about their external appearance or their intention to be loved, nor did they have any notion of their grace and beauty. So I put sound vibrations to work that could penetrate through the rudimentary covering and stir the soul, awakening new images, and on the aromas that contributed to the vibrations.

Ebramar smiled mischievously.

— I see that the tentacles of the past still surround you; before anything else, you took care to develop the fair sex... I agree that the feminine soul should embody ideals in all their forms. Well, that is beside the point! The problem is that you have awakened these people too much from their embryonic slumber, and sowed in them refined desires and sensations beyond their level. This will give rise to passions and pernicious struggles, the consequence of which is cosmic catastrophe.

Have you forgotten that the colossal forces you unleash are a double-edged sword? You know that music, its rhythm and sounds, must be scrupulously dimensioned with the density of the astral body, in order to avoid damage; in the case of the human masses, this basic principle must be even stricter, because excessive excitement can lead to imbalance and all kinds of harmful effects, the list of which would be too long.

Musical vibrations, due to their action on the astral body, can be both therapeutic and harmful, causing skin diseases, madness and even death.

Scents are both beneficial and treacherous, and it is no coincidence that the production and use of certain scents, especially strong ones, were secrets of the temples of our old planet.

As for the light, it needs no comment. Even a poor mortal knows that without it life perishes and that it is capable of blinding and killing. In our magic, we learn to deal carefully with these two very powerful forces.

— You are right. I thank you for the warning and will try in future not to get carried away and act according to the principles of reasonableness and caution.

The next day, on their last visit, the masters were taken to an island; it was so far away that only the sky and the ocean could be seen. There Narayana had set up a very original correction colony. The most incorrigible offenders were sent there for serious crimes and were subjected to moral coercion, based exclusively on the combination of sound vibrations, aromas and colors, inside specially adapted enclosures in caves and cells.

Thoroughly re-examined , the results of this system were , however, contradictory. There were indisputably positive cases of moral recovery: a high number of highly dangerous criminals became emotionally balanced, certain nefarious instincts, ignominious vices and all kinds of perversions were eradicated. Sometimes, however, the treatment resulted in dementia, idiocy, strange illnesses and sudden deaths.

In the evening, Supramati went to Ebramar's chamber and found him thoughtful and worried. They exchanged some views on the inspection and, above all, on Narayana's method of recovering delinquents.

He is overstepping the mark by conducting dangerous experiments. How much more nonsense will he have perpetuated if I am not here with you? Undoubtedly, everything he does is original and ingenious, like himself, but now he is overdoing it, I repeat. He needs a friend to curb his excesses and guide this powerful force, inspired by the best of intentions.

— I agree. With your permission, I will be happy to stay here with him and take on the role of high priest and hierophant. He confided in me that he would be happy to see a magician, hierarchically superior to him, heading his initiation school and the priestly caste.

Ebramar held out his hand, looking at him with gratitude in his eyes.

— I approve of your offering and appreciate your sacrifice, the result of your love for me. I understand that you have prepared legislation for your future kingdom that is a wise as it is erdudite, and it would be a sacrifice on your part to give up such a broad and interesting activity.

— It is not a sacrifice, it is a great happiness to give you, my great teacher and benefactor, even a minute of joy, to take your mind off any worries , just when you are about to leave us.

Besides, it will be a way of repaying Narayana. I owe him what I am today; have to thank for having you as my mentor. As for the activity of enlightener in the country assigned to me, it can be carried out by another magician. There is no shortage of worthy and capable people, thank God!

Ebramar stood up and hugged him.

— Thank you, Supramati! You really gave me a minute of great happiness, proving that you have mastered any human pettiness. I will be talking to the mentors later today, and I have no doubt that they will approve of the choice. Your replacement will be your eldest son, Sandira, whose upbringing I took care of from birth. You will pass on all your projects to him. But here comes our fan, he added, interrupting Supramati's expressions of gratitude.

In fact, in the adjoining room, Narayana's light and hurried footsteps and his voice asking permission to enter were heard.

As soon as he had sat down, he said:

I can see from your radiant but cloudy expressions, master, that you did not like my correctional methods . In fact, I was already anticipating the scolding, so I left the visit to the island as the ultimate surprise.

— Since you yourself knew beforehand that your work would not please, let me make a few comments. In general, the technique used deserves praise, however... They could only be implemented a hundred thousand years from now and, even then, among a generation of people who are evolved, both physically, morally and intellectually.

As proof of this, let us review the facts. The cures observed, or rather the moral recoveries, were rare, and all took place among the descendants of earthlings – the offspring of somewhat evolved races; the best results were precisely those of people belonging to the families of the lower-level initiates, that is, those who had already achieved some intellectual and physical progress, albeit premature. As for the bulk of the aborigines who have undergone treatment, you will agree that the results are pitiful. In cases where the sound vibration technique predominated, there were many sudden deaths as a result of a rupture between the physical body and the astral body which was insufficiently flexibe and dilatated .

Strong aromas, acting on an obtuse and dense brain, incapable of absorbing them, lead to idiocy or madness. An evolved brain, accustomed through intense mental work to the rapid and constant exchange of substances, would have absorbed the aromas and assimilated the beneficial effects.

As for colors, whose power is gentle but dangerous, they can trigger skin diseases and other strange manifestations.

— Ah, I made a mistake; I never thought it would be so difficult to scale knowledge with its application! — exclaimed Narayana, visibly disappointed. — Poor my successors, it is they who will suffer the consequences! — he said, half pityingly, half debauchedly.

— No one is free from making gaffes during his arduous ascent. But, in order to protect you from occasional future mistakes, I leave you here a mentor, a loyal friend; his enlightened love and enormous knowledge will help you. Supramati has accepted the role of high hierophant, which you wanted a higher wizard to perform, announced Ebramar.

— Do you want to stay with me, Supramati? But you were making the final preparations to be the king and the legislator of an already elected people! — Narayana exclaimed in surprise.

— Someone else will do it. Since Ebramar considered me worthy of this position and there is no one to replace me, I will be your advisor as soon as he leaves. Besides, as your successor, I have certain obligations towards you, Supramati added jovially.

With his characteristic rapture, Narayana threw himself towards Supramati and hugged him tightly.

— Thank you, thank you, my friend and my best successor! I cannot find words to thank you; my happiness would be complete if it were not for the weight of the imminent separation from Ebramar. I cannot come to terms with the idea of never seeing him again, or of only reaching , even mentally, those distant spheres where he will remain as a perfect being!

— You are wrong, Narayana, to consider me a perfect being - Ebramar observed with a melancholic smile on his lips. — Only in this inferior land can I appear to be something elevated due to our ridiculous vanity in calling ourselves children of Reason or Light; after leaving them and being in a higher planetary system than ours, many unexpected things may happen, such as me becoming a lowly ignoramus before the workers who will be my teachers and enlighten me.

My knowledge will be of little use there, as I will have to research and learn to control a cosmic apparatus that is much more complex than our elements, which are still very crude and heavy. In the higher systems, the cosmic matter is so complex in its composition that I will have to undergo a complete course of scientific learning.

Yes, my children, the dwelling place of the Omnipotent is inconceivable, grandiose, and enigmatic, and in the crackle of uninterrupted creation and immeasurable devastation, billions of workers swarm through unfathomable space. Never before had anyone imagined the breadth of that Wisdom and Omniscience that seem to have infused themselves into the tiniest of particles. Even the light from a star, that travels incalculable distances before reaching our heavy atmosphere thousands of centuries later, is not the work of chance. An arcane messenger from a perhaps extinct world, she carries with her the cosmic substances that we need here...

Ebramar fell silent and his inspired gaze seemed to stare at a distant vision.

Just imagining the arduous distance to be traveled and the enormous work to be done, an oppression gripped the hearts of their listeners – like atoms, lost in the immensity of humanities, whose heel of time tramples them like ants on their way ; they even seemed as if they were hearing the crackling of the wheel of eternity.

Casting a glance at the disciples, Ebramar understood their spiritual state and said affably:

— Of course, we would get dizzy just imagining the infinity that surrounds us, but we must vigorously shake off this weakness and realize that among the billions of souls we are quite blessed by fate. We have learned many laws, ignored and inaccessible to the profane; we have already left behind the arduous transmigration of the inevitable ascent . Which leads the indestructible spark from its atom to the radiant central point, where the Ineffable dwells, of Whose particle we are composed.

So, hold your heads high, my friends! I am leaving you to climb another step; however, I promise not to waste any time and to prepare myself properly to receive you, my dear disciples, in the same way as my loyal mentors are waiting for me now. Undoubtedly, my being will be governed by different ethereal conditions; but the bond that unites us will never be broken.

— Master," murmured Narayana deafly, "I have a request to make . I would like to witness your departure, and I would consider this moment to be the one of the most cherished and sacred memories. Can I have this grace? Perhaps I am not worthy of it, or I will not be able to bear that alien light.

— I promise you that you will be with me in that solemn hour, and that you will see me free myself from the earthly shell. Work hard to unite yourself with me and bring the time closer when, my children, I will welcome you to my new home.

The next day, the magicians set off with Narayana to visit the kingdom of Abrasack.

CHAPTER XVI

The aircraft was rapidly approaching Abrasack's domain. The wizards were traveling without having warned him nor had their messengers been sent to ask the masters to inspect the kingdom. As neither of the two monarchs received an invitation, Udea refused to accompany the magicians and preferred to return home with Ariana.

Narayana joined Ebramar's group, referring to his inalienable right to participate in verifying his former disciple's successes.

From the height of their flight, they could see a marvelous panorama below. A flowing river rolled in its bed and, on both banks, wide strips of fertile land and lush vegetation stretched out, flanked on the horizon by a jagged range of bare mountains.

In the wide estuary, a few islands could be seen; one of them – the largest and all granite – stood sentinel.

Continuing its dizzying flight, the ship soon began to land softly; then we could see a huge city spread across two banks of the river . Its enormous buildings, surrounded by vast gardens, were lost in the distance.

All the magicians were gathered on the bridge when the ship slowed down. Suddenly, Narayana, dropped his telescope and started laughing.

— Masters, they are waiting for us! There's even an anchorage for our ship. Ha ha ha! Bravo, Abrasack! That is what an organized police force means!

Now we could see a sea of human heads bobbing on the shore, and the enturage lined up around the harbor, where the ship finally docked. A vast staircase covered in colorful mats led up to an elevation, where Abrasack stood with Avani and a large family; five sons and three daughters. They all wore richly embroidered linen robes; their faces expressed great resolution and developed minds.

All the people prostrated themselves as Abrasack and his family respectfully greeted the magicians. They were then taken by litter to the palace, where a magnificent lunch awaited them. The magicians praised the king for having guessed their unexpected arrival, thereby proving that he had magnetic communication with the divine city.

The next day, the magicians gathered in Abrasack's workroom.

Sitting in the center of the semicircle formed by the magicians, the king outlined the contours of his kingdom on the map, before the inspection of the country and its institutions began.

Abrasack's handsome, manly countenance had changed a lot in recent centuries; now it reflected a serene dignity and that consciousness of strength that power and the habit of command provide.

— Allow me, dear masters, to give a brief account of what happened from the moment I landed with my companions in this barren and swampy land, where a numerous, rude, wild and rebellious people lived. It was clear that the natives had not the idea of laws, obligations, divinities or any other serious concern. To be able to shape this human clay, that I was given, I had to dilute it with a dose of fear. With the powers I had at my disposal, I tamed them and subjected them to my will. Later, I installed them mixed on both shores.

According to the general plan, future civilization should be based on three pillars: religion, with its rituals; ruthless royal power, shrouded in divine mystery; and finally, the social laws, which could keep the people within the desired limits, ensuring them a path of progress for many centuries to come.

The power of the monarch, assisted by a Council of Initiates, would be at the heart of the entire governmental system.

You, dear teachers, readers of other people's thoughts, for whom a crude soul represents no mystery, will believe that it was neither pride nor vanity that moved me to elevate regal virtue to an inaccessible height, and surround it with divine adoration.

No, I have always considered the monarchy, due to its simplicity, to be the most perfect and appropriated system of governing peoples, even though the king, naturally, must correspond to these ideals. To this day, mine overflow with the exalted desire to justify the trust placed in me in my intentions to provide these people with the greatest possible benefits by merging with them in their interests. You will judge for yourselves whether I have succeeded in this, but my greatest fear has always been I would become a mediocre monarch, one of those who permeated our extinct Earth at the time of its decadence.

My laws are strict. Aware of the harm caused by injustice, I have taken care to put truth above all else; before justice, everyone is equal, whether they are my children or the last of the peasants.

The most precious human material at my disposal was undoubtedly the group of earthlings revived thanks to the primal substance. Of course, not all of them were able to make full use of their brain's capacity, although it was quite flexible, but their bodies were developed and their organs well specialized.

Suddenly, cases of death began to occur among these semi-immortals. According to our initiated scientists, immortality was due to the particularly harmful emanations of the primitive earth, which absorbed and destroyed the link created by the elixir of long life between the physical and astral bodies.

This left me heartbroken. As the frequency of cases increased, I foun myself fated to remain among the savages without my instructors, artists, craftsmen, in other words; deprived of an indispensable superior race.

If the spirits of the primary species began to incarnate among us, it would be impossible to take care of their rapid evolution, and civilization would have come to a standstill for a long time.

I confess that, at that time, I almost weakened and I almost asked you for help. Knowing that I had full autonomy, I kept looking for a solution together with my initiates and, finally, I found it. It was necessary to delay the most evolved desincarnate spirits in certain places and force them to be born in appropriate conditions.

You know that magic makes it possible, and you are also aware of the number of disasters that occur as a result of accidental births, when inferior beings, with low instincts, take up residence in social conditions above their ethical and intellectual level. It is not enough to be born heir to a throne to know how to govern. Such meddlers abhor everything that is superior to them, living in the midst of the sam nullities or uneducated and debauched rabble, whose omission is the cause of general ruin.

I paid special attention to education. I made sure that every child learned that there was a divinity behind them, who had given him the great gift – life – and that they should respect this divine gift in everyone, and never take it from someone else for free, because it would be impossible to give them their life back . Man must preserve his existence with a correct, balanced and hygienic way of life. Any disease, as a result of abuse, perversion, lack of cleanliness, gluttony, etc., is considered criminal and severely punished by law; parents are held responsible if their children fall ill as a result of their negligence.

— Ah, what a wonderful idea! I will use it in my kingdom, interjected the fiery Narayana, drawing a laughter from the magicians.

Such unexpected interferation interrupted Abrasack's speech and a lively exchange of ideas began about what he had just told them.

The next day was dedicated to inspecting the city. Abrasack took his visitors to a huge building, which housed numerous statues of personalities who had distinguished themselves in life through wisdom, knowledge, and the practice of good . They called it the Temple of Glory; there, servants of the sacred caste took turns on duty to tell the visiting public about the lives of the great men and their immortalized deeds. Admission was free. In the case of the higher castes, they were obliged to attend the temple with their children from an early age, so that they could be initiated into the fundamentals of a useful and dignified life and become aware that the slightest injustice or dishonest act would deprive them of securing a place among the elect, venerated by the people.

The magicians were very interested in the method Abrasack had devised for selecting souls to fill the ranks of their higher caste. Narayana expressed his impatience to see the "living necropolis" as soon as possible, which, according to his opinion, would be the most interesting thing about his former disciple's kingdom.

— Hang in there! The "living necropolis" is my main work and I have left it until last.

— How did you resolve the burial issue? — Ebramar asked.

— I have to confess that the problem gave me a lot of headaches. Due to the intense heat and very humid climate, I knew that simply burying the bodies could generate dangerous miasma;

digging graves in granite rocks was a huge and unproductive job. Nor did I want to incinerate the corpses, giving the damaging consequences for the astral body, the destruction of the physical body by fire. So, I opted for another formula.

Aborigines – who stand out from the general masses, who are sufficiently evolved to receive certain initiations and who are capable of becoming useful beings in future existences, such as junior officials, artists, or masters of trades – have a special burial, along the lines of the superior race. We make their spirits incarnate within families of greater intellectual development, mixed by marriage with representatives of the superior race.

As for the basic mass – still on the threshold of evolution – I have established a simpler form of burial for it.

In the estuary of the river, whose waters supply the country, you may have seen a series of volcanic islands. On one of these islands, we excavated a gigantic underground temple, with halls, tombs and galleries, where the dead of the capital and the surrounding area are taken.

Similar temples are spread throughout other regions of the country. The family of the deceased brings the body of the deceased to one of these temples, leaves it there for seventy days and pays a small fee for the initial expenses. A special caste of priests and servants take care of these temples. The body is taken to a circular cave, where a dry and warm environment is artificially maintained; in the center of the enclosure is a huge, botomtless reservoir filled with a resinous and acrid liquid. A sheet is impregnated with this liquid and the body of the deceased is wrapped up in it, like a mummy, and then immersed with the other corpses in the reservoir. A sign on the chest of each of these wrappings identifies the deceased and the date of death.

On top of tall braziers they burn resinous herbs impregnated with special essences, which spread a smoke with a suffocating smell. Every two days, the smoking material is replaced with a new material; the reservoir is filled with the liquid that has been absorbed by the corpses. The servants, or rather the lowly priests, who are in charge of this work, wear special robes and cover their faces with masks to protect themselves from the noxious gases in the environment.

After seventy days, the once robust bodies shrink to the size of a doll; their faces are still very recognizable, hair and nails remain intact. The corpses look like flexible wax figures. I must say that, with the passage of time , they deteriorate, becoming brown or yellowish, resembling plant roots.

But when they are taken out of the cave, their appearance is pleasing ; the family is given a flask of essence with which, after a certain time, the body must be rubbed to preserve its well-groomed appearance. The family members come with cases and, in this sort of more or less decorated coffin, 1 they can take the deceased home or bury them on the island. Many wealthy families build a sort of niche with drawers inside the walls of their homes, luxuriously furnished, to become their family tomb. Aromatic essences are smoked there and funeral rituals are performed. It is said that sighs, moans, and even screams are sometimes heard in these small tombs.

It also happens that terrified relatives empty those tombs and take the dead to remote valleys, cliffs or deserts, where they plante them as tubers, because, according to popular belief, the damp earth mitigates the suffering of the poor dead.

Magic is already part of our civilization; so, we have sorceresses who offer their services to the families of the deceased. They say that a very strange flora grows in those unusual sepulchres: the corpses, buried in the damp earth turn into real roots, which emerge in tufts of dark green leaves; on moonlit nights, a bluish shadow of a human head hangs over them. Sorceresses swear that the shadows communicate with each other; the roots of these strange plants are considered to be powerful talismans, associated with subjected demons, used in the service of those who possess them.

Abrasack was silent. A minute later, one of the wizards commented:

— What the sorceresses say is true. In spite of some positive aspects, their method is cruel, because it allows them to partially maintain a link with the astral. I will tell you how to avoid this danger later.

Abrasack thanked them.

The next day, the magicians began the detailed inspection of the country and its institutions, avoiding making any judgment on what they saw, leaving that for the end of the inspection.

Finally, the day come for Narayana to visit the necropolis of the living, which he had been waiting for impatiently. A large boat painted black, with a high, curved bow, reminiscent of the Egyptian one, was waiting for the magicians. Twelve rowers glided it glide down the river with the speed of an arrow.

Soon, they approached the funereal island, whose granite massif loomed ominously over the foaming waves, crashing thunderously on the craggy ledges, bristling like bristles.

Maneuvering between the reefs, the boat entered a long tunnel, sometimes illuminated by resinous torches; after numerous turns, the boat came to an inner lake, surrounded by bare and pointed rocks. On the shore of the lake, facing each other, there were two entrances: on the porticoes two identical inscriptions were drawn in hieroglyphics : " Die to be reborn".

The boat docked next to one of the entrances; the wizards climbed a ladder until they found themselves inside a spacious, vaulted hall, from which rocky galleries led off in different directions, disappearing into the distance.

— The bodies are embalmed here; this whole part of the island is used to prepare the mummies," explained Abrasack. — No one is allowed to pass beyond this hall, except the next of kin who accompany the dead person, or, when the mummy is ready, to say goodbye . If you wish, dear masters, I can show you the whole process, and perhaps you would like to prescribe some modifications.

With the magician's acquiescence , Abrasack took them to the place where the holy priests worked especially to embalm the bodies.

Having seen everything, Abrasack returned with the visitors to the first hall and invited them to cross over to the opposite bank, where the "necropolis of the living" , a genuine city of the dead was located.

They all returned to the boat, crossed the lake and docked near the opposite entrance; there, on the steps, the access was protected by black basalt sphinxes; in the wide-mouthed stone vessels, resinous substances were burning.

Through a wide corridor, which ended in ten steps, there was a large underground temple , whose vault was supported by massive quadrihedral columns. At the back , on heavy pedestals, stood two enormous sphinxes carved out of the rock. Their eyes, set in the rock, glowing with phosphorescent light, as if they were searching the room vivaciously In a deep depression between the two sphinxes, at the height of a few steps, stood a kind of stone altar, supporting a standing human figure, as if wrapped in a long blanket.

From the side walls, they distributed lighted torches to numerous galleries. The priests and priestesses stood next to the altar and the sphinxes, carrying silver harps . They were all dressed in white robes, with belts and cloaks. Aromatic essences were burning in the tripods.

After a solemn chant in honor of the distinguished visitors, Abrasack pointed to the two sphinxes and said:

— The mummies are taken to the sarcophagi through the door on the left, while the astral body, summoned to incarnate, comes through the door on the right.

The magical funeral takes place in this temple, where the "look-alike" is initially confined to this place and is later taken to the new fleshy shell.

As Abrasack approached, the door of the left sphinx opened silently, and through a long, slightly sloping gallery, they came to a series of tombs arranged to the side, faintly illuminated by bluish lights. On the walls, in a succession of niches, we could see numerous mummies in a upright position and, in the center, some others, full. Entering one of them, the one that was full, Abrasack stopped and pointed to a series of sarcophagi:

— Here rest my former comrades - he said, slightly moved. — I summoned them from space and gave them primal matter, but out of sheer ignorance and presumption, I did not administer the right amount. Instead of living as long as I did, I saw their lives extinguished two centuries later; their friendly and brave souls, however, will one day return to work for the benefit of my people. Through complex rituals, which I will describe to you later, we manage to evoke the astral forces of the celestial region where the polar star is located, which we incorporate into the "look-alikes", temporarily incarnated in mummies. Our deposits are real underground cities populated by living astral – powerful and really dynamic forces – which give us the control over the earth's pole, necessary to solidify our country.

To maintain the life of the "look-alikes", we use very powerful aromas; magical spells enable the action of nutrients and provide the astral beings with a comfortable life in a pleasant environment – just as you see here, in the artistic and sculptural reproductions on the walls of the tombs. They communicate with each other; in fact, I have built a special place for them, a chamber up there, where moonlight penetrates through openings, and in whose radiations they bathe, refreshing the astral body and strengthening the spiritual forces.

Every day at midnight, a beep goes off, announcing to those who rest here that it is time to wake up. The time is drawing near, and you will be the witnesses to this event.

Now, do you see that little side cave with two red granite sarcophagi? I have reserved the place for myself and Avani; my successors, however, will occupy the regal chambers. Now I will take you to where the earthlings rest. There you, Supramati, will find those you entrusted to me, sticken by premature death.

Narayana looked surprised at Supramati, but said nothing and followed the others through a narrow gallery to the cave indicated .

It was a long underground space full of mummies, both in niches and in long tanks made of wood or stone.

The magicians and Abrasack stopped in the center, examining the surroundings. A few moments later, the air was cut by a trembling metallic sound, as if hundreds of little silver bells were ringing all over the place, nearby and in the distance In an flash, the bluish light that illuminated the room faded and fatuous flames appeared over the niches and tanks, shedding faint flashes of light.

At that moment, the mummies seemed to move and become covered with a gray mist, which densified oscillating and began to take on human shape, wrapped in a cloak; some figures were dark, others light and phosphorescent. It was now possible to distinguish that they were men and women, and even children; their faces, with their fuzzy outlines , were happy and surprised. Hovering above the ground, the beings headed for the exit.

— They are going to the moonlight chamber, Abrasack whispered, inviting the wizards to accompany him.

The moonlight chamber was a large enclosure carved out of the rock. Through the openings in the vault, wide beams of moonlight poured down in silvery flashes on the waters of a reservoir, burrowing in the center of the cave . All around was strange vegetation, dotted with dense shrub flowers and even some trees. Banks of moss were hidden under the shadows; all that vegetation seemed solid, immovable: a true garden of shadows.

In front of the wall, on some tables, there were flat, widemouths vases filled with a colorless liquid, and a dish with a fine red powder; a resinous yet pleasant smell permeated the air, like the essence of flowers, and served as food for the astral bodies.

The figures that crowded in hurried to bathe in the reservoir and then drank the liquid from the pots and absorbed the dust; all those delicacies did not seem to run out. Meanwhile, the shadows thickened, the faces became animated and the blurred eyes rekindled.

At that moment, the magicians and Abrasack were preparing to leave the chamber; Ebramar signaled for Supramati and Narayana to follow him.

They headed back towards a huge underground temple, shrouded in gray semi-darkness. On either side of the right sphinx door stood seven priests and priestesses, all wearing white robes and holding crystal harps In front of the door stood a tall triptych, around which, in a semicircle, seven high-level adepts prostrated themselves. The flickering pink flames illuminated their stern and concentrated countenances, and their white robes, glowing in pectoral insignia.

When the wizards and Abrasack took their seats to see what was going to happen, one of the adepts made a sign and immediately a slow, harmonious chant was heard, accompanied by the trembling sounds of harps.

The melody was strange, sometimes soft and fast, sometimes slow and deep, with notes that tore at the soul and made your hair stand on end.

After a while, the door between the sphinx's paws slid open silently and a misty shadow appeared from the dark back to the gallery, hovering before the triptych, whose flames immediately went out. A clear phosphorescent thread emerged from the spectre, to be lost in the dark dephts of the gallery.

The fiery outlines of the cabalistic signs were drawn in the air and the burial chamber immediately shook with the roll of thunder. A shimmering bolt of lightning zigzagged through the air and broke the radiant thread, while a phosphoric mist, reverberating all the colors of the rainbow, tinged with fiery flashes, enveloped the suspended shadow and took the shape of a missile that, crackling, projected itself into the air, losing itself in the shadow of the vault.

— The spirit was transferred to the body of a newborn child ; the adepts recorded, in arcane documents, a new chapter in the history of the new individual. To the deeds done, the birth records and subsequent deaths, they will add a note of the new reincarnation, the name of the new family and an opinion of what may be expected of him in terms of his contribution to the good of the people, his success in the arts, science, and so forth.

While Abrasack was speaking, some lamps lit up; after a brief conversation with the adepts, discussing the phenomenon that had taken place, the magicians left the mortuary island.

The next day there was a solemn meeting in the great hall of the palace. The magicians told Abrasack their thoughts on their enlightening activity.

After a detail discussion on the aspects of government and social life, and given some warnings about future changes, the chief hierophant gave the floor to Ebramar.

— Despite a few isolated slip-ups, we can only praise his colossal work, which, however, has not prevented him from expanding his knowledge and perfecting himself, Ebramar said. — His method of embalming, the establishment of the schools of initiation, the progress in arts and crafts are testimony to his serious and tireless work.

Your laws are rigid, sometimes severe, but clear and fair; your people are wise, obedient, and hard-working, accustomed to seeing earthly life as a preparation for the afterlife, and they will flourish for a long time; the civilization they founded will be particularly long-lived. What you have achieved by using in practice such a complex undertaking reincarnation - i.e., subordinating one of the most terrifying laws of the invisible world to human will and control - is a proof of the most intrepid flight of your intelligence and your iron will. Through science, you have defied the forces of fate.

Pale with emotion, Abrasack knelt down; tears of happiness and gratitude welled up in his eyes when Ebramar touched him with the magic sword and a wide blue stripe shone on his forehead.

Then, Ebramar kissed him; the magicians repeated the gesture and greeted him; then they all went to the great temple, where a solemn mass was said for the graces received.

The next day, the magicians said goodbye and the spaceship took them back to the divine city.

EPILOGUE

The city of the Magicians has changed little over the last few centuries. With its majestic temples, magical palaces, its vast gardens – an oasis of plants and flowers – the city was a true corner of earthly paradise. The palaces of Udea and Narayana, empty for a long time, once again welcomed their owners. A few weeks ago, all of Ebramar's disciples gathered at his house to spend their last days in that land with the great magician.

Never before had Ebramar lavished so much kindness and attention on his spiritual children. Together with everyone, or alone with someone, he would have long conversations, teaching and giving advice that would be very useful in the future. Everyone listened appreciatively, deeply engraving the valuable instructions in their hearts, but their eyes could hardly hold back the tears, and a bitter feeling overwhelmed their hearts.

Even Ebramar resented being separated n from his spiritual family, his children of light, but the great worker needed to rest. To every being created by the Ineffable, sleep is a gift to be able to endure the trials of the flesh and gather new strength to face the long road, and this condition applies to everything.

After so many millennia of existence dedicated to the extraordinary work that lit up his forehead with seven magician's torches, Ebramar longed to immerse himself in the light of rest in order to regain his strength and, later on, to continue the journey of ascension to yet another level, which cannot even be sensed by the reason of earthly humanity. He knew that the light, immanent in him, would reach those regions and those who were dear to him, not only those who cherished him, but any being, no matter how miserable – what would he say of those who were close to him!

One afternoon, after lunch, everyone gathered on the terrace of Ebramar's palace and the conversation went on longer than usual. The great magician was silent and thoughtful, his gaze roaming over those present.

— I must tell you, my children, that today's meeting is the last; the hour of our separation has already sounded, he stammered in a deaf voice.

Seeing that everyone paled, he added:

— I realize, my friends, that the human weakness of the fear of separation still inhabits you. I know that you would like to see me near, which is a certain selfishness on your part, even if it is motivated by love. Do you know that the life of a magician is a constant tension of volition? So, I am exhausted from wanting and I am looking forward to resting; I must strengthen myself so that later I can get on my way and continue my work; the road ahead of me is still very long...

There are so many mysteries I must research, so many powers to acquire and so many powerful forces to learn that I need to renew my spiritual strength.

So, dear children, let me rest in that abode of heavenly beauty, of sleep without fatigue, bathing in harmony and light, enjoying absolute peace and quiet, full aware that I have earned this rest. Do not evoke me, nor disturb the bliss of my magical sleep, with your anguished thoughts or regrets.

— Master, can we at least know where you are going? — said Supramati. — Could you tell us, so that our hearts and thoughts can address reassuring prayers to you?

I am going to go to the star we call the "Star of the Magi"; you know it, celestial scholars . It always appears at the moment when a great missionary, a son of light, after having rested there and prepared for his exalted mission, descends to earth to wrap himself in the heavy garments of the flesh and accept a bloody and painful end. This blessed star will send me a ray and I will ascend there.

Ebramar stood up; everyone who was there, one by one, approached him, then he blessed them all and said a friendly word to each one.

When it was Narayana's turn , the magician put his hand on his head.

— Be reasonable and firm, my "prodigal son", and never let pride or any other human weakness hinder the fruits of the victory you have won. I leave you Supramati, as my most precious legacy, and he will be for you a reliable and affectionate mentor.

Finally, Nara approached him; Ebramar gazed enigmatically and thoughtfully into those clear eyes, full of love.

— Now I can set the time of my retreat. I will stay away in the tabernacle, for final preparations; the high hierophant will instruct you on the time, when you should gather at the gates. Only you, your consorts and those appointed by the great hierophants will be able to take part in the event. As soon as I leave, you may leave now.

He made a gesture and became invisible.

Deeply moved, Ebramar's disciples decided to spend those nine days in absolute fasting and continuous prayer. They all withdrew in silence in order to prepare for the moment when they would gather in one of the caves for a solemn combined vigil.

Nara stood last, with Supramati and Narayana, and signaled for them to stay.

— I would like to pass on Ebramar's wish. He wants you to bury everything that is left of him. In the tomb already dug near the sanctuary. I also want to fast, but alone, and I will do so in Ebramar's burial chamber; I will join you later. And now, my friends and faithful companions of life through the centuries, forgive me if I have not always been humble and patient enough, and ... whatever happens, remember me well, and she held out her hands to both of them.

— Are you thinking of leaving us? — Supramati asked, barely containing his perturbation, while Narayana looked at her in a mixture of sadness and surprise.

— It is not a question of leaving you, but of getting rid of this body that I have been carrying around for so many centuries, and returning to my home; besides, staying here without my master and benefactor would be too difficult. You understand, of course.

— Of course, we understand, but it is just that the news of your withdrawal was so sudden... Supramati murmured.

— I am still not sure that I am going, although Ebramar once admitted the possibility of this release – not to accompany him, of course, because I am not worthy – but so that I can rest in space. He did not tell me when it would happen, but it does not hurt to hope, she added, saying goodbye.

Finally, the day set by Ebramar arrived and, with the coming of night, the final preparations began. The wizards, the magiesses and all those who had been invited by the great hierophants dressed in fine gala robes and stood in line along the gallery that connected the gates of the sanctuary with an isolated promontory among the granite rocks, in the depths of which the underground city had been excavated. In the center of the promontory was a golden pedestal, around which blue lights flickered; on its four sides stood the great astrologers who spoke the language of the stars.

At around two o'clock in the morning, a thunderous roar echoed off the walls of the underground temples ; the gates of the sanctuary opened, an intense light poured in and Ebramar appeared, as if wrapped in a transparent sphere. Seven beams of light formed a kind of radiant crown over his head; an expression of joy and bliss shone on his handsome countenance, and he clasped the magic sword to his chest. His feet did not touch the ground, and he seemed to float over the gallery, like an apparition; then everyone began to follow him.

When he reached the pedestal, Ebramar stopped, or rather, hover over it, those present then sang an imposing and majestic hymn.

Silence followed; even nature seemed to be waiting. There was not the slightest movement in the air; it was a wonderful night, warm and fragrant; only an almost imperceptible crackle betrayed that something extraordinary was happening.

The four astrologers then began a marvelous hymn in a mysterious language, understandable to the stars. Suddenly, a golden light shone in the sapphireblue sky and grew closer and larger, flooding the promontory with brilliant rays.

The air was filled with translucent, radiant beings, the protectors of that new land, the Spirits of the Spheres, . Finally, the four groups of elemental spirits – servants of the powerful initiate – and the four igneous films, which merged on Ebramar's chest, were bound together.

Raising his magic sword, the great magician smashed those links with one blow, saying:

— I thank you, the higher elemental spirits, for your loyalty, submission, and service .

At that moment, Ebramar's gaze stopped on those standing there.

— I salute you, my teachers, friends and disciples, and I thank you all.

— Go and rest, friend and tireless worker, in the abode of the Ineffable, said the chief hierophant, raising his hand.

At the same moment, a sparkling bolt of lightning seemed to strike Ebramar's chest and ignite the flames of his crown. All those present, with the exception of the astrologers, fell to their knees, and a terrible spectacle unfolded before their eyes.

Ebramar's earthly body was consumed in flames, and the radiant astral that had been freed was projected upward by the golden ray.

At the same time, the cloak of one of the magicians ignited, her body fell to the ground and a sleek specter i resembling a silver butterfly emerged from it. It was Nara, who was following her beloved master. A minute later, the specter faded; the luminous beings blurred into a mist and the lightning was extinguished.

All that remained of the golden pedestal was a handful of phosphorescent ashes , which the disciples respectfully collected in a crystal urn, topped by a crucifix.

Nara's body had not been consumed, but it had become light, flexible and incredibly transparent, giving it an astonishing resemblance to an iridescent wax statue.

Ebramar's burial chamber, although not large, was lined with admirable sculptures and sapphire-colored inlays; a light, whose origin was unknown and which resembled moonlight, illuminated it softly.

At the back, in a deep niche, on a blue block in the shape of an altar, rested the urn with Ebramar's ashes. Nara's body, shimmering in pale blue flashes and emanating a fragrant smell, was buried next to Supramati and Narayana under the altar with the urn.

Only the higher initiates and Ebramar's disciples were allowed to enter the burial chamber, where Nara's urn and body lay, to perform religious services.

The door, which had no key or padlock, opened by itself, only for the worthy; an ordinary mortal would not be able to cross the threshold.

One evening, about seven days after Ebramar had left for the Star of the Magi, on one of the terraces of Supramati's palace stood two men in white were standing, leaning aginst the railing.

One of them, apparently the master of the house himself, so absorbed in his thoughts, that seemed not to notice his surroundings. Narayana, who was beside him, apparently did not even notice him. His serious gaze wandered meditatively, either at the marvelous picture of nature, or at the blue-lazuli firmament, densely sprinkled with stars and resembling a curtain woven in gold.

— Can you answer a question that puzzles me so much? I know that on several occasions you accompanied the master to different worlds; did he ever show you this Star of the Magi where he is now ? If so, please tell me, if there is no obstacle: what shape is it?

Supramati remained silent for a while, but a smile was on his lips and his eyes seemed to be gazing at a radiant vision.

— It is true, I have seen that wonderful place and I will be happy to share my impressions. That world is flooded with light, impossible to imagine: it is a region of incredible beauty and luxuriant vegetation, which cannot be described or compared with anything we know. Everything there vibrates, everything is harmonious sound, soft scent, a range of unprecedented colors, the combination of which generates the mysterious light I told you about.

There, lulled by waves of ether, the spirits of the magicians rest in total relaxation and bliss.

That haven of tranquility and light, in which spirits immerse themselves in "Manvantara", gave rise to the mistaken notion of nirvana. They imagined it– look at that! — the spirit plunges into cosmic light, losing its individualism and merging with the Divinity. What is certain is that nirvana is a well-known form of rest, a state of repose from which the soul emerges invigorated to work in the region of eternity.

A mortal is not given the ability to see the path and know the goal for which the soul of a great initiate strives; the region where the march of perpetual motion ends, directed behind the flaming walls, ruling the cosmos - that is a mystery of the Ineffable.

We, my friend Narayana, who have climbed an insignificant ladder of knowledge and goodness, see at our feet a pulsating human anthill; we watch in sadness the blind and ignorant mob, suffering as a result of the instincts of the flesh and hating each other, tear each other apart or kill each other, only to gain some fleeting earthly goods, never attained. Human beings do not realize that they have come to earth as temporary guests, that death sweeps them away as sand is swept away by a strong wind; they forget the great commandment of Love – the only commandment that makes peace possible. "Love one another" - which the Son of God advocated.

How blessed we are, what a wonderful grace we have, to understand divine laws and to be able to shake off the worst of human weaknesses and misconceptions, Narayana whispered, overwhelmed with jubilant praise and raising his eyes to the celestial vault, Supramati shook his hand.

— So let us continue towards the light, let us show the way to our brothers and sisters, wandering in the darkness, confined in the human "earth", and let us work tirelessly to make ourselves worthy of the sacred mission entrusted to us: that of being the legislators in this young earth.

JOHN KEELY'S STORY

ABOUT JOHN KEELY ...The ethereal force discovered by John Worrel Keely from Philadelphia... is not a hallucination... The phenomena presented by the inventor [at the end of the 19th century]... have been surprising, almost miraculous, not in the sense of supernatural, but in the sense of superhuman. If Keely were allowed to do so, he could reduce an entire army to atoms in the space of a few seconds as easily as he reduced the body of a dead ox to that form [of atoms].

He was what in Kabbalistic language is called a magician from birth... He was unaware and would continue to be unaware of the full extent of his powers... he attributed them to a erroneous origin... that is why he could not fully develop them... because he did not have the ability to communicate what was only a inherent capacity of his own special nature. And so he could not transfer the secret to anyone…

About the "Keely engine", the inventor himself explains:

" Anyone who examines my machine, if they want to have even an approximate idea of its modus-operandi, must discard any idea of machines that work by virtue of the principles of depression and aspiration, by the expansion of steam or other similar gas. My machine has no pistons or eccentrics... My system, in all its parts and minutiae, is based on sympathetic vibration.

John Ernst Worrell Keely (1827 – 1898), from Philadelphia, was a researcher into the secrets of sound. He spent 50 years of his life developing and perfecting inventions that used the vibrational sympathetic force or etheric force to make objects levitate.

His laboratory demonstrations impressed scientists and onlookers alike. Keely wanted to produce his "machine" on a commercial scale, but the project failed because Keely's invention only worked in conjunction with the peculiar vibrations of the operator's own body; in other words, it was not enough to have the machine, it was necessary to "train" operators in a capacity that Keely possessed, but he did not know how, why, what kind it was or how to develop the faculty in other people, a technique that, it seems, was well known among Tibetan monks. More recently, Edward Leedskalnin claimed to know the secret of the building of the pyramids and other megaliths. He lived in a palace called Coral Castle, near Miami, Florida. The castle was built by Leedskalnin himself with gigantic coral blocks of coral weighing more than 30 tons.

In 28 years, working alone, without using modern construction machinery, he cut and fitted together around 1,100 tons.

He carried out this work with extreme discretion, always at night, avoiding publicity and keeping his construction techniques absolutely secret, despite visits from engineers and government agents. However, on one occasion some teenagers who managed to spy on him claimed that they saw him move the huge coral blocks, making them "float like hydrogen balloons". Everything indicates that Leedskalnin had discovered a way of manipulating gravity.

Keely Engine Company

John Worrell Keely (1837 – 1898) from Philadelphia was a carpenter and mechanic who announced in 1872 that he had discovered a new principle for producing energy. The vibrations of a simple tuning fork had given him the idea and the means to extract etheric energy.

Keely persuaded several engineers and capitalists to invest in the idea, forming the Keely Motor Company in New York in 1872. He soon had a capital of one million dollars, mainly from wealthy businessmen in New York and Philadelphia. He used the money to buy the materials needed to build an engine based on his theories.

He had soon built an etheric generator, which he demonstrated to amazed audience in 1874 in Philadelphia. Keely blew into a nozzle for half a minute, then poured five gallons of tap water into the same nozzle. After some fine adjustments, the pressure gauge indicated pressures of 10,000 pounds per square inch. This, Keely said, was evidence that the water had been disintegrated and a mysterious steam had been released into the generator, capable of moving machinery.

A spectator at Keely's demonstrations described the power of the machine. "Great ropes were broken, iron bars broken or bent, driven through twelve-inch planks, by a force that could not be determined."

Keely predicted that his discovery would make other forms of energy obsolete. A quart of water would be enough to send a train from Philadelphia to San Francisco and back. A gallon would propel a steamship back and forth from New York to Liverpool. "One bucket of water has enough of this steam to produce a force sufficient to displace the world from its course."

Keely and the group of directors of Keely Motor Company.

Keely lived in high style, like the boss of any big company. To his credit, he spent most of the money invested in research equipment. He did most of the experimentation, building his own device. He was unwilling to entrust the secret to those who could not or would not understand , especially physicists and engineers. Skeptics noticed that the equipment could never function as it should unless Keely was present.

Work proceeded slowly. To keep the shareholder's spirits up, Keely organized public demonstrations. These were masterpieces of performance. He demonstrated a marvelous machine, a "vibrating machine" or hydro-pneumatic pulsating vacuum engine. It was a work of art by the engineer, made of shiny metal and copper. The machine was connected to another machine called a "liberator," a complicated array of metal wires, tubes and tuning forks. Keely explained that he was extracting a "latent force" from nature, the vibrating energy of the ether. [Keely often used a harmonica, violin, flute, sitar, or pitch pipe to activate his machines]. Some said it was worth the price of being fooled to hear the eloquent language Keely used to explain his theory. [He was said to have considerable musical talent and knowledge].

A central idea of Keely's theory of nature was the notion that musical tones could resonate with atoms, or with the ether itself. He even drew this musical diagram to help people understand the details of this theory. [There are those today who use this as an indication that Keely was ahead of his time, anticipating the theory of quantum mechanics].

Biographers have described Keely as a "mechanical experimenter," "inventor and impostor," "perfidious teacher," " deadbeat," and " scandalous brat." Keely's lack of formal scientific education . Keely's lack of formal scientific education did not upset his supporters, nor did it intimidate Keely himself from proclaiming his theories as "scientific." Keely expounded his ideas using an elaborate theory of "etheric force," seasoned with eloquently profound terms such as: "sympathetic balance, quadruple negative harmonics , etheric disintegration." His backers were properly impressed. He looked with condescending pity at those who did not seem to understand.

Some disappointed shareholders withdrew their support as Keely's experiments were repeatedly delayed. Keely declared that he had already proved that his theory could be implemented for useful purposes, and made big promises about the economic benefits of etheric energy over coal and other energy sources. But he resisted demands from investors to produce a marketable product. Shareholders were unhappy with Keely's insistence that more experimentation was needed to "perfect" the machines. Fortunately, close to bankruptcy, Keely acquired a wealthy backer, Mrs. Clara S. J. Bloomfield-Moore, the widow of a Philadelphia paper manufacturer.

She granted him more than $100,000 for expenses and promised him a salary of $2,500 per month. she became active promoting Keely in newspapers and books and seeking out scientists who could validate his claims. She suggested that he share his secret with Edison or Tesla to accelerate their development, but Keely refused. At least he agreed that the scientists could observe the demonstrations.

E. Alexander Scott, an electrical engineer, witnessed such a demonstration. When Keely showed him the etheric force making a weight rise and fall in a closed jar of water, Scott was not impressed. Keely used the sound of a sitar to activate the globe releaser, which then transmitted the etheric force through a wire to the water container. Scott suspected that the weight was hollow, so that a minimal change in water pressure could make it rise or fall, in the same way as a Cartesian diver. The wire, he suggested, was a hollow tube that transmitted air pressure to the water chamber. To refute the idea, Keely cut the wire to prove that it was solid. But Moore discreetly took a similar piece of wire from the workshop and later discovered that it did indeed have a thin, hollow center.

Other demonstrations showed that the etheric force was great enough to lift enormous weights. He could also fire his " vapory gun," demonstrated at Sandy Hook, Long Island.

Scientific American magazine followed Keely's career with some fascination and amusement. They were not impressed, reporting that all the demonstrations they witnessed could easily have been produced with hidden sources of compressed air.

Keely continued to research for fourteen years, ocasionally organizing demonstrations to placate impatient shareholders. Mrs. Moore was concerned about Alexander Scott's negative report, and by impolite opposing articles in newspapers and magazines. So, she sought a second opinion from the British physicist Prof. W. Lascelles-Scott. He spent a month in Philadelphia carrying out his research, finally informing the Franklin Institute that "Keely has demonstrated to me, in a way that is absolutely unquestionable, the existence of a hitherto unknown force."

As physicist Lascelles-Scott and engineer Alexander Scott obviously disagreed, they were brought together to witness further Keely's demonstration. Mrs. Moore suggested that the definitive test would be to cut that wire that Scott claimed was actually an air line. This time, Keely vehemently refused. Lascelles-Scott returned to England, and Mrs. Moore, her faith shaken, reduced Keely's salary to $250 a month.

After Keely died on November 18, 1898, suspicious skeptics and newspaper reporters made a thorough examination of his laboratory. Some of Keely's machinery had already been taken by "believers" who hoped they could make it work. A Boston electrician, T. Burton Kinraide, took the engine to his home in Jamaica Plains . Part of the device ended up in England. No one could make it work as it did in Keely's laboratory. The secret was not in the machines; the secret was in the laboratory itself.

Engineer Alexander Scott and Mrs. Moore's son, Clarence, examined the building, accompanied by the press and photographers. False ceilings and floors were opened, revealing mechanical straps and connections to a silent water engine in the basement (two floors below the laboratory). A system of pneumatic switches under the floorboards could have been used to switch the machinery on and off. A three-ton sphere was found in the basement, apparently a reservoir for compressed air The walls, ceilings and even apparently solid beams revealed hidden pipes. The evidence of large-scale fraud was obvious and undeniable.

What is really remarkable is that Mrs. Moore had persuaded several apparently respectable scientists to observe Keely's demonstrations, and some of them said they were impressed, and even convinced that Keely had made revolutionary scientific discoveries. Why were some so easily fooled by Keely's obvious (though very elaborate) frauds, which were correctly guessed by more perceptive and skeptical observers? Of course, it must be said that Keely never allowed anyone to examine his machines, test them independently, or even look inside them. Even today, fraud artists promoting energy machines can find some trained engineers or physicists willing to publicly declare that they have found no fraud or deception in the machines and are convinced that new scientific principles are at work. Yes, these are the "qualified witnesses" at work.

Keely had kept his company running for 26 years without ever putting a product on the market, paying a dividend or revealing his secrets. That is his only undoubted achievement. He never divulged his secrets to anyone, as far as we know. A close friend reported that he had once asked Keely: "John, what do you want for an epitaph?" His reply, "Keely, the greatest humbug [entertainement fraud] of the ninereenth century."

The term "humbug" is associated with the American showman Phineas Taylor Barnum (1810 – 91), who wrote a book "Humbugs of the World" and was renowned for deceiving the public with fraudulent and exaggerated "wonders." Barnum and Keely never met, but they could have been soul mates.

The Keely case is generally recognized as one of the most successful scientific frauds. Even today, there are those who believe that he has been "framed" and that his "secrets" are yet to be discovered. A website, Keelynet, is dedicated to continuing and expanding his work, following his hidden theories of physics and matter.

Zibia Gasparetto's Greatest success stories

With more than 20 million titles sold, the author has contributed to the strengthening of spiritualist literature in the publishing market and to the popularization of spirituality. Learn more of the author's successes.

Romances Dictated by the Spirit Lucius

The Life Force

The Truth of each one

Life knows what it does

She trusted in life

Between Love and War

Esmeralda

Thorns of Time

Eternal Bonds

Nothing is by Chance

Nobody is Nobody's

God's Advocate

Tomorrow Belongs to God

Love Won

Unexpected Encounter

On the Edge of Destiny

The Sly One

The Morro of Illusions

Where is Teresa?

Through the Doors of the Heart

When Life chooses

When the Hour Comes

When it is necessary to return

Opening for Life

Not afraid to live

Only love can do it

We Are All Innocent

Everything has its price

It was all worth it

A real love

Overcoming the past

Other success stories by André Luiz Ruiz and Lucius

The Love Never Forgets You Trilogy

The Strength of Kindness

Under the Hands of Mercy

Saying Goodbye to Earth

At the End of the Last Hour

Sculpting Your Destiny

There are Flowers on the Stones

The Crags are made of Sand

Books of Eliana Machado Coelho and Schellida

Hearts without Destiny

The Shine of Truth

The Right to be Happy

The Return

In the Silence of Passions

Strength to Begin Again

The Certainty of Victory

The Conquest of Peace

Lessons Life Offers

Stronger than Ever

No Rules for Loving

A Diary in Time

A Reason to Live

Eliana Machado Coelho and Schellida, Romances that captivate, teach, move and

can change your life!

Romances of Arandi Gomes Texeira and The Count J.W. Rochester

Lancaster County

The Power of Love

The Trial

Cleopatra's Bracelet

The Reincarnation of a Queen

You Are Gods

Books of Marcelo Cezar and Marco Aurelio

Love is for the Strong

The Last Chance

Nothing is as it Seems

Forever With Me

Only God Knows

You Make Tomorrow

A Breath of Tenderness

Books of Vera Kryzhanovskaia and JW Rochester

The Revenge of the Jew

The Nun of the Marriages

The Sorcerer's Daughter

The Flower of the Swamp

The Divine Wrath

The Legend of the Castle of Montignoso

The Death of the Planet

The Night of Saint Bartholomew

The Revenge of the Jew

Blessed are the poor in spirit

Cobra Capella

Dolores

Trilogy of the Kingdom of Shadows

From Heaven to Earth

Episodes from the Life of Tiberius

Infernal Spell

Herculanum

On the Frontier

Naema, the Witch

In the Castle of Scotland (Trilogy 2)

New Era

The Elixir of Long Life

The Pharaoh Mernephtah

The Lawgivers

The Magicians

The Terrible Phantom

Paradise without Adam

Romance of a Queen

Czech Luminaries

Hidden Narratives

The Nun of the Marriages

Books of Elisa Masselli

There is always a reason

Nothing goes unanswered

Life is made of decisions

The Mission of each one

Something more is needed

The Past does not matter

Destiny in his hands

God was with him

When the past does not pass

Just beginning

Books of Vera Lúcia Marinzeck de Carvalhoç and Patricia

Violets in the Window

Living in the Spirit World

The Writer's House

Flight of the Seagull

Vera Lúcia Marinzeck de Carvalho and Antônio Carlos

Love your Enemies

Slave Bernardino

the Rock of Lovers

Rosa, the third fatality

Captives and Freed

Books of Mónica de Castro y Leonel

In spite of everything

Love is not to be trifled with

Face to Face with the Truth

Of My Whole Being

I wish

The Price of Being Different

Twins

Giselle, The Inquisitor's Mistress

Greta

Till Life Do You Part

Impulses of the Heart

Jurema of the Jungle

The Actress

The Force of Destiny

Memories that the Wind Brings

Secrets of the Soul

Feeling in One's Own Skin

World Spiritist Institute

www.ingramcontent.com/pod-product-compliance
Lightning Source LLC
LaVergne TN
LVHW041748060526
838201LV00046B/942
9798869184214